# LIFE IN FREEDOM

# LIFE IN FREEDOM

*Liberation Theologies from Asia*

## Michael Amaladoss, S.J.

ORBIS BOOKS

Maryknoll, New York 10545

The Catholic Foreign Mission Society of America (Maryknoll) recruits and trains people for overseas missionary service. Through Orbis Books, Maryknoll aims to foster the international dialogue that is essential to mission. The books published, however, reflect the opinions of their authors and are not meant to represent the official position of the society.

**Library of Congress Cataloging in Publication Data**

Amaladoss, M. (Michael), 1936–
   Life In Freedom : liberation theologies from Asia / Michael
Amaladoss
      p.   cm.
   Includes bibliographical references and index.
   ISBN 1-57075-124-2 (alk. paper)
      1. Liberation theology.   2. Theology, Doctrinal—Asia—
History—20th century.   I. Title
   BT83.57.A465   1997
   230´.0464´095—dc21
                                                                    96-29694
                                                                    CIP

# Contents

## PART TWO
## RELIGIONS FOR LIBERATION

# Preface

The story of how I came to write this book is interesting. It will also help the reader understand the focus and limits of this book. The theology of liberation is popularly identified with Latin America. Asian and African theologies—in Christian circles—have been inspired by the Latin American model, though they have acquired their own particular accents. While Latin American theologians focus on poverty caused by economic and political oppression, Africans are more sensitive to the denial of their identity by cultural oppression, and Asians are concerned with religiosity and religious pluralism and their impact on the struggle for liberation.

In Asia, one can identify various theological streams. Besides liberation theologians, there are some who see evangelization as proclamation leading to a change of religious allegiance. Others are interested in inculturation and the building up of the local church. These are also sensitive to the problems and tensions of interreligious dialogue, particularly in the area of spiritual paths, methods of prayer, etc. Asian bishops and theologians have tried to reconcile these diverse streams by describing evangelization as a threefold dialogue with the poor, the great religions and the cultures of Asia. But tensions and mutual suspicions continue.

Asian liberation theology has been criticized for being a pale imitation of the Latin American model. Its use of a marxist framework for the analysis of society, which has no positive role for religion, has not been welcome in Asia. More recent liberation theologians have been trying to distance themselves from such an image.

It is in this context that I received an invitation from *Lumen Vitae,* an International Catechetical Institute in Brussels, Belgium, to give a course of lectures in 1993 on 'Liberation Theologies from Asia.' Preparing for this course opened my eyes to new horizons with which I had not been fully familiar. In 1985 we had a seminar on 'Towards an Indian Theology of Liberation,' in which we explored liberation elements in other Indian religious traditions. So I cast my net wider than 'Christian' liberation theologians. It was also a chastening experience for me to realize that some theologians of other religions, such as Gandhi in India and Buddhadasa in Thailand, theologized and wrote about liberation themes long before the development of liberation theology in Christian circles. Face-to-face with an abundance of material, I decided to limit myself to authors whose reflection arises out of some involvement in liberation movements.

The aim of this book is to help its readers share my exciting discoveries.

In this book, I have limited myself to Asia: west, south, east and southeast. I have

*xi*

not taken into account the vast amount of writing on the economic, political and social aspects of liberation. I have focused on people who have reflected on the problems of liberation from a religious perspective, but in view of socio-political actions or movements.

I have divided this book into three parts. In the first part, I introduce the reader to various liberation movements in which Christians are involved: the Minjung theology of Korea, the theology of struggle in the Philippines, the Dalit theology of India and feminist and ecological movements. In these last two movements, we see Christians involved with the believers of other religions.

In the second part, I take up different religions of Asia. For Hinduism, Buddhism, Christianity and Islam, I have identified some theologians whose reflections I have found interesting. Given the situation in China, it has not been easy to identify people who have written about Confucianism from the background of experience. I also thought it important to include a chapter on cosmic religions.

In the third part, I have tried to reflect on liberation as an inter-religious and integral project.

Many of the theologians I have identified are voluminous authors. My brief reports and summaries can only introduce them to you and invite you to explore further. For this purpose you may find the select bibliography at the end of the volume interesting.

My lectures at *Lumen Vitae* included one on the art that liberation movements have produced in Asia. I have to confess that it is not complete enough for publication, since I have not had the time or opportunity to explore this theme in other countries besides India.

Asia still remains a continent of poor people. Practically all the countries have embraced a liberal model for the economic development of their countries. The consequences that we already see are small groups of rich people, many poor, and a growing gap between them. It is significant that many of the theologians presented here have reacted critically to both liberal capitalism and marxist socialism. When I started preparing this book, I had thought of calling it *The Third Way* between liberal capitalism and marxist socialism, but marxist socialism had collapsed, and capitalism had emerged as the only available alternative. There are, however, people who think that capitalism should not be left to the vagaries and monopolies of the free market but must be made socially responsible. For this purpose, the critiques and vision of these Asian theologians are very relevant and of enduring validity. I invite you, therefore, to discover them through the following pages.

I have the pleasant duty to thank the directive group at *Lumen Vitae*, particularly André Fossion and Etienne Vandeputte. I am also grateful to two batches of students at *Lumen Vitae*, not only from Asia but also from Europe, Africa and Latin America, who have encouraged me by their interest and comments. Special thanks are due to S. Arokiasamy, S.J. for his patient reading of the text and encouraging remarks.

# PART ONE

# LIBERATION MOVEMENTS

# 1

# Minjung Theology of Korea

Minjung theology is the reflection of the poor Christians in Korea on their experience of life. The Koreans say that the word 'minjung' is untranslatable. It is made up of two characters: *min* meaning 'people' and *jung* meaning 'mass.' It is the ordinary people. But as used by theologians, it refers to people who are oppressed—economically, politically, socially or in any other way. One could be rich but politically powerless or socially marginalized. Anyone who is in any way oppressed belongs to the minjung. The oppressors are the elite and the powerful, who could be native and/or foreign. In a colonial situation, for instance, the whole people is minjung. But even in such a situation, there will be some locals who collaborate with the colonial power. One can see that the minjung do not quite correspond to the 'proletariat' of the Marxian tradition. Besides the minjung, who are economically, socially and politically oppressed, there are the culturally and spiritually rich, the carriers and agents of the cultural tradition. They are masters of their own destiny. Their creativity breaks out in various ways and could even be revolutionary. They have been created in the image of God and made masters of the earth (Gn. 1:26f). They are, therefore, living a contradiction which is the origin of dynamism manifested in various ways.[1]

## THE ORIGINS

Minjung theology emerged in the 1970s. In 1961 the Methodist Church in Korea organized the Urban Industrial Mission, in which evangelists became workers in factories. This gave them firsthand knowledge of the oppression that the workers suffer. This was a period of fast economic growth in Korea. Industrial capitalism was flourishing, easy loans were available and export was promoted. But this happened at the expense of the poor workers who migrated from the villages and worked long hours in very poor conditions for very poor wages. Women and children were particularly vulnerable. Any attempt to organize the laborers and demand justice was brutally suppressed. This experience provoked the Christians to reflect on the meaning of the Good News in this situation. When a strong dictator, Park

Chong-hee, supported by the military and a brutal secret service, took over in 1971, the Christians, particularly the professors in the universities, were dismissed from their jobs and imprisoned. Many of the early minjung theologians have spent time in prison. It was from this minjung experience that minjung theology emerged.[2]

## THE MINJUNG AND *HAN*

Minjung experience is characterized by *han. Han* is the feeling of resentment, depression, repressed anger, helplessness, just indignation, etc., which is combined with the desire for a better future. Suh Nam-dong has described it:

> On the one hand, it is a dominant feeling of defeat, resignation, and nothing-ness. On the other, it is a feeling with a tenacity of will for life which comes to weaker beings. The first aspect can sometimes be sublimated to great artis-tic expressions and the second aspect could erupt as the energy for a revolu-tion or rebellion.[3]

*Han* is not a onetime feeling, but a prevailing mood. It is both individual and col-lective. It is not just an objective situation of oppression but people's lived experi-ence of oppression.

Two illustrations of *han* will give us some experiential idea of it. Miss Kim Kyong-suk was involved in trade-union activity and was killed during a demon-stration at the age of 21.

> According to the letter she left for her mother and younger brother, in her eight years of experience as a factory worker, she had innumerable nose-bleeds from exhaustion, and she sometimes worked three months without being paid. She had to live on, struggling with near-starvation, inadequate clothing, no heat in winter; and often she had only small thirty-won cakes to eat for a meal.[4]

She was even unable to go to church on Sunday. In her death, she embodies the *han* of 8 million Korean workers. Kim Chi-Ha gives us another illustration of *han,* but in a story form: *The Story of Sound* (1972). Here is a summary.

> Ando was a young man who lived in a small rented room in a slum area in Seoul. He was unsuccessful in anything he attempted. Whenever he tried to stand up on his two feet, he saw visions of a crime he was about to commit. In order to avoid the crime, he had to run endlessly. He had to run all day and all night. As a result, Ando was restless and tired all the time.
> But his trouble was more than just running and restlessness. He had bad luck in whatever he did and wherever he went. If he earned one dollar, ten dollars were taken away from him. He was robbed and beaten wherever he went until finally he was near starvation. Thus, one evening he stood up and said, "Damn it! This is a doglike world!" Because he said this, he was taken away and beaten by the police. He was then taken to court where he was pro-

nounced guilty. His head and legs were chopped off, but he survived with his trunk only. The court issued him a sentence of five-hundred years in prison. In the prison house Ando hit the walls by rolling his trunk. Every time he hit walls, it made a bumping sound which made the powerful people shiver and the wealthy people tremble. This was the sound coming from the Minjung.[5]

## HAN AND DAN

The way of resolving the tension of *han* is through *dan*. The author of the previous story, Kim Chi-Ha, describes *dan*.[6] It has two levels: personal and social. At the personal level, it is self-denial. One detaches oneself from dreams of a comfortable and easy life, seeing them as without depth and delusions that pass away. At the social level, one sublimates the experience and in this way cuts the vicious cycle of revenge. It can lead to social transformation. The process is described in four stages.

The first stage is to realize God in our heart. This realization motivates us to worship God. The second stage is to allow the divine consciousness to grow in us. The third stage is to practice what we believe in God. This stage marks our struggle to overcome the injustice of the world through the power of God. The final stage is to overcome the injustice through transforming the world.[7]

Korean mask dances, known as *mudang,* seem to be one way of achieving *dan* at the personal level.[8] The mask dance is a popular form, supported by music and involving dialogue, even with the audience. The group is spontaneous and improvises. There is a lot of satire, vulgar jokes and even sex-related dirty words. The story normally concerns monks who misbehave or noble men who act stupidly. They are portrayed in an unfavorable light and are made fun of. People have a good laugh in a world of fantasy that is close to the real world. The experience can be therapeutic. With reference to the mask dances, minjung theologians speak of a critical transcendence. By looking at life symbolically and in a humorous manner, people learn to step back and realize the relativity of their experience. People can laugh at themselves, too, and in the laughter, the tensions of *han* are released. Even when the people engage in collective action for transformation, this sense of critical transcendence makes them less self-righteous.

Self-transcendence rather than self-righteousness makes it possible for the minjung to insert a wedge (grace) into the vicious circle of the ruled becoming the same kind of oppressive rulers by seeking revenge.[9]

Korean women theologians suggest that women are the *han* of the *han*—the oppressed of the oppressed. But they have developed their own way of handling *han* through folk wisdom that helps their survival. Lee Oo Chung names three elements of this wisdom: present-centered optimism, the conviction in one's work, and the love of neighbors. There is no dichotomy here between the body and the soul, between this world and the next.[10]

## A MINJUNG READING OF THE BIBLE

This is the experiential context in which minjung theologians read their Scriptures. The experience of Jesus offers them a paradigm. Jesus identifies himself with the minjung. In a study of Mark's Gospel, Ahn Byung-mu points to a special category of people called the *ochlos.*[11] The *ochlos* were not just 'people,' which would have been *laos,* but the unorganized crowd that was constantly around Jesus. They were differentiated from the disciples and the ruling classes. They followed Jesus, but they could also be easily won over by the leaders and shout against Jesus. They were the despised tax collectors and those considered sinners either because they were engaged in occupations that were not approved of or because they were sick in various ways and sickness was considered a consequence of sin (Mk. 2:15-16). Jesus accepted them without any conditions. He ate with them and healed them of their infirmities. He did not seek to organize them and become their leader; he proclaimed to them the coming liberation of God's rule, thus giving them a new hope. Because of his option for the minjung, Jesus was put to death, but by rising again from the dead, Jesus gave them assurance of new life.

In the Old Testament, the Exodus is an obvious paradigm for a process of liberation, but the minjung appear in various forms.[12] In the creation story (Gn. 1:28-30), God blesses them and tells them: "Be fruitful and multiply, and fill the earth and subdue it; and have dominion over all other living things." If we remember that this text was written during the exile, then we can understand its power as a memory of God's promise when they were actually poor, marginalized and oppressed in a foreign country. The minjung are also the oppressed people in Egypt whose liberation by God is narrated in the story of Exodus. This story is also kept as a living and encouraging memory when it is narrated at every paschal feast. The minjung are also the oppressed people to whom the prophets Micah and Amos brought God's promise of liberation. In this case, they are not oppressed by foreigners, as in Egypt, but by their own people. To them too the prophets proclaim liberation.

## MOSES AND JESUS: A CONTRAST

Though both the Exodus event and the life, death and resurrection of Jesus are paradigms for the minjung, there are significant differences between them. Suh Nam-dong outlines these:

> In terms of the minjung, Moses was a heroic leader. Jesus was a resister who kept company with the minjung. In the case of Moses, the revolution was a success. But in the case of Jesus it seems to have failed, if we evaluate it in the same terms as that of Moses. Actually, if we use the term of "revolution" for Jesus, we must recognize the fact that the style of his revolution is different from that of Moses. In the case of the Exodus, the revolution occurred only once at a historical point, while the event of the Crucifixion-Resurrection was aimed at permanent revolution. In the case of a one-time revolution,

the minjung are the objects of salvation (salvation from outside). In the case of permanent revolution, the minjung become the subjects of salvation (self-reliant salvation). Moses answered the cry (aspiration) of the people; but Jesus was the very cry (aspiration) of the people themselves. In this sense, Jesus is truly *a part of* the minjung, not just *for* the minjung. Therefore Jesus was the personification of the minjung and their symbol.[13]

## MINJUNG HISTORY AS SALVATION HISTORY

Starting with the life and action of Jesus as a symbol and type of God's saving action in the world and in history rather than the only liberative self-manifestation of God, the minjung theologians re-read the history of the people to discern in it the ongoing action of God. Hyun Young-hak has stated their perspective very clearly.

As Christians we have to start with the premise that God, as Lord of History, has worked in and through our history and that God, as revealed in the life, death and resurrection of Jesus Christ, has a special concern for the under-dogs, namely the minjung. Otherwise, the Christian God would have no place in our history, in the events of our time, or for that matter in the future.[14]

Looking back on Korean history, they discover, first of all, that the minjung have always been oppressed by one or another power, foreign or indigenous. Koreans lived under the shadow of the Chinese and the Japanese. When they were not directly colonized, they were ruled by their own national elite, who were cut off from and exploited the people. They are particularly sensitive to Japanese colonialism from 1895 to 1945. But throughout this history of oppression, the minjung have periodically revolted against their masters. Suh Nam-Dong has chronicled these events, and it is not necessary for us to enter into detail.[15] The inspiration for this liberative activity of the minjung comes from various sources.

## AN INTER-RELIGIOUS LIBERATIVE TRADITION

In the early history of Korea, the Buddha Maitreya is seen as a liberative figure. In Buddhist cosmology, the history of the world is divided into different aeons. During each aeon, a Buddha appears. Among these, Buddha Siddharta, or Amita, is the Buddha of the present world. If we pray to Buddha Amita, we will enter his western paradise after death.[16] But if we pray to Buddha Maitreya, who is the Buddha of the coming world, he will help us realize the new world.[17] In Korea, while the rulers promoted Amita Buddhism, the people believed in the coming of the Maitreya, and this belief gave rise to many messianic movements, thus contributing to the revolutionary practice and belief of the minjung. It is significant that while Amita Buddhism supplanted Maitreya Buddhism in China and Japan, the latter survived among the minjung of Korea.[18]

Another source of liberative activity among the minjung is the practice of shamanism. The mask dances we referred to earlier belong to this tradition. Shamanistic activity continued among the minjung even when the rulers tried to promote Confucianism or Buddhism or even among the Christians. It remains a popular way for the release of *han*. Minjung theologians give shamanism a positive symbolic interpretation rather than reject it as superstitious. They relate it to the power of the Spirit, as we shall see later.[19] Shamans are often women, and shamanistic practices relate to nature, to the seasons, to the body and its sickness, to life and to problems of relationships. Through shamanism, minjung theology also integrates feminist and ecological concerns.

The Donghak religious movement was founded in 1860 by Choe Je-u (Choe Messiah). It is an indigenous religion, though it may have been influenced by Catholic literature that was appearing in the early 19th century when Catholicism was being severely persecuted. Its basic teaching was that humanity is heaven. This leads to a demand of egalitarianism in ethical practice. One Korean commentator compares it to the *advaita* or nonduality of Indian tradition.[20] The movement believed in an apocalypse when the world will be destroyed and a new era will emerge. This belief led the minjung to revolutionary actions, playing a powerful role in the Donghak Peasant Rebellion of 1895 and the March First Independence Movement of 1919.[21]

The final source, to which the minjung theologians pay most attention, is the liberative influence of Christianity. This is particularly noticeable during the period of the Japanese occupation and at the present time.[22] Though Christianity came to Korea earlier, the impact of Christianity on the minjung is dated from 1876, when the Bible was translated into Korean. While Catholicism used Chinese, the Protestants used the popular, spoken language of the minjung to translate the Bible. The Bible became the book of the minjung, and its liberation stories inspired them. One good evidence of this is that the Japanese banned the circulation of the books of Exodus and Daniel.[23] The minjung saw their own history in the history of Israel in Egypt.

In the interim period, the missionaries tried to keep Christianity apolitical.[24] But after the division of Korea and the rise to power of the military-technocratic complex, the Christians woke up again to protest against oppression, and their persecution by the politico-economic and military power only sharpened their reflection and their recourse to their Christian convictions for inspiration in their struggle.

## MINJUNG AND MESSIANISM

It is in this liberative tradition of the minjung that the minjung theologians place themselves. They see the movement of the minjung in messianic terms, but they give a particular meaning to messianism by calling for the millennium.

First of all, they distinguish the messianism of the minjung from the false political messianisms of the powerful and the elite. They point to three inadequate political messianisms in the history of Korea.[25] The first is the messianism of the colonizer. The Japanese, for instance, claimed to act in the best interests of the people, trying to impose shinto worship on them. The minjung, of course, refused to accept this salvation of the colonizer. Then the Marxist regime of North Korea promised liberation through the dictatorship of the proletariat. The minjung rejected this socialist heaven under the patronage of the party that dominated and determined everything, where people lost their freedom. After the division of Korea, the elite and the powerful of the South offered a new, technocratic paradise that turned out to be a paradise for the few, built on the blood and sweat of the minjung. In all these political messianisms, the people were treated as objects. They were invited to share in a future in which they would continue to be at the bottom of the social and economic scale, with no real participation in shaping their own destiny. The future would not be created *by* them; it would be made *for* them by the powerful. Political messianisms tend to be totalitarian and absolutist, based on a theory of contradiction in which the enemy has to be destroyed. They promise a paradise realizable in history. Kim Yong-bock's comparison of the proletariat and the minjung is quite illustrative of the differences.

> This difference between the minjung and the proletariat entails different views of history. Minjung history has a strong transcendental or transcending dimension—a beyond history—which is often expressed in religious form. There is a close relationship between religion and the minjung's perception of history. Even if minjung history does not involve religious elements in an explicit manner, its folklore or cultural elements play a transcending function similar to religion in the perception of history.[26]

The minjung theologians also reject the otherworldly messianism of religions that promise a paradise after death. We have mentioned earlier the western paradise of the Buddha Amita. The Kingdom of God in the Christian tradition, according to them, tends to be similarly alienating. Suh Nam-dong contrasts the minjung Millennium to the Kingdom of God.

> While the Kingdom of God is a heavenly and ultimate symbol, the Millennium is a historical, earthly, and semi-ultimate symbol. Accordingly, the Kingdom of God is understood as the place the believer enters when he dies, but the Millennium is understood as the point at which history and society are renewed. Therefore, in the Kingdom of God the salvation of the individual persons is secured, but in the Millennium is secured the salvation of the whole social reality of humankind. Consequently, while the Kingdom of God is used in the ideology of the ruler, the Millennium is the symbol of the aspiration of the minjung.[27]

It is suggested that in the early church there was a change from the historical and eschatological thinking of Hebrew culture to the cosmological and metaphysical worldview of Hellenism. With Constantine, the faith itself is co-opted by the ruling elite and the Kingdom of God becomes a nonpolitical symbol.

The Millennium of the minjung is therefore neither historical, like the earthly paradises promised by the political messianisms, nor is it otherworldly, like the religious messianism of the Kingdom. It is historical and yet transcends history. Earthly paradises are promised by the powerful. The minjung have no part in them. The otherworldly paradise will only make them passive. Often there is an unholy alliance between these two types of messianisms. The hope of the minjung is concrete and historical; they work at transforming society. But at the same time they do not have a blueprint or the power to realize this transformation with certainty in history. Their struggle is therefore a process, a permanent, unfinished revolution toward a community of justice, communion and peace.[28]

## MINJUNG, JESUS AND THE SPIRIT

The hope of the minjung has its foundation in the event of Jesus. But Jesus identifies himself with the minjung that is the subject of its own history and becomes its servant. The action of the minjung therefore is not based on power, but powerlessness. Or we should rather say that it is not the oppressive political and military power of the elite, but the creative power of the minjung. It is nonviolent. It is the power of the Holy Spirit. As Kim Yong-bock expresses it:

> The minjung are the permanent reality of history. Kingdoms, dynasties, and states rise and fall, but the minjung remain as a concrete reality in history, experiencing the comings and goings of political powers. Although the minjung understand themselves in relation to the power which is in command, they are not confined by that power. The minjung transcend the power structures which attempt to confine them through the unfolding of their stories. Power has its basis in the minjung. But power as it expresses itself in political powers does not belong to the minjung.[29]

Korean women theologians see Jesus as the compassionate mother who bears the suffering of all, a "symbol of females and the oppressed," though he has a male physical form; a shaman who liberates them from *han,* symbolically female, since shamans in Korean tradition tend to be female.[30]

The Holy Spirit, seen as present and active in the minjung in all places and at all times, enables minjung theologians to adopt an inclusive perspective that transcends what is normally spoken of as Christocentrism and ecclesiocentrism. The Jesus event is central, but it is also paradigmatic. Jesus himself becomes a cosmic figure,[31] so what happens in the life of Jesus becomes symbolic of the cosmic and universal activity of the Spirit in the minjung. If the Spirit's power is present in the minjung, then ecclesial structures become secondary, too. This perspective also makes possible the integration of some elements of Korean shamanism, which is built around the activity of the spirits.[32]

## SIGNIFICANT CHARACTERISTICS

As I conclude this brief and rapid survey of Minjung theology, I would like to highlight four characteristics that seem significant to me.

First of all, minjung theology is rooted. It is based on the history of the people.

The Bible, especially the Jesus event, is used as a key to re-read their own history as a people. Theology itself is seen as the social biography of the minjung. The social biography of the minjung is interpreted politically in the light of the Jesus event, but the purpose of the interpretation is not just to understand history (past), but to make it (future). The political interpretation is set in the dynamic context of the ongoing history of the minjung.

By being rooted, minjung theology becomes inclusive; it includes the earth, the body, life, the community. It perceives God and God's Spirit active everywhere and at all times in their history. This is not grand theory about the cosmic Christ or about the all-embracing plan of God or about the universal activity of the Spirit. It is a simple experiential affirmation that God has always been present in the history of the minjung. Such a simple affirmation, however, liberates Christ and the Spirit.

Both the rootedness and the inclusivism of minjung theology are shown in the place given to experience and its expression in story and symbol, in dance and ritual action. There is a silent distancing from the 'word' that objectifies and alienates. Once the focus is on the experience and the symbol, it becomes unimportant whether the story is real or imaginary, provided it is a symbolic expression of the lived experience of the people. The borderline between myth and history is crossed. To put it another way, the materiality of history is transcended without being denied. This approach also makes possible the integration of symbols, myths and rituals of popular religion. Since they are symbolic, they need not be branded superstitious or their integration syncretistic.

The minjung is action and future oriented. It is committed to history. The minjung and their theologians who have verbalized their experience have protested against oppression, agitated for change and suffered as a consequence. But at the same time there is a detachment and distancing. There is inner freedom. There is no compulsion of power. While the goal is clear, the process is more important than the result. It is very kenotic in Christian terms. But, at the same time, one cannot fail to see also a Buddhist, and in general an oriental, sensitivity.

# 2

# A Theology of Struggle
# from the Philippines

A theology of struggle has emerged in the Philippines over the last fifteen years. The Philippines is the only Christian country in Asia. It is 94 percent Christian, of whom 84 percent are Catholic. Muslims make up 4 percent. Though it is an Asian country, it resembles Latin America in many ways. It is not merely predominantly Catholic, it is the only country in Asia which has a past as a Spanish colony. This has affected not only its culture and popular religiosity but has also given it a particular type of agricultural feudal system.

## THE SOCIO-ECONOMIC AND POLITICAL SITUATION

The Philippines is a developing country in which the gap between the rich and the poor is great and increasing.[1] The poor, however, are of different types. First of all, there are the rural poor from the big plantations with export-oriented crops. These plantations are owned and managed by a rich minority. The peasants working on these plantations are poor, landless laborers, poorly paid and oppressed in many ways by the rich landowners. Land reform has always been one of the demands of the peasants, but the landowners either control the government or are supported by it, and any effective reform has been resisted.

The second group of poor people are the tribals. As the big landlords extend their plantations with government support or tolerance, many of the tribals are displaced from their own ancestral lands. They not only lose their lands and their livelihood, but their land-based culture and way of life are also affected. The replacing of natural forests with artificial plantations using chemical fertilizers and mechanized farming contributes to ecological destruction.[2]

A certain kind of rapid development and modernization leads to the growth of cities when impoverished rural populations migrate to the cities looking for employment. Thus we have the slums, with their urban poor eking out a living in a variety of ways but living in poor housing without proper sanitation and other facilities.

*12*

Their children are generally too poor to profit from the educational and other opportunities in the cities. Their nearness to the more affluent neighborhoods makes the injustice of the situation all the more blatant.

To these could be added other problems such as the exploitation of child labor, the oppression of women, sex tourism, etc. As in other poor developing countries, there is also the problem of international debt and the domination of international institutions such as the IMF and the World Bank, who impose on the debtor nations economic policies and structural adjustment programs that are not, to put it mildly, social minded and friendly to the poor. These policies only focus on increasing the gross national product, which in practice helps the rich become richer and the poor become poorer. This affects both the rural and urban poor, since it keeps salaries low and cuts funds available for community and social programs.

While the theology of struggle was in its formative stage, there were two other problems. One was the presence of American military bases, symbols of foreign domination and militarization. The other was the dictatorial rule of Ferdinand Marcos, who suppressed civil liberties and oppressed anyone involved in the conscientization and organization of the poor. Marcos was thrown out by the EDSA revolution of February 1986[3] in a demonstration of people's power. While the experience was positive in many ways and has restored some individual political rights, the aftermath has shown its limitations. It has also unmasked the entrenched structural nature of the problems at the economic, social and political levels. Even the political gains are limited, since the people's power has been hijacked by the traditional political class of the rich, who are looking after their own interests—in 'democratic' ways, of course. One could say that the theology of struggle itself has gained in clarity thanks to the experience.

## THE CHRISTIAN RESPONSE

Christians who felt challenged by their faith and the poor and wanted to get involved with the poor in their struggle for liberation faced special difficulties. The Communist Party's National Peoples' Army sponsored armed struggle for the liberation of the poor. Vigilante groups sponsored by the rich landlords fought the National Peoples' Army and terrorized the poor who demanded their rights. The national army was engaged in fighting the National Peoples' Army and minority rebel Muslim groups. In this situation, Christians who opted for the poor were quickly and conveniently identified with the Communists and were accordingly subjected to condemnation by both the church and the state. Such Christians had to struggle to keep their separate identity. In a concrete situation, they may share with the Communists a practical concern for the poor, even if they do not share their ideology. Their practical concern for the poor and social justice sets them against the government and its policies. It is in this situation that the theology of struggle emerged, as dramatically illustrated by the following story.

Edicio de la Torre, a priest at the time, found himself in prison, sharing stories with his companions about why they were there. Some were social activists, trade unionists, student leaders, etc. Ed. de la Torre's reason for being in prison was that he was doing Filipino theology—the theology of struggle.[4]

## A THEOLOGY OF STRUGGLE

Socially concerned Christians in the Philippines were certainly influenced by the Latin American liberation theology of the 1970s. One means of such influence was the participation by Filipino theologians in the Ecumenical Association of Third World Theologians. In 1976 there was a seminar in Baguio City on "Religion and Development in Asia," one of whose animators was François Houtart, who at that time was sharing with Asians methods of analyzing society and moving from merely development-oriented to liberation-oriented social action.[5] This started, particularly among religious, a movement of people who devoted themselves to the building of Basic Christian communities, programs of conscientization, etc. Their efforts to seek inspiration and justification for their involvement with the poor as well as for the action of the poor themselves, to explore a spirituality to accompany and sustain their action, and to do so in the Filippino cultural and religious context gave rise to the theology of struggle.

The coining of the term is attributed to Fr. Louie Hechanova. In a talk he gave in 1982, he said:

Some kind of liberation process is going on in our country in which Christians are involved and out of which faith reflections are beginning to emerge. To be more accurate, I am more inclined to describe what is going on as a struggle towards liberation. The faith reflections that have arisen could probably become the basis for a "theology of struggle."[6]

Liberation is the goal toward which the people are moving. No one knows what form it will take, or even when it is going to come, but at the moment what is going on is the struggle toward liberation. Everyone is called to get involved in the struggle.[7] The reflection focuses more on the conditions and requirements of the struggle than on the goal of liberation. Ed. de la Torre relates this theme with the traditional idea of the Christians being the church 'militant.'[8]

The theology of struggle is not 'about' the struggle, but 'of' and 'in' the struggle.[9] It is the reflection of the people who are actually struggling, namely the poor and the oppressed and those who have chosen to struggle with them. It is a popular theology, primarily expressed in the spontaneous prayers of the basic communities, in popular liturgies and songs. The *koreo* is a liturgical-cultural production of song, mime, readings and dance, often held in the streets rather than in churches. It starts with the life situation of the people. People have an occasion to express their outrage at their oppression, seek sources of empowerment, and in that search discover the God-in-them, the God-with-them, the God who would set them free.[10] The EDSA revolution of February 1986 was one such 'celebration,' with religious symbols such as the crucifix, images of Mary and candles; prayers such as the recitation of the rosary and the celebration of the Eucharist; singing of hymns; encouraging speeches by leaders; discussions with the soldiers.

## POPULAR EXPRESSION

The following songs, psalms and prayers illustrate the flavor of this popular theology. A farmer prays:

Lord of History, we offer you this soil as a symbol of the land we till. For a long time, we have aspired to own this land, so we can provide a good future for our children . . . Help us in our struggle, Lord. Give us the courage to continue with our attempt to have a strong peasants organization, so we can continue our struggle for this land.[11]

Social analysis can take the form of a psalm.

Woe to you
Who enact oppressive legislations
who fabricate dictatorial amendments,
who promulgate tyrannical decrees—
1081, 1834, 1835, 1836
1877, 1877-A, 2045
and myriads of secret laws,
who sign lopsided agreements
with alien vultures and predators,
depriving the poor of their due
and trampling the rights of the people,
increasing the number of widows
and multiplying the legions of orphans.

What will you do on the day of judgment
when the risen masses will end
your reign of greed and terror?
to whom will you run for help?
(US? CIA? WB-IMF? ASEAN?)
Where will you stash your loot?
(Batac, Switzerland, California?)
For all this, the wrath of Yahweh is not turned back,
the spirit of the Lord will subvert you unceasingly
till the end.[12]

The intimations of martyrdom are not far away, but they do not bring fear or discouragement.

I fear not death's spectre
Nor lament the bestial holocaust
Deprived of a proper resting place.

It matters not if my children
my wife, friends and kin
see me not breathe my last,
for they know the form of death,
wickedly devised by the powers-that-be
that awaits those who struggle
that divine justice may reign in the land.[13]

## A DESIRE FOR CHANGE

Ed. de la Torre suggests the basic attitude that is required for getting involved in the struggle. He distinguishes between people who suffer but do not struggle, people who suffer and therefore struggle, and people who struggle and therefore suffer.[14] Suffering unjustly is the key to the struggle. People who suffer but do not struggle may be passive for many reasons: they may be afraid; they may be resigned; they may consider their suffering as fate; they may even have interiorized the idea that suffering is the will of God for them; they may have been taught that struggle leads to hate and violence and therefore is wrong; or they may have been made to believe that to struggle is to be a Communist and an atheist. People who choose to struggle, even in the face of the suffering it may bring in addition to the suffering they already have, do so because they believe that justice is their right and that they are called to build a better world. As a popular song has it:

Long have I lived with illusions
That life is ruled by fate
Like a wheel turning round
One is up, one is down.
By why are we always poor?

Long have I lived believing
That fortune comes unexpected
Or bestowed by God
Ah these are all speculations.

I've thrown my dreams away
The heaven of the poor
We will have to build
Here on earth.[15]

## A NEW SPIRITUALITY

It is struggling toward this goal that provides the basis for a new spirituality. The Reign of God acquires a human and earthly face and serves as a criterion of discernment that helps us judge what are traditionally considered spiritual exercises.

Bending on one's knees
doesn't constitute holiness—Pharisees do.

A thousand ejaculations and halleluias
don't make a man holy—Charismatics do.
A brilliant exhortation of the calibre of St. John Chrysostom
doesn't add a single cubit towards godliness—
Demagogues do.
It is the collective witness,
the collective idea of martyrdom,
the collective struggle that makes man
fully human, fully alive, wholly holy.
To be human, to preserve life, to uphold its sacredness—
That is the quintessence of spirituality.[16]

Such spirituality, of course, can find expression in common reading of and reflection on the Bible, in songs and novenas, in Eucharistic celebrations, and so on, provided they embody the struggle from which they emerge and to which they lead. God is encountered in the community that struggles, so that the struggle becomes sacramental. The Bible is read with new eyes. When one reads the parable of the Good Samaritan, for example, one normally thinks of the Samaritan. But one could also stop to think about the thieves: Why are there thieves? How can we have a world where thieving will not be necessary?

The struggle situates itself dynamically between two poles: the experience of suffering and the hope of a new world. Suffering is real enough. The new world, however, is neither a dream nor an ideological utopia, because for a Christian it is God's promise. In a booklet with the suggestive title, *Where Are We Going! Heaven or New World?* Carlos H. Abesamis explores the answer of the New Testament to this question and concludes:

For me, *to inherit eternal life* used to mean: the soul, filled with sanctifying grace on this earth, will enjoy a life of seeing God forever in heaven, after death. . . . Similarly, for me, *salvation and to be saved* used to mean: to save my soul for heaven. Now I know that biblical salvation and eternal life refer to that fullness of life in the age-to-come—where I and every human being, having vanquished death, will participate in a new history of life-giving justice, joy, compassion, seeing God, being sons of God, and where God will be all in all. Today, working for eternal life is working towards that fullness of life for each human being—and for all humanity—on our journey towards the definitive age-to-come.[17]

On this journey God is with us. God is not a presence somewhere beyond or above. God is in the community, within each one's heart, empowering them in their struggle. God is struggling with the people. Reflecting on the EDSA revolution, many people ascribed it to a 'miracle.' In an imaginary dialogue with God, Ben Moraleda reflects that if by 'miracle' is meant that God somehow intervened from outside as some sort of a *deus ex machina*, then such a perspective is insulting both to God and to the people. God's presence and power were felt, not in some mysterious or magical manner, but concretely and tangibly . . . in the sweat of the Filipino peasant . . . in the grim determination of the worker . . . in the hunger and shame of the urban poor . . . in the anger of the tribal . . . in the defiance of the freedom fighter in the hills . . . and at an opportune moment . . . in the fearless men, women and children . . . in the courage and humility of a woman, Cory Aquino . . . in the confusion and disgrace of armed men . . .

This experience leads to a prayer:

And we know we can become like this—a truly nationalist people seeking and fighting for justice, freedom and national sovereignty, because *YOU*—who planted this desire in the hearts of the world, and who continue to urge and embolden us from within our core—*are with us, within us and among us, today and always.*[18]

## JESUS AND THE STRUGGLE

Jesus Christ has a privileged place in the struggle. His passion, death and resurrection become a paradigm of the struggle and hoped-for victory of the people. The *pasyon*, or the passion play, narrating the passion of Jesus in the context of the history of salvation, becomes an occasion for the workers and peasants to identify their own sufferings with the redemptive suffering of Christ. A popular confession of faith reads:

I believe that our country—like Christ—is also crucified by the selfish landlords who sit on thrones like kings. Even if land was created for all, for this was heaven's wish, our peasant's fate is one of landlessness. . . .
I believe that Christ rose from the dead. This will also happen with the oppressed. They will rise up, they will dream dreams. All will fight. The struggle will continue. In their struggle they have one wish: that they too will join in the attainment and establishment of the Kingdom.[19]

Edicio de la Torre painted a crucifixion with one hand open and the other clenched into a fist.

I thought how people are at the start—one hand open, begging for some relief from those above them, but clenched fists against each other, competing for what trickles down. At the end of the organizing process, the clenched fists are directed to their proper target, upwards. The open hands receive each other as companions in a shared struggle.[20]

Such a Christ is not an answer to all our questions, as traditional theology would have it. On the contrary, Christ is the question that should provoke us into committing ourselves to the struggle. The answer will come from the people, from us whose task it is to try to build a new world.[21]

## SEARCHING FOR A NEW ECCLESIOLOGY

Such a movement toward commitment and community focused on the people seems to go counter to certain tendencies in the church. This leads the theology of struggle to search for a new ecclesiology. The question can be agonizing:

> But why is it that the Church you called into being
> in this world has become a hard rock
> of an institution?
> It has massed vast capital and the least of
> our brothers are forgotten.
> Why is it full of forms, O Lord,
> but devoid of content?
> It thrives on dull celebrations,
> business-like operations,
> plastic relations.
> Oh, its heart is parched,
> not even a mist of poetry dwells in it.
> Lord, forgive me for these things that burn in me.[22]

The church is divided between those who want to struggle with the poor and those who see such struggle either as political activity in which the church should not be involved or as leading to a compromise with marxist movements. The former group was often suspected, persecuted and marginalized by the latter. Another unspoken division may be between the church of the poor and that of the middle and richer classes. At the EDSA revolution, the church chose to be political. But once the political dictatorship was overthrown, the search for justice was perceived as hobnobbing with the atheistic ideology of communism. The struggling Christians therefore are looking for a church of the people, a prophetic and serving presence in the community, open to other Christians, believers and all people of good will who are also struggling for the Reign of God in solidarity with groups of people everywhere who share the same dreams and visions.[23]

I have pointed to the difficult situation in which Christians who opted for the poor found themselves between the Communists and the National People's Army on the one hand and the forces of the rich and the government on the other. Some left the church and joined the Communist movement. Others tried to keep their independence, though foreseeing the possibility of a critical collaboration with the Communists on particular issues. This tension was also seen at the level of reflection. Some activists, without becoming Communist, analyze the situation in terms of the class struggle and consider some violence as inevitable in the context of the oppressive structural violence.[24] Others, however, advocate active nonviolence. Francisco F. Claver, for instance, while not excluding violence in self-defense as a last resort, speaks of the violence of the meek that does not kill, which comes from the strength and the gentleness of Christ and is shown in civil disobedience, striking for better wages, and so forth.[25]

## STRUGGLE AND CELEBRATION

The Filipino people like to sing, dance and celebrate, so their struggle too takes the form of celebration.[26] Their protest takes the form of a song. Liturgies and prayers are an integral part of demonstrations. As the protest comes out of a deep conviction and hope, there is strength, but no bitterness. Their very togetherness in struggle brings out their sense of community and joy of living. The very fact of their coming out to struggle is a reason for hope and celebration. Here one can see a spirit of freedom, even in the midst of involvement that the Minjung theologians called transcendence.

## NEW SOCIAL ANALYSIS

There have been developments at the level of social analysis which do not seem to have been integrated yet into the mainstream of the theology of struggle. At the time the theology of struggle emerged, the social analysis that was used was based on marxist theory and focused on the economic and political dimensions of society. There was a positive approach to religion and spirituality, particularly at the popular level. That is part of the genius of the people. In more recent times, however, there have been noteworthy attempts to broaden the framework of analysis. Brendan Lovett speaks of the centrality of culture, mostly with reference to the destruction of culture by modernity.[27] He also proposes a fivefold hierarchy of values, borrowing from Lonergan: vital, social, cultural, personal and religious.[28] This does not seem to have had any impact on the theology of struggle.

Francisco F. Claver points to the relationship between social structures and cultural values.

Social structures are the sum of permanent and stable relationships that make it possible for people in a society to interact in the economic, political, social and other aspects of life, in a more or less ordered and predictable way. Cultural values define what a people perceive as good and worth striving for. These values underlie the norms, goals, worldviews that move a people to act as they do, as well as the rules that guide patterns of social interaction and structuring.[29]

The process of social change involves change in both social and cultural areas. In practice, change may be more rapid in one or the other area, and this can lead to tensions. The impact of modernity has brought about a cultural crisis in many developing societies. More importantly, the kind of development promoted by many international institutions focuses mainly on material-technological aspects, ignoring basic values in the sphere of life, social relationships, ecology and women. A struggle for holistic human development cannot ignore the crisis of these cultural values, but these concerns, in the Philippines, seem to be attended to more by the feminist and ecological movements.

## LIBERATION AND ZEN

Another interesting development in the Philippines is the development of Zen in the context of the movement toward liberation, although its impact may be limited to a few and it does not seem to have affected the mainstream of the theology of struggle. Ruben Habito explains how the practice of Zen can contribute to a sharpened awareness of and commitment to social change. This reflection is the result of his experience with socially aware groups in the Philippines.

> Well-guided practice leads to its fruition in the experience of personal liberation in seeing one's true nature as empty. It leads to the attainment of wisdom, of seeing things as they are, without a tinge of ego-centered attachment. This very wisdom is the seat of compassion whereby the sufferings of all living beings become one's very own. And it is this identification with the suffering of concrete living beings in this very real world that is the firm basis of the at-one-ness and solidarity with the exploited and oppressed in their aspirations and struggles for a just and peaceful world, as we unite in a common endeavour to liberate ourselves from the violent and unjust structures of society.[30]

## THE STRUGGLE CONTINUES

The EDSA revolution has been called an exodus experience. But the hoped-for land reforms have not come, the poor continue to suffer, and there is no real popular participation in politics. There is disillusionment on the one hand; on the other, people realize that the struggle for justice is ongoing. The exodus was not the end, but the beginning of the long march through the desert toward the promised land. The struggle therefore continues, but with new hope born out of experience. This hope finds expression in the following prayer.

> We ask for faith
> to see that death and prison are not forever
> that life and freedom will prevail

> We ask for faith
> to celebrate even while we mourn
> knowing that death and prison
> are already signs of a people's struggle
> for freedom and life.

> We raise our voices in prayer
> through the bars, boldly
> believing that there will be an answer
> as our people awaken.[31]

# 3

# Dalit Theology in India

The Indian term 'Dalit' means 'broken,' 'trampled upon,' 'oppressed.' Dalit theology is the emerging theological reflection of more than 125 million people in India who are broken by the caste system.

## THE CASTE SYSTEM

The caste system is a way of organizing society.[1] A caste is an endogamous group—people who belong to a caste do not enter into marriage alliances outside their caste. A caste is hereditary: one is born into a caste. A caste is normally characterized by a particular occupation: farming, soldiering, commerce, etc. Society is made up of the hierarchical ordering of different castes. In India there are more than 4,000 castes. The caste is known in India as *jati*.

The hierarchical ordering is done according to a scale determined by ritual purity and pollution. There are four broad categories, called *varnas*. The *Brahmins* are on the top as the most ritually pure. They are the priests and scholars. After them come the *Kshatriyas*, the warriors who govern. They are followed by the *Vaisyas*, who engage in commerce. The last group is the *Shudras*, the servants, workers and peasants. Beyond the pale of society organized by the four *varnas* are the outcasts, the untouchable. They are fully polluted, especially by their occupations: they remove dead animals, work with leather, do cleaning jobs, etc. The Dalits are the untouchables and outcasts.

No one knows how this way of ordering society came about. The Dalits may have been conquered peoples reduced to slavery. They may have been simply the poor who were forced to eke out a living doing menial jobs. At some stage the Brahmins, the priests and scholars, assured their own social domination by evolving an ideology and legitimizing it with a creational myth.[2] According to this, creation emerges from the sacrifice of the primal person or *purusha*. Different classes of people emerge from different parts of the body: the Brahmins from the mouth, the Kshatriyas from the arms, the Vaisyas from the thighs and the Shudras from the feet. The Dalits are even outside this scheme, really at the bottom of the social order.

Once the scheme was worked out, it was interiorized. Continuity was assured through the principle of heredity and endogamy. There are hierarchies within each *varna,* according to occupations or economic status. For example, among the Brahmins the scholars are superior to the priests. Once the system was in place, there may be some mobility within a *varna* according to changes in economic or political status, but there is no change in the *varna* scheme itself.[3]

## THE DALITS

The Dalits at the bottom are really oppressed, broken. One can say that it is a cumulative oppression. Economically they are poor. When they are not engaged in traditional menial jobs, they are landless laborers who may end up as bonded laborers if they become victims of unfair lending practices by the landlords. Politically they are powerless. In villages they are at the mercy of the rich and the powerful. Even at the national level, they are a minority of 15 percent who carry no weight, even in a democratic society. Socially they are marginalized. They live outside or on the edge of the villages. They have no real equal social relationship with others. Common facilities such as village wells and temples are out of bounds for them, in practice if not in theory. Religiously, they are ritually impure. They have their own gods and goddesses who end up as servants of the higher gods in popular mythology. It is a culture of discrimination and oppression, accepted as social order and imposed with force. The women are particularly vulnerable, treated and violated with impunity as objects. Personally the Dalits interiorize all this and vacillate between unwilling submission and impotent anger.[4]

The social system is so strong that even other religions—Islam, Sikhism and Christianity—have succumbed to it. They do not legitimate it as Brahminic Hinduism does, but they meekly accept it as inevitable, at least at the social level. Many Dalits who left Hinduism to join other religions, hoping to escape the discriminations of the caste system, experience not only disappointment but tension because of the evident gap between a religious rhetoric of equality and a social praxis of discrimination.[5]

The caste system has not been accepted passively in the course of Indian history. There have been protest movements.[6] Buddha, in the 6th century before the common era, proposed his way of liberation to everyone, irrespective of caste. Bhakti movements have always protested the caste system. The Buddha suggested: "A man becomes not a Brahmin by long hair or family or birth. The man in whom there is truth and holiness, he is in joy and he is a Brahmin."[7]

Chokhamela, a bhakti poet from Maharashtra, laments:

If you had to give me this birth,
  why give me birth at all?
You cast me away to be born; you were cruel.
O God, my caste is low; how can I see you?

> When I touch anyone, they take offence.
> Chokhamela wants your mercy.[8]

> The only impurity is in the five elements.
> There is only one substance in the world.
> Then who is pure and who is impure?
> The cause of pollution is the creation of the body.
> In the beginning, at the end, there is
> nothing but pollution.
> No one knows anyone who was born pure.
> Chokha says, in wonder, who is pure?[9]

Given the strength of the social order and praxis, the equality religions preached was limited to the religious field. The accessibility of God to all was affirmed, but with no further social consequences. The devotion and God-experience of some Dalit saints is acclaimed, but such admiration is not translated into the social sphere.

During the struggle for independence from colonialism, the quest for democracy and independence raised hopes of liberation in the Dalits. Thanks in good part to the movement of Dr. Ambedkar, a Dalit leader, in the democratic Constitution of the Indian republic, untouchability has been legally abolished. They have reserved seats in the central and state legislatures and in government educational institutions and jobs. While a small minority may have profited by these provisions to better their economic status, social discriminations continue. One might even say that they have become worse. On the one hand, because of the rising awareness, the Dalits feel the oppression all the more strongly. On the other hand, the feeble efforts of the Dalits toward liberation seem to provoke more violent oppression by the dominant. Atrocities against the Dalits have only increased.

## DALIT LITERATURE

Contemporary Dalit literature pictures this situation graphically. Waman Nimbarkar speaks of the interiorized shame:

> When I knew nothing, I knew
> My caste was despised (low, despicable?)
> The Patil had kicked my father,
> Cursed my mother.
> They did not even raise their heads
> But I felt this 'caste' in my heart.

> When I climbed the step to school
> Then too I knew my caste was low.
> I used to sit outside, the others inside.[10]

Arun Kamble contrasts an Untouchable and a Brahmin:

> If you were to live the life we live
> (then out of you would poems arise).

We: kicked and spat at for our piece of bread
You: fetch fulfillment and name of the Lord.
We: down-gutter degraders of our heritage
You: its sole depositary descendants of the sage.
We: never have a paisa to scratch our arse
You: the golden cup of offerings in your bank.
Your bodies flame in sandalwood.
Ours you shovel under half-turned sand.

Wouldn't the world change, and fast,
If you were forced to live at last
This life that's all we've ever had?[11]

## DALIT CHRISTIANS

The Christian Dalits have become particularly sensitive to their multiple oppressions.[12] On the theory that the caste system is a Hindu phenomenon, the special benefits and reservations of opportunities for advancement and jobs are denied to them. Within the church, in spite of a rhetoric of equality proclaimed in Scripture—St. Paul declaring that in the risen Christ there is neither Jew nor Greek, neither male nor female, neither slave nor free (cf. Gal. 3:28)—and celebrated in the Eucharist, there are continuing social discriminations: different places in churches and cemeteries in some villages, denial of rightful participation at the levels of authority, and refusal of equal access to common resources. In wider society, the fact of their conversion to Christianity has not liberated Dalits from the oppressive socio-cultural order expressed in terms of endogamy and hierarchy.[13]

The fact that the Dalit converts to other religions have not been able to escape the oppression of social discrimination shows that the caste system is primarily a socio-cultural structure, not a religious one. Brahminic Hinduism justifies this system in terms of a myth and a ritual order of purity and pollution. Other religions, such as Christianity and Islam, do not justify the system but accept and tolerate it. This does not excuse them for not trying to change an unjust social order. There have been unsuccessful reform movements within Hinduism itself. Just as social discrimination and oppression are compounded with economic and political oppression, economic development and political participation are necessary conditions of social change. But they would not bring about social change automatically, as Dalits who are economically and politically upwardly mobile have found out by experience. The goal of liberation is therefore socio-cultural change.[14] The question for reflection is: How can religion bring this about?

## LIBERATION MOVEMENTS

Though the protest of Dalit Christians against unequal treatment, especially within the church community, is not new, a movement for liberation and theological reflection accompanying it is rather recent. This movement can be better understood in the context of wider and older movements in the country, which emerge contemporaneously with the movement for political liberation from colonialism.[15] Let us then take a brief look at these movements, especially from the point of view of the theological reflection accompanying them. I shall limit myself to a typological look.[16]

E. V. Ramaswamy Periyar launched a movement against social discrimination. In practice it became anti-brahminism and anti-brahminic Hinduism. He vocally advocated an atheistic humanism, though it was more anti-brahminic-Hindu than anti-God.[17]

Bhimrao Ambedkar was a Dalit. He declared that he had no choice in being born a Hindu but that he will not die as one. He became a Buddhist, encouraging his followers to do the same. It was, first of all, an option against Hinduism. Secondly, it was also an option against Christianity and Islam, seen as foreign to Indian culture and tolerant of the caste system. His Buddhism was moralistic and humanist.[18]

Both Periyar and Ambedkar are making a theological statement. They are not so much atheist as against religions and rituals that justify or tolerate social discrimination. This is a form of negative theology. The following poem expresses this well.

> On my birthday, I cursed God.
> I cursed him, I cursed him again.
>
> . . . . .
>
> Would you chop a whole cart full of wood
>     for a single piece of bread?
> Would you wipe the sweat of your bony body
>     with your mother's ragged sari?
> Would you wear out your brothers and sisters
>     for your father's pipe?
> Would you work as a pimp
>     to keep him in booze?
> Oh Father, Oh God the Father!
> You could never do such things.
> First you'd need a mother —
>     one no one honours,
>     one who toils in the dirt,
>     one who gives and gives of her love.[19]

Another stream of religious reformers reject the dominant brahminical stream in Hinduism but rediscover an older (*adi*) Hindu tradition that they claim has been suppressed by the present dominant tradition.[20] This older tradition was egalitarian, humanistic, anti-caste and anti-ritual. It is represented by leaders of protest and bhakti (devotional) movements. This can be seen as the reclaiming of a popular-prophetic stream of Hinduism against the dominant-elitist one. Part of their *credo* reads:

I believe that God is only one and . . . formless . . . Neither is there any book of His; nor does he incarnate, nor is there any image of His . . .

I believe that the religion of saints is the original religion of India; being full of humanism, it is beneficial to mankind. Spiritual experiences of such ascetics as Sadasiva, Rshbhadeva, Mahavira, Buddha, Kabir, Ravidas, Dadu, Namadeva, Tulsisaheb can deliver me.

I believe that all human beings are equal, and brothers. . . . Humans become high and low by their own virtues and vices. Human heart alone is God's temple, hence to practise equality toward the entire humanity is the 'supreme' religion.

I believe that according to the teachings of Kabir all the Brahmin's scriptures are based on selfishness, falsehood and injustice.[21]

Some other reformers attempt to re-interpret Hinduism itself. Shree Narayana Guru affirmed the unity of all humanity. He said:

One *jati* (caste), one religion, one God, for man of the same blood and form, there is no difference. Animals of the same caste alone procreate. Viewed thus all humanity belong to one caste.[22] God is the universal father of all and all life is His life, all activity is His.[23]

Mahatma Gandhi denied that the caste system is an element of true Hinduism. He considered it a satanic institution and a sin that Hinduism must expiate. His perspective too was *advaitic* or non-dual. "No matter by what name we describe Him, God is the same without a second and if we are all children of the same Creator, naturally there cannot be any caste amongst us."[24]

## DALIT THEOLOGY

It is in the wider context of these theological reflections in Indian tradition that we must set the reflection of Indian Christian theologians. Dalit theology is still in formation, and there are many voices.[25] I shall limit myself to presenting some typical trends. Some affirm that Dalit theology can be done only by the Dalits, who have experienced the oppression. A. P. Nirmal, for instance, speaks of a methodological exclusivism.

The 'Christian' for this theology is *exclusively* the 'Dalit.' What this exclusivism implies is the affirmation that the Triune God—the Father, the Son and the Holy Spirit—is on the side of the Dalits and not of the non-Dalits who are the oppressors.[26]

It is questionable whether the division of everyone into Dalit and non-Dalit and the vision of God, who is the God of all, as opting not only preferentially, but exclusively for the Dalit is a useful approach, even if it is methodological. Others do not think so. They feel that while the Dalits are the oppressed, the oppressive structures involve everyone who belongs to the caste system. The Dalits will not be liberated if the whole caste system as a hierarchical ordering of society is not changed. Challenges to the system can come not only from the Dalits, but also from others who are in solidarity with them. As K. Wilson has said:

> Christian dalit theology does not forbid Christian dalits from working with non-dalit authentic Christians, the renascent Hindus, the reformed Muslims and humanistic forces from various other faiths and ideologies, on a common human platform and thus hasten the process of establishing a human and humane culture which is why "the Word became flesh."[27]

It would be good to keep in mind this broad humanism, rooted in the incarnation of the Word and open not only to all Christians, but to all people of good will, of all religions and ideologies.

In developing a Dalit theology, A. P. Nirmal takes as a starting point the creed in Deuteronomy 26:5-12.

> And you shall make response before the Lord your God. A wandering Aramaen was my father; and he went down into Egypt and sojourned there, few in number, and there he became a nation, great, mighty and populous. And the Egyptians treated us harshly and afflicted us and laid upon us harsh bondage. Then we cried to the Lord, the God of our Father, and the Lord heard our voice, and saw our affliction, our toil and our oppression, and the Lord brought us out of Egypt with a mighty hand and in outstretched arm, with great terror, with signs and wonders; and he brought us into this place and gave us this land, a land flowing with milk and honey.

The figure of the 'wandering Aramaen' recalls the status of the Dalits as 'no people' who become 'God's people.' Since the Aramaen stands for the whole people, he is the image of the vision that the Dalits should have of themselves as a community. The sufferings of the people recall the oppression of the Dalits, so Dalit theology is characterized by pathos. The 'mighty arm' and 'terror' point to the need on the part of the Dalits to agitate for their rights. The land of milk and honey is the reward, not the goal of the struggle for liberation. The goal is human dignity as people created in the 'image of God.'[28] Dalit theology is also doxological. For the Christian Dalits, the move to Christianity from Hinduism is a liberating exodus experience. This experience guarantees an exodus hope for full liberation.

## A DALIT GOD

A. P. Nirmal then goes on to develop the idea that the Christian God is a Dalit God.[29] The Dalits are the servants of society; the Christian God is a God who serves. The Suffering Servant of God of Isaiah is the image of this servant God. "Servitude is innate in the God of the Dalits. . . . Since we the Indian Dalits are this God's people, service has been our lot and our privilege." Jesus Christ is also a Dalit. His genealogy (Mt. 1: 1-17) has some questionable characters such as Tamar (Gn.

38:1-30), Rachel (Jos. 2:1-21) and Solomon. As a Son of Man, he has nowhere to lay his head (Mt. 8:20) and suffering and death are his lot (Mk. 8:31; 9:12; 10:45). He also identifies himself with the Dalits of his day, eating and drinking with the publicans, tax collectors and sinners (Mk. 2:15-16). His Nazareth manifesto (Lk. 4:16-29) and his defense of the rights of the Gentiles in the cleansing of the temple (Mk. 11:15-19) confirm his dalitness. The final symbol of this is Jesus in his passion and on the Cross, feeling totally forsaken, even by God. The Holy Spirit will recreate the Dalits as she recreates the dry bones (Ez. 37). She also chooses the oppressed gentiles as members of the new people of God, even before the Apostles do (Acts 10:38).

The theme of God and Jesus being on the side of the Dalits has also been explored by others. A text such as Isaiah 3:15 could be applied to the Dalits: "What do you mean by crushing my people, by grinding the face of the poor?"[30] A psalm like 140:1 could be read as the cry of the Dalits: "Rescue me, Yahweh, from evil men."[31] Dhyanchand Carr suggests that in Matthew's Gospel Jesus is portrayed as opting for the despised Galilean crowds against the more sophisticated and self-righteous elite of Judea and the diaspora. Matthew also suggests, in the figure of the Canaanite woman (Mt. 15:21-27), that even the elite can obtain the Lord's favor by humbling themselves. Thus Matthew's Gospel offers paradigms for a Dalit theology.[32] Samuel Rayan sees in Jesus, rejected by his people and condemned to die outside the gate, a type of the Dalit people.[33]

## TABLE FELLOWSHIP

The table fellowship of Jesus, to which he invites the outcasts of his day—the publicans and the sinners (Mk. 2:16-17; Lk. 15:1f; Mt. 21:31f)—can be seen as a symbol of Jesus' saving action reaching out particularly to the outcasts of society like the Dalits.[34] There are no obligatory ablutions, as was customary among the elite Jews; no special places of honor; no food conditioned by ritual taboos. Jesus is there as a servant rather than a presider. But in the symbol of table fellowship, we notice a slight shift in connotation. Community with God finds expression in community with people. Table fellowship is the forerunner of the Eucharistic meal. The Eucharistic banquet celebrates the community of the new people of God. It is an affirmation of equality in community. God's saving love is reaching out to all peoples, irrespective of their economic, social or ritual status. These status differences not only become irrelevant but must disappear in the new community of the Reign of God. But this is not an easy process. Paul had to warn the Corinthians about despising the poor when they came together for the Eucharist, feasting by themselves while the poor were starving (1 Cor. 11:20f). He also had to oppose Peter for excluding gentiles from fellowship to satisfy Jewish purists (Gal. 1:11-16).

## A NEW COMMUNITY

The image of the new community of the Reign of God gives rise to another strand in Dalit theology. The stress is not so much on the option of Jesus for the outcast, but on his call to everyone to a new fellowship in which all are equal and there is no discrimination. It is a goal celebrated ritually in the Eucharist but to be progressively achieved at the social level.[35] Such a theological approach requires a shift in sociological perspective. The starting point is still the Dalit experience of oppression, but the focus is not merely on the oppression and God's option for the oppressed, but on the new community of freedom and fellowship, love and justice, which is the new people of the Reign of God to which God calls *all* peoples. Sociologically, though the Dalits are outcasts, they belong to a social order that is structured by the caste system, and true liberation of the Dalits will go hand in hand with the liberation of everyone from the caste system.[36] If God opts for the Dalits, it is in view of leading them and others to a new community of equality. The Dalits will have to play a role in this transformation by prophetically challenging their oppressors, not by withdrawing into themselves as God's specially chosen people, with the risk of giving a positive value to their dalitness.

K. Wilson takes a different type of communitarian approach. Starting with the reflection that Dalits are not merely Christian, but also Hindu, Marxist, Buddhist, etc., he suggests that we must take a human rather than a Christian approach, calling to his support the mystery of the incarnation. "No other example is more effective to testify to the human *dimension* of Christianity than the *example* of God's choice to take upon himself the form of a human being."[37] By stressing the human dimension, Wilson also transcends caste divisions. He asserts:

> Reality reveals that the real problem of Dalits is not caste, but the problem of their right to be human on their native Indian soil.... The Dalit issue has to be tackled as a changeable human condition, and certainly not as a caste issue.... It is the human right of every individual in the world to live in dignity worthy of his or her humanity.[38]... The need of the hour is for Dalits to set aside forthwith the problem of caste and bring forward the question of their human rights, i.e. the right to be human. The kingdom of God which is within every human being must be brought out. This unfoldment is the task of Christian theologians vis-a-vis Dalits.[39]

## LIBERATING PRAXIS

What can Christians do to bring about the new community of the Reign of God? Christian action has to have a double focus: the Christian community itself and the wider community.[40]

In the Christian community, every discrimination should be immediately abolished at the religious level. At the social level, making use of the Eucharist and Reconciliation as strong forces of inspiration, the church could promote inter-dining and intermarrying among the different castes, particularly with the Dalits, since these are the occasions in which caste discrimination is practiced. At the economic, political and personal levels, the Dalits should be built up through development and conscientizing projects. Religious communities are meant to be counter-cultural. Unfortunately, they are as caste-ridden as the wider church, so the religious could make a special vow of community to counter, consciously and spiritually, the caste system in the context of the Reign of God.

In the wider society, Christians could support the affirmative action programs of the government in the economic and political field, encouraging particularly political participation. It could focus its own efforts in moral and social education and action in dialogue and collaboration with people of good will in all religions. Here again, inter-dining and intermarrying movements could be launched. Nonviolent opposition against injustices and atrocities and peaceful agitations oriented to conscientization of the oppressors could also be encouraged.

# 4

# The Awakening of Women in Asia

Over the last twenty years or so, the women of Asia have suddenly woken up to their plight in life and society. Women's movements have sprung up everywhere, even at popular levels. They protest against their oppression and seek liberation. A good way of understanding the many ways in which women are oppressed is to look at the story of an average woman's life.[1]

## A STORY OF OPPRESSION

Even as a child is conceived, the family is looking forward to a male child. In some places, modern tests are used to identify the sex of the fetus, and a female fetus may be aborted. If a female child succeeds in seeing the light of day, she may still be killed in some areas because she is seen as a burden. Even if the child is not killed, she is made to feel unwelcome by the wider family and even by her father.

As she grows up, she is socialized into a male dominated or patriarchal society. The girl feels herself the weaker sex. She does not have the same freedom as the boys have. She is supposed to be submissive, passive, dependent, emotional, earthy. She is made to stay at home and help the mother in household jobs. She may be denied the chance of going to school. If she studies, she is directed toward service jobs.

As she grows into puberty, she is in danger of being sexually abused, even by her own people. If she is poor and has to go out to work, she is at the mercy of everyone and is paid less than her male counterparts. She may be lured into sex tourism or prostitution, often for economic reasons.

When the time comes for her to be married, her family has to buy her a husband by paying exorbitant dowries, often falling into irretrievable debt in the process. Even then, the husband's family may not be happy, and she may be subject to constant harassment and occasional 'accidents' that lead to her death.

If she is a working woman in an urban situation, she has a double load, as she has to work at home as well as in her place of work. Her work at home is not quantified, and even the Marxists would not consider her as producing surplus value by her labor. If she is poor, she has to go to superhuman lengths to secure basic necessities such as water. She is likely to be abandoned by her husband and left to fend for herself. Sometimes she may be a migrant domestic worker in the city, slaving for a family and subject to various harassments.

If she is in a rural setting, contemporary development projects that deplete natural forests, lower the rainfall and the water tables, produce pollution of all sorts and soil erosion make her job of gathering or producing the basic necessities of life—water, food and fuel—more and more difficult. They require more time and effort, and she has to go longer distances to find them.

In a patriarchal social order, she has no power or decision-making ability. She is an unequal partner in life. In Chinese and Indian traditions, she is dependent on her father in childhood; in adulthood, she is dependent on her husband; in old age, she is dependent on her son. Producing male heirs or work-hands is perceived as her principal task. Otherwise she is a servant of the family, subject to all sorts of domestic violence, physical as well as psychological.

In the religious sphere, she has no dominant role or authority. The dominant gods are male. Their representatives are also male. The woman is often considered ritually impure, because of her menstruation. She is the temptress, in the image of Eve. The submissive, chaste, hardworking, even suffering wife is held up as the ideal. Not living as a woman, but espousing virginity, is her only way of gaining a certain respect. Religious devotion and ritual are sources of alienating consolation for her. The phenomenon of possession in popular tradition is a way of releasing tension without in any way addressing its causes.

The concrete manifestations of these attitudes and situations may vary from country to country and culture to culture, but the oppressive structures are similar everywhere. A group of Asian women summarizes these oppressions in the following words.

We have come to the realization that these women suffer from triple oppression—as citizens of developing countries in an unjust world economic system, as workers and as women. Women are treated as inferior in society, denied their rights to participate in decision-making and to develop as full human beings. The low status of women is derived from their relationship with the male members of their families. Often women are victims of rape and other forms of violence. As part of the most exploited and oppressed groups, industrial women workers suffer as cheap, docile and dispensable labor. Women in the sex industry, often related to tourism and military bases, are used as commodities and are considered as social outcasts. Indigenous minority women have been deprived of their ancestral land and cultural identity. Urban poor women live in constant threat of eviction and economic dislocation and are denied their basic rights to proper housing, facilities and services. Rural women are forced to work long hours at home and in the fields and are often paid unequal wages, if paid at all.[2]

## VARIOUS TYPES OF WOMEN'S MOVEMENTS

In the face of such oppression, various types of women's movements have started in Asia.[3] Three of them seem rather prominent. There is a stream of what we may call liberal feminism among educated middle-class urban women. They model themselves on similar movements in the West. They focus on women's rights and gender equality with regard to salaries, jobs, leadership positions, and so on. They also campaign against particular issues such as the dowry problem. At the level of the church, for instance, they may demand priestly ordination for women.[4] A second stream is represented by the women's sections of leftist political movements. They tend to be limited to working women. Even work is defined narrowly as industrial labor; it would not include domestic or farm work. A third stream is made up of popular movements. Many of these have come up in recent years: farm workers, fisherwomen, slum dwellers, factory workers, unorganized urban workers, and so forth. They tend to focus more on basic issues of life: food production and marketing, ecological destruction, water and land issues, freedom from violence, and compulsion in personal and family life.

In terms of analysis, the first group tends to accept the existing structures but fights for equal individual rights within the system. The Marxists take a class approach that focuses only on industrial labor. The more popular movements are sensitive to the patriarchal structure that finds expression in socio-cultural organization, in scientific and industrial development models, in political power relationships, and in religious structures. They are not insensitive to issues of individual rights and gender equality, but everything is seen in a holistic, interconnected manner. One important element of such an integrated approach is the experienced link between the exploitation of women and the exploitation of nature. Vandana Shiva has expressed this well, pointing to some of the themes and directions of the struggle that oppose such exploitation.

> Indian women have been in the forefront of ecological struggles to conserve forests, land and water. They have challenged the western concept of nature as an object of exploitation and protected her as Prakriti, the living force that supports life.... Their ecological struggle in India is aimed simultaneously at liberating nature from ceaseless exploitation and themselves from limitless marginalization. They are creating a feminist ideology that transcends gender and a political practice that is humanly inclusive; they are challenging patriarchy's ideological claim to universalism not with another universalizing tendency, but with diversity; and they are challenging the dominant concept of power as violence with the alternative concept of nonviolence as power.[5]

Here we can see the themes of protection of life, liberation of nature and women, an inclusive humanism that transcends gender differences, insistence on diversity and the power of nonviolence. Underlying these themes is a vision of an alternate way of life and social organization. It is quite possible that popular women's movements do not always spell out clearly all these implications, but a close look at the movements themselves does indicate that these implications are not absent.

The images and structures at the religious level normally reflect the cultural vision, though religions do play a prophetic role of challenging current cultural structures. But culture and society normally succeed in domesticating mainline religion, marginalizing protest movements. We shall take up this point later. God is seen as male—Father. Even where there are goddesses, they are dependent on their male counterparts as their consorts.[6] Men are also the ritual mediators and control the roles of authority and priesthood.

## WOMEN AND NATURE

Today there is a growing perception that this domination of the masculine stereotype is also characteristic of the relationship of people to creation. The world is seen as an object to be used and exploited, without considering its proper processes of life and ongoing renewal, and thus leading to its progressive impoverishment and destruction. Science and technology become instruments of a practical rationality that is guided by the unbridled pleasure principle of consumerism and the profit-oriented processes of production and marketing that this gives rise to. Especially in a rural setting, where people live closer to nature, women have a close relationship to nature, not only analogically as producers of life, but as producers of food and users of natural resources, all of which are polluted, if not destroyed, by industry and commerce. One can see the close relationship between the liberation of women and the liberation of creation or nature from masculine domination. Gabriele Dietrich contrasts production of life and production of profits:

> We have to affirm the production and protection of life as the basic objective around which society needs to be organized. The present production and protection of profits which is the organizing principle of society runs directly counter to basic survival rights of the poor, of women and of nature.[7]

Aloysius Pieris makes the same link in a more 'religious' language. "Feminism is the summons from the universal human conscience to all humankind to restore the sacramental praxis in a world desecrated by instrumentalism."[8]

Women and creation are not only dominated and exploited by the masculine approach that objectifies and instrumentalizes them; they also share a common lot as the oppressed and are mutually related as producers and defenders of life. We shall explore the ecological dimension of this holistic vision in the next chapter. Here we shall limit our attention to the feminist perspective, without isolating it from its holistic context.

## A NEW SOCIO-CULTURAL ORDER

The liberation of women in such a holistic context would involve neither the participation of women in men's power positions nor the substitution of feminine domination. What we need to move toward is a new socio-cultural order that would be neither patriarchal nor matriarchal, but simply human. Human does not mean a nondescript neuter perspective that is neither masculine nor feminine. It means a holistic order that recognizes the true identity and freedom of both the masculine and the feminine and promotes their reciprocal relationship and collaboration in the creation and sustenance of life and society. Feminists are rightly afraid that talk about complementarity and family values may not challenge the existing patriarchal structure, only suggest minor adjustments within it.

For instance, the woman's role in giving birth and nurturing gives her a special place in the family and society. It also gives her a special responsibility in society. It is necessary not only to recognize and affirm her identity, but also to respect her dignity and freedom as a responsible human being and welcome her participation in decision making concerning all matters that pertain to life in society. On the other hand, some feminists talk about the rights of women in an isolated way within the existing structures. Movements of women have also discovered that it is ineffective to campaign against particular evils oppressive of women, such as dowry, easy divorce, and unequal property laws, unless there is a change in general awareness and social structures.[9]

## A HERMENEUTIC OF SUSPICION

How can religion help in the liberation of women? What is the role of theological reflection? The relationship between religion and culture is dialectical; religious meanings find expression in cultural symbols and structures. In this process, religions take on the negative aspects of cultures. On the other hand, religious meanings, in so far as they are ultimate, transcend cultural structures. This transcendence finds expression in Scriptures, anti-structural ritual elements, or in the words and actions of prophetic persons or groups. Prophecy is often triggered by the painful experience of an unjust situation that leads the sufferers to look closely at the traditional doctrines, symbols, rituals and structures and seek to re-interpret them in terms of the primordial, precultural or counter-cultural religious experience. This process is sometimes called the hermeneutics of suspicion. Nowhere does this seem more necessary than in what concerns women, given the pervasive nature of patriarchy in socio-cultural symbols and structures. It is not my intention to present here a thoroughgoing critique. Many have done so. I am also limiting myself to the Asian context and to what Asians—women and men—have said.

## OPEN FOUNDATIONAL TRADITIONS

Even a brief look at various religions shows how cultures have domesticated more open foundational traditions. Hinduism has patriarchal perspectives in the Vedic tradition. But in the Upanishadic period of reflection, the Absolute Brahman is neither male nor female. Its appropriate symbols are life, breath, light, sound, and so on. In the Bhakti tradition, not only is the Absolute seen as male and female, but women can become devotees. The Buddha opened up the path of renunciation to both male and female disciples. He showed the same openness to different castes, too. Christ's treatment of women was not bound by the prevailing cultural norms; Mary Magdalene was the first witness of the resurrection. Mohammed says:

Whosoever performs good deeds, whether male or female, and is a believer,
We shall surely make them live a good life and We will certainly reward them
for the best of what they did. (16:97. Cf. 33:35)

Women, like the wife and daughter of the Prophet, also played key roles during the
life of the Prophet.[10]

Cultures generally are in contrast to such open perspectives.[11] Starting with the
point of view of sexuality as something ambiguous, if not evil, woman is seen as the
temptress. They are also considered dangerous and ritually impure because of their
monthly bleeding. Even in tribal traditions, the witches are usually female.[12] It is as
if one recognizes their generative power and is afraid of it. They are objectified as
objects of pleasure. There may even be a hidden admiration when they are seen as
courtesans, intelligent and artistically accomplished. But they are used and socially
marginalized. The woman that is approved of is either chaste, unquestioningly submissive to her husband, or a virgin. In Indian tradition, Sita, the wife of Rama, is
held up as a role model. She is not only loyal to her husband, even when she is carried away by Ravana, but is ready to be tested in the fire, at the bidding of her husband, to dispel any doubts about her chastity in the mind of the people. Even after
the test, she is banished from the country and is finally swallowed up by the Earth,
her parent. This ending is perhaps a mild counter-cultural note. In the Tamil epic
*Silappadikaram*, we have the contrast between Madhavi, the courtesan, who finally
renounces the world, and Kannagi, whose chaste anger burns up the city of Madurai as revenge for the unjust killing of her husband. In Christian tradition, the contrast will be between Eve the temptress and Mary the virgin Mother.

## COUNTER-CULTURAL FIGURES

Indian historical tradition honors rebel figures such as Andal, Mirabhai and
Mahadeviakka, who defy cultural stereotypes and feminine role models by defying
social norms.[13] They declare their freedom from socio-cultural conditioning by
offering themselves to God in defiance of society—including, in some cases, the
husbands to whom they may have been married—and by overcoming the many
obstacles put in their path. Sexuality is acknowledged and made noble—not by
denial, but by being directed to the Lord—not in some mystical way, but in a very
emotional, human way. For example, Mira was married to a Rajput prince, but she
rejected marriage, became a disciple of the Dalit saint Ravidas and a devotee of Lord
Krishna.

Mine is the lifter of the mountains,
   the cowherd and none other.
O Sadhus! there is no other —
   I have seen the whole world.
I left brothers, I left kindred,
   I left all I had.
Sitting near the sadhus,

I lost worldly shame.
I looked at the devotees and I was one with them;
I looked at the world and wept.
With tears I watered love's creeper and it took root.
I churned the milk, drew out the ghee
and threw away the whey.
Rana sent a cup of poison:
I drank and stayed ecstatic.
Mira's attachment is strong —
What was to happen has happened.[14]

Mahadeviakka was devoted to Shiva. She left her husband and joined the company of the saints. She is said to have roamed around naked, covered only with her long hair, defying tradition.

Her nakedness becomes a symbol of defiance of accepted social norms. She exclaims:

People,
male and female,
blush when a cloth covering their shame
comes loose.
    When the lord of lives
lives drowned without a face
in the world, how can you be modest?

When all the world is the eye of the lord,
onlooking everywhere, what can you
cover and conceal?[15]

This is obviously a counter-cultural, prophetic stand that is not to be taken as the norm for everyone. But it does call into question accepted perspectives and values regarding women. It is taken in this way by contemporary Indian women.

We can see in this a model for the numerous religious vocations that the church has in Asian countries. It could be a gesture of freedom, in many cases. The freedom could be made still more meaningful if female sexuality is not denied but accepted and made fruitful in free, multi-faceted generativity oriented to promoting life.

## GOD, MALE AND FEMALE

Among Christian women in Asia, attempts to valorize the place of women in religious vision and praxis have focused mainly on the image of God, the example of Jesus, the figure of Mary and women in society.[16] Before looking at these briefly, one clarification may be useful, since my summary will be selective. The purpose of theological reflection is to provide us an alternate vision that can challenge the present unjust situation and inspire and animate our present and future praxis. It will be helpful to keep this goal in mind. It is sometimes said that many societies were originally matriarchal, but moving from a patriarchal to a matriarchal social order, even if it can be done, is not going to solve the problem of sex discrimination. The same could be said regarding attempts to revive and promote a goddess religion or female shamanistic cults. They may cater to needs for security or release of tension. As an Indian song has it:

> In this country, they say,
>> there are goddesses without number —
> But not a single link of our chains
>> could they loosen.[17]

They are eventually alienating and not helpful to the liberation of women. Similarly, in a Christian context, focus on the caring and nurturing aspects of Mary as mother or identification with the suffering Christ may meet emotional needs without being liberating.

The Christian image of God as Father is experienced as very patriarchal, but a careful reading of the Bible shows that feminine images are also used in talking about God. R. J. Raja summarizes a brief survey of feminine imagery with reference to God in the Old Testament:

> Israel saw her God not only as a Father (Is. 63:16; 64:7), husband (Is. 54:5; 62:5), protector (Is. 41:14; 43:14), warrior (Ex. 15:3), king (Ps. 98:6; 99:4), etc., but also as a mistress (Ps. 123:2), a midwife and a nurse (Ps. 22:9-10; 71:17; Is. 46:3-4; Hos. 11:3-4), a woman in travail (Is. 42:14; 46:3-4) and a mother (Num. 11:12; Jer. 31:20; Is. 49:14-15; 63:9; 66:12-13; Hos. 11:3-4; 8-9; Ex. 19:4; Dt. 32:11; Ps. 27:10; 131:2). Should we not then accept YHWH as the Mother and Father of our very being and acclaim Her/Him and pray to Her/Him as such?[18]

In the Indian Shaivite tradition, when the Absolute is seen as male and female—*Shiva* and *Shakti*—the female is the active, dynamic principle.[19] *Shakti* means energy, power. This power in the form of *Kali* or *Durga* can also be salvific as destructive of evil.[20] From this point of view, when we think of the feminine in God, the focus is not merely on the birthing, nurturing and compassionate aspects, but also on power as creative and salvific. This may correspond to some contemporary reflections on the Spirit as feminine in God. This is also linked to the idea of the Spirit as immanent (intimate?) compared to the Father as transcendent.[21] But I think that such attempts to ascribe sexual characteristics to the different Persons of the Trinity is ambiguous at best. The Spirit's role in the incarnation, overshadowing Mary, is often perceived as masculine. Aloysius Pieris speaks of earth and water as feminine and fire and wind as masculine symbols.[22] Traditionally not only water, but also fire and wind are used as symbols of the Spirit. So I think that it is best to speak of God as masculine and feminine. The best image of this is the Indian *ardhanarisvara*—the figure of Siva, male and female. But in terms of language and symbol, one should feel free to use both masculine and feminine symbols, as occasion suggests. It is perhaps significant of a patriarchal mind-set that people who have no problem in using masculine symbols about God object to the introduction of sex in God-talk as soon as feminine symbols are used.[23] Such a free use of symbols will also conscientize us to the fact that all our talk about God is always symbolic.

Such an approach to God as male and female would be critical of the spiritual tradition that images God as male and the human as female. This simply reflects a traditional patriarchal social order. It is significant that in Indian devotional tradition God can be imaged not only as Father and Lover, but also as Mother and Beloved. In this manner, all human relational and emotional relationships become capable of symbolizing the divine-human relationship.[24]

## JESUS IN THE CONTEXT OF FEMINISM

With regard to Jesus, many suggestions have been made.[25] Suffering women can identify with the suffering Jesus and see their pains and oppression as somehow having a redemptive value in union with the sufferings of Jesus. Some focus on the Lordship of Jesus that puts down every form of domination, including male domination. Some see feminine qualities such as nurturing and compassion in the life and miracles of Jesus. Others use more symbolic language to see Jesus as mother or beloved. I would rather focus on three other perspectives.

From a theological point of view, the insistence that in the incarnation the Word of God took on human nature, which it wanted to transform, and not merely the male sex, is worth exploring. Secondly, feminist theologians also point to the important roles played by women in the story of Jesus: Mary, the mother of Jesus; the rich women who accompanied and supported his ministry; and the apostolic function of women like the Samaritan woman or Mary of Magdala, who was the first witness to and apostle of the resurrection. Jesus' treatment of women—the Samaritan woman, the woman taken in adultery, the Canaanite woman, Mary of Magdala, and Martha and Mary of Bethany—shows that his attitude to women and their role in his work was much more positive and egalitarian than was warranted by the culture of his time.[26] One has the impression that even the apostles and evangelists did not quite appreciate this.

Finally, a poem by Gabriele Dietrich[27] makes a powerful link between the blood of the Cross, the bleeding women and the Eucharist.

> I am woman
> and my blood
> cries out:
>
> Who are you
> to deny life
> to the life-givers?
> Each one of you
> has come from the womb
> but none of you
> can bear woman

when she is strong
and joyful and competent.
You want our tears
to clamour for protection.
Who are you
to protect us
from yourselves?
I am a woman
and my monthly bloodshed
makes me aware
that blood
is meant for life.
It is you
who have invented
those lethal machines
spreading death:
Three kilotonnes of explosives
for every human being
on earth.

(Then follow paragraphs that evoke the suffering and bloodshed imposed on women in abortion, rape, birth control and domestic labor.)

I am a woman
and the blood
of my sacrifices
cries out to the sky
which you call heaven.
I am sick of you priests
who have never bled
and yet say:
This is my body
given up for you
and my blood
shed for you
drink it.
Whose blood
has been shed
for life
since eternity?
I am sick of your priests
who rule the *garbagriha,*
who adore the womb
as a source for life
and keep me shut out
because my blood
is polluting.
I am a woman

and I keep bleeding
from my womb
but also from my heart
because it is difficult
to learn to hate
and it might not help
if I hate you.

I still love
my little son
who bullies his sister
He has learnt it outside,
how do I stop him?
I still love
my children's father
because he was there
when I gave birth.
I still long
for my lover's touch
to break the spell
of perversion
which has grown
like a wall
between women and men.
I still love
my comrades in arms
because they care
for others who suffer
and there is hope
that they give their bodies
in the struggle for life
and not just for power.
But I have learned
to love my sisters.
We have learned
to love one another.
We have learned
even to respect
ourselves.

I am a woman
and my blood
cries out.
We are millions
and strong together.
You better hear us
or you may be doomed.[28]

This is a significant and powerful statement that needs no commentary.

## MARY AND WOMEN

In Catholic circles, particularly, Mary is also seen as a model of the new woman. For women, it is easier to identify with Mary than with Jesus.[29] One should, however, be careful about two tendencies. In popular piety, people often attribute to Mary all the feminine characteristics—caring, nurturing and compassion—that they are reluctant to attribute to a 'male' God. Secondly, attributions of titles such as 'Mother of the Church, Mediatrix and Co-redemptrix' may make us forget that they are talking of a secondary, unequal role in the project of salvation. There is always an ambiguity about whether Mary represents the ideal woman or is the symbol of humanity in its salvific dialogue with the divine. However, the images of the Mary of the *magnificat* and Calvary, of the mother who was an example even to Jesus as he grew up, and of the Mary of the upper room, around whom the disciples were gathered on the day of Pentecost, inspire many women.

## WOMEN IN SOCIETY

The final point I wish to indicate is the rediscovery and reaffirmation of the equal dignity of women in life and society as willed by God. In the biblical creation story, the affirmation that God created humans as male and female in the image of God, and so equal in dignity, is found side by side with another story that sees woman as a helper to man.[30] The role of women in the biblical history of salvation is not often highlighted. Besides the women we referred to in the life of Jesus above, we have the midwives who save Moses, the prophetess Miriam, and women like Judith. The genealogy of Jesus in the Gospel of Matthew mentions four women who stand out for their lack of conformity to current cultural norms in the working out of God's will. In the New Testament, Jesus talks of transcending sexual roles in the Reign of God and himself becomes human rather than male in his resurrection, since in the risen there is no longer Jew nor Greek, slave nor free, male nor female (Gal. 3:28). In spite of the reservations of Paul, women seem to have played an important role in the early church. This 'hidden' tradition is a challenge to the contemporary church.

In a wider cultural context, the liberation of women is really the liberation of the feminine in all of us.[31] The masculine and feminine are two complementary elements in a totality, variously symbolized as *yin* and *yang*, love (*agape*) and wisdom (*gnosis*), contemplation and action, cosmic and metacosmic. As Aloysius Pieris points out, *agape* without *gnosis* is blind; *gnosis* without *agape* is violent.[32] When both elements are integrated in a totality in a harmonious way, we move from looking upon the woman, the body, and the earth as instruments and consider them as symbols. This holistic perspective will become clearer still as we look at the liberation of the earth in the next chapter.

# 5

# In Harmony with the Earth

People all over the world have become sensitive to the ecological crisis, which can be summarized in a few words. Technology in the hands of humans is interfering in the natural processes of the cosmos in such a way that it is progressively deteriorating. This provides an unhealthy environment for all forms of life now, and earth may well become uninhabitable in the future.

## THE ENVIRONMENTAL CRISIS

Human energy needs for heat, transportation, all kinds of machines—from household appliances to big factories—are largely being met by the burning of non-renewable energy resources such as fossil fuels—coal, gas, and oil. The richer countries use most of these resources: 20 percent of humanity uses 80 percent of the world's fossil fuels, with no controls on their use. The supply of these fuels is not unlimited and may at some future date be exhausted. Water, wind, and the heat and light of the sun are renewable resources, but their use has not been widely developed.

The use of fossil fuels and industrial chemicals has unwelcome side effects.[1] They release gases such as carbon dioxide into the atmosphere, which is injurious to health and progressively reduces the supply of oxygen so essential for life. These gases also conserve heat and produce global warming that may lead to flooding due to the melting of the earth's icecaps. It might also interfere with the normal growth of vegetation, which requires a fine balance of temperature. One particular consequence of these unwelcome chemicals and gases in the atmosphere is the depletion of the ozone layer that protects the earth from ultraviolet rays. An increase in such radiation can be detrimental to life processes on the earth.[2]

Large-scale destruction of forests causes another set of problems.[3] Forests are usually destroyed for large-scale animal farms, for sale of the wood, or for developing vast plantations of cash crops like sugar cane or special types of trees used in industry, such as eucalyptus. A forest is a fine blend of macro and micro, plant and animal organisms. When a forest is cut down, these organisms are destroyed. Forests also have a role in the ecological balance of the earth, since they contribute to the regulation of rainfall. Where there are not enough forests, clouds do not condense into rain and there is less rainfall. This affects water resources as the water table keeps going down. Lack of water affects agriculture. Without the thick cover offered by the trees and vegetation of the forest, fertile topsoil is likely to be washed away by rain or floods from the mountains, which contributes to increasing desertification.

Big factories also contribute to environmental pollution.[4] Apart from smoke and water pollution, the accidents in Bhopal (poisonous gas) and Chernobyl (nuclear radiation) have made the whole world aware of the hazards that poisonous gases and nuclear radiation can cause to humans and agricultural products.

Chemicals in artificial fertilizers and pesticides may affect humans who eat treated agricultural products. Agricultural biotechnology, while it may increase production, interferes with the normal process of food production, upsets the nutritional balance, and also unjustly limits the rights of peasants.[5]

People have become aware of these hazards, and 'green' movements have forced governments and industries to take some preventive steps to protect the environment. The 'green' movements, largely a phenomenon of the richer first world, seem to concern themselves mostly with the environmental problems that affect the quality of their own lives. They do not seem to bother much about the global situation. Neither do they question the cultural attitude that leads to such environmental destruction or the unbridled consumerism that makes it inevitable.

## PEOPLE'S MOVEMENTS IN ASIA

People in Asia are aware of global environmental problems, particularly of tragedies like Bhopal, but not being big consumers, they do not feel too concerned about macro-problems such as global warming or ozone layer depletion. This does not mean they are insensitive to ecological issues; their focus is on concrete, local issues that affect their day-to-day life. Gail Omvedt points out that while environmental degradation is experienced at the level of *consumption* and tolerated because of people's instinct for economic survival, "it destroys the *conditions of production* of peasants, fishworkers, hunters, and gatherers; it affects their production process itself, not merely the 'quality' of their daily lives."[6] One could go further and say that consumption by the rich causes the environmental problems of the poor. Agrawal describes it graphically:

> A resident of Delhi who uses shirts made of cotton which has been produced in a field in Maharashtra heavily sprayed with pesticides leading to multiple resistance in mosquitoes; electricity from a dam in the Himalayas that has destroyed forests and blocked migration of fish; paper produced in Madhya Pradesh by a factory that has polluted the local river and logged forests in an ever-widening circle, disrupting the life of tribals; cereals from Punjab where food is produced using a technology that drains soil fertility.[7]

If one sees what happens in Delhi as 'development,' then one is forced to ask: Development of what, for whom? and at whose expense? It is from this point of view that one can see a number of people's movements across Asia in the recent years. Rather than offer a catalogue of places and persons, I shall indicate the major issues that people are worried about, with an occasional reference to a particular movement for purposes of illustration. For each issue, one can point to concrete examples in many countries such as India, the Philippines, Malaysia, and Indonesia. While the local circumstances are different, the orientations are the same everywhere. It is significant that in all these cases, the movements have a popular character. They are basically protests to defend life, even if the enlightened leadership later spells out the global ecological implications.

## DEFENDING THE FORESTS

The *chipko* movement in northern India is well known.[8] In the Himalayan foothills, women foiled the efforts of tree-felling crews by hugging trees. There are similar movements elsewhere where people are defending their forests.[9] In defending the forest, these people's motives are not primarily 'ecological.' Their concerns are vital. They are defending their way of life and their resources. For people living near a forest, it is a source of firewood, wood for their houses, fruits and roots, and water fountains. In many cases, it is also the abode of their gods in sacred groves.[10] With experience, they find out that once the trees are cut down, the rains wash away the topsoil and there is eventually less rainfall and slow desertification. They soon learn from experts that the forest is a complete ecosystem consisting of a network of organisms and plants. One can replant trees for commercial purposes, but one cannot recreate a forest.

Whereas a forest is for the benefit of the whole community, commercial plantations do not serve the needs of the community and are only profitable to the few individuals who plant them.[11] Some commercial trees, such as the eucalyptus, can be detrimental to the soil. People also know the difference between cutting down a few trees, allowing time for reforestation, and the wholesale felling of trees that destroys the forest altogether.[12] Here we see a triple problem. A natural resource essential for the life of the people is destroyed by interference with its natural growth and renewal. The real profit of the operation goes to the commercial interests who cut down the trees to feed their paper mills or plywood and match factories. In some cases, the community itself is divided. Men seem to look at the immediate financial gain of jobs and are not averse to joining the felling crews. But women are much more sensitive to the significance of the forest for their lives; they are the ones who go looking for firewood, water, or wild fruits and herbs.

## PROTECTING THE SEA

One of the issues that has been highlighted in India and in the Philippines recently is the problem faced by traditional communities of fisherfolk.[13] In an effort to 'develop' fishing techniques and increase the quantity that can be taken to market, two new kinds of technology were introduced. One is a net made of synthetic material that is not only strong but more thoroughgoing in catching even smaller fish. Another is the use of trawlers that reach out faster, broader, and deeper to catch whatever is available. The quantity of the fish caught and the cash income is certainly larger, but this income goes only to the few rich people who can invest in mechanized boats. The majority of the poor fisherpeople, for whom fishing is their livelihood, supplying both their main food and a meager income, see their income drastically reduced. The new nets do such a thorough job that they catch everything, even small fish. They also destroy the sea environment and fish eggs, so fish reproduction is interfered with and the fish become depleted.[14]

The poor fisherfolk get less fish to eat and sell; women lose their traditional job of making and repairing nets. The fisherfolk, especially the women, have been at the forefront of a movement agitating against the introduction of modern mechanized fishing.[15]

There are three issues here. A few people get rich at the expense of the majority of the people, who not only become poorer but also see their traditional way of life ruined. Secondly, nature's resources, meant for all, are monopolized by a powerful, rich minority, often with political support. Thirdly, the new techniques of fishing ruin nature—the sea and its capacity to carry on its normal reproductive process—by interfering with and even destroying the natural conditions in which this takes place. The use of this technology does violence to nature when people only look at the profits, without bothering about what happens to the sea, much less to the fisherfolk.

## DAMNING THE DAMS

A third kind of development project that has provoked people's movements is the building of dams.[16] Governments propose to build dams to promote irrigation of wastelands and produce electricity. Building a dam inevitably submerges land in the valley and displaces the people living in these areas. The people who promote the dam do not show much interest in resettling the affected people or paying them adequate compensation. Those who profit from the new irrigation scheme and the power generated by the dam are not the people who are displaced.

In addition, the people affected are often tribals; uprooting them from their land destroys their identity and community.[17] There is also a political aspect to this, because the interest of the tribals may not be considered the interest of the nation. The history of colonialism has been the history of appropriation of the best lands from the tribals in the cause of development—for others—through dams, mines, commercial plantations, etc.[18] People have resisted such projects, sometimes successfully. Sometimes it has been shown that the area to be irrigated is less than the area that will be submerged. At other times, people have shown that a smaller dam will be more ecological and more useful to the local people.[19] Besides ecological issues, these dam projects, like similar development projects, highlight the problem of the tribals, their land, and their way of life, which national governments do not respect and are ready to sacrifice in the 'national' interest—which always turns out to be the interest of the rich landlords or urban dwellers.

## PEASANT MOVEMENTS

Agriculture is another area where certain kinds of modern development projects cause ecological concern.[20] In order to increase agricultural yield, chemical fertilizers and pesticides are used. These not only contaminate the produce, they also destroy the natural capacities of the earth by increasing salination and destroying microorganisms that are normally a part of the process of agricultural growth. The result is that the natural renewal rhythm of the earth is interfered with and even permanently destroyed. Agriculture is no longer a natural process. It becomes an artificial, 'scientific' project, carried on with new strains of seed developed in the laboratory, supported by fertilizers and pesticides. The close, natural, experiential contact of the peasants with the earth is destroyed. With the development of mechanized agriculture and the growing salination of the land, the poor are forced out of their land, increasing the population of the urban slums. Urban ecologists may only see the harm done to their food by the chemicals used in agriculture, but the real drama is that of the peasants and, even more, that of the earth.

## POLLUTING THE ENVIRONMENT

The final area of growing ecological awareness that I would like to point to is the environmental pollution caused by industries, big and small.[21] Events such as Bhopal and Chernobyl are, fortunately, not too frequent. But people are more and more aware of smaller industries, such as tanneries, that pollute the air or water sources in their neighborhood. Popular agitation against nuclear power plants is also becoming more frequent.

What is common to all these popular movements is that they concern grass-roots issues of life. They may later develop into proper ecological movements, under the guidance of better-informed people, but they start as basic life problems. In this manner, they also remain relevant. They arise from the communities of the poor and the tribals. They may be guided later by middle-class leaders, but they remain the protests of the poor against the rich who exploit resources common to all for their own benefit and convenience. In every case, they contest what is imposed on them as the inevitable consequence of modern economic and scientific development. What is affirmed in the process are the strong links between people, land, and nature and the quality of life. Let us unpack these issues a little more in detail.

## HAVING OR LIVING

In the modern world, human well-being or success in life is seen in terms of having rather than being. Consumerism is the basic orientation. One is supposed to be better off if one has more things to consume. This desire to have leads to a spirit of possessiveness. Possessiveness is egoistic. Egoism leads to individualism, where the other is seen as the enemy against whom one is competing, either for scarce resources or a bigger share of the cake. Human effort is therefore focused on producing things that can be consumed. There is an emphasis on quantity rather than quality. Valuing production goes with valuing technology and industry on the one hand and monetization and marketing on the other. Technology and industry make possible the production of more fancy goods in greater quantities. A money economy (rather than bartering) and a system of markets facilitate distribution of products. Banking services not only keep the money supply flowing in appropriate and profitable ways, but makes money itself into a product that can be increased in the speculative activities of buying and selling. In such a context, development is seen as the more efficient production of goods. Income is measured in terms of money and products.

This way of looking at life contrasts with the traditional way of life, where humans lived in harmony with nature and nature supplied their needs. Even when humans produced their food through agriculture, hunting, or fishing, they respected nature and its processes of regeneration. Life was lived in community and solidarity. The earth was seen as the gift of God, given in common to all, and people were not allowed to appropriate it for selfish purposes. People were not against attempts to understand nature or the use of technology, but nature was understood in order to be better in harmony with it. The technology used was appropriate to the purpose. People were close to the land, the earth. Those who were using it for agriculture, for example, were respectful and apologetic. A people's way of life and culture were conditioned by the land they lived on and the nature that surrounded them. This may be a typological description of an ideal situation, but one can still find it among tribal peoples.

One can contrast this with the 'modern' way of life, which looks upon humans as workers. Humans have to produce; only productive work is appreciated. A way of life that centers around subsistence is not even considered.[22] Normal agriculture is not considered productive work, unless one produces agricultural goods for marketing. The normal work of women in the family—bringing forth and nurturing children and meeting the survival needs of the family through cooking, house maintenance, and so on—is not considered productive work. These tasks cannot be quantified and marketed. Subsistence farmers, like most tribals, and women at home, are not considered wage earners. Even the Marxists are not interested in them;[23] their proletariat are industrial laborers. Normal agriculture is not considered scientific. It becomes modern—industrial and scientific—when seeds are artificially developed and chemical fertilizers and pesticides are used. Fishing becomes scientific when outboard motors and nylon nets are used for deep-sea fishing. One can understand why it is women and the tribals who protest against this 'modern' way of life based on 'productive' work.

## SCIENCE, TECHNOLOGY AND VIOLENCE

A certain exploitation of the weak by the strong was not absent in ancient societies. To dominate a land was to dominate its people. The powerful profited from the work of the poor and the powerless by enslaving them. In a patriarchal society, the men dominated the women, exchanged them as possessions, and used them as a domestic work force.

In modern times there are new developments. Some would consider them a change in kind, while others think they are only a change in degree. One could discuss this, but what is important is to see that there is a change.

I think the basic change is the way people approach the world of nature.[24] It becomes something to be dominated and exploited, an object 'out there.' It is 'liberated' from both God and humans. God may be its creator, but God is not needed to understand and dominate it. The world is thus seen as an autonomous machine, and science seeks to unveil its secrets by discovering the causes of phenomena. Technology tries to use such knowledge for the production of goods.

Science has always claimed to be objective, but what it actually does is objectify nature. In order to study nature, science analyzes it under experimental conditions, abstracting each element from the natural and historical circumstances in which it is found. Some would claim that this is doing violence to nature.

When this knowledge is used to manipulate nature or produce goods through technology, this produces even more violence. It is one thing to discover nature's laws in order to live in conformity with nature, to better use its resources, or to protect oneself from it in cases of disaster or sickness. It is another to use those laws to do violence to nature, to interfere with its normal functioning, to exploit it greedily and unjustly. Contemporary biotechnologies show how far such interference with natural processes can go. This illustrates the ecological problem. A certain objectification of nature for purposes of study may be inevitable, given the nature of human intelligence, provided the process is not abstracted from the overall context of life. But where objectification leads to instrumentalization, we have introduced a dichotomy, not only between nature and God, but also between nature and humans.

This 'scientific' attitude that objectifies and dichotomizes is also extended to other components of life and the human community. Women are objectified as objects of pleasure and instruments of human reproduction. Prostitution and sex tourism, rape, the use of women as sex objects in the media and advertising dehumanize them. Contemporary biotechnologies increasingly devalue the role and freedom of women in human reproduction and make it a mechanical, commercial process.[25] One can now see why people see the 'rape' of the earth or the sea as going hand in hand with the rape of women and why the protection of the earth goes together with the liberation of women. Positively, both nature and women collaborate in the production and nurture of life. Negatively, both nature and women are exploited by the same objectifying and instrumentalizing scientific-technological mentality.

## OBJECTIFICATION AND DEHUMANIZATION

Such exploitation of nature and women also leads to the dehumanization of people, since it leads to the objectification and instrumentalization of people and the body. A scientific-technological outlook often tends to be materialistic, with no use for the spirit or transcendence. The human and the social also become objects of 'scientific' study. One seeks to condition and control them by the media and market forces. In such a world of objects, community has no meaning. The other is seen as a means to be exploited or used for one's own advantage. The law governing human relations is 'each one for oneself.' This is egoism on the one hand and isolation on the other.

The sense of community also suffers. The scientific-technological approach to reality privileges the faculty of knowing above love and emotion. Objectivity requires detachment. Science has no feelings. One can produce and sell weapons of mass destruction that maim and diminish people and engage in war games without worrying about their human consequences—feelings do not enter into the process. One can promote production and development without bothering about the consequences to poor peasants, tribals or fisherfolk. One can play the market, hoping it will adjust itself, without worrying about its impact on the oppressed. Even the Marxists ideologically only see workers and classes, not the people behind them.

The scientific-technological approach seems to believe in limitless growth. Bigger is better. It does not respect diversity of cultures and conditions. It does not believe in democracy, either: there is only one possible approach—the scientific one! It becomes increasingly global in its outreach. Combined with the liberal-capitalist ideology, this approach concentrates economic power in a few multinationals, forcing even national political authority to become subservient. The rich become richer and the poor become poorer. International bodies such as the International Monetary Fund, the World Bank and the World Trade Organization, meant to promote development and help the poor, share the prevailing ideology and are controlled by the richer economies. As a result, they only succeed in promoting maldevelopment and increasing poverty, destroying ecological and cultural diversity in the process.

One can now see the links between movements that defend nature, those that struggle for the liberation of women, and others that support the interests of the nonindustrial poor such as tribals, peasants, fisherfolk, and urban slum dwellers. These people are not fighting for better wages or participation in management or ownership, but for a different way of life, one based on a different way of looking at nature, humans and society. What is at issue is a conflict of cultures, if we understand culture as consisting of a worldview, attitudes, values and way of life. Liberation then becomes a struggle not primarily for economic and political change but for a cultural change, even if economics and politics provide the arena in which the struggle is lived out.

What kind of support can religions give to such a struggle? As in previous chapters, I shall limit myself to an account of current reflection.

## A SEARCH FOR INTEGRATION

Given the various dichotomies that have given rise to the 'modern' approach to nature, one can speak of liberation from such a perspective as a process of re-integration. This can be seen in its various dimensions. It is not helpful to hierarchize or prioritize these dimensions, even if we have to speak of them one at a time. They are mutually dependent and supportive.

The basic, englobing theme that one would stress is the theme of life in its various aspects. Humans cannot think of themselves as living beings without realizing they are spirits-in-bodies. No religion is merely materialistic. One need not engage in apologetics to prove this. It is much more a question of becoming aware of one's rootedness in one's body and one's ability to transcend the body. The body is not something that we have. We *are* our bodies, though we are not *only* our bodies. Our bodies mediate our relationship to the world and to others. It is in and through the body that we express ourselves and are present to others. The body also mediates our relationship to the earth. The body is of the earth. To destroy the earth is to destroy our bodies. The ideal, rather, is to live in harmony with the earth.

The Dravidian cultural tradition in India, for example, has worked out an elaborate homology between nature and humans. Nature is divided into five spheres: the mountain, the forest, the cultivated fields, the seashore and the desert. A particular emotion corresponds to each sphere: an aspect of man-woman relationship, a special musical mode, a tutelary deity, etc. For example, corresponding to the respective five spheres listed above are lovers' union, patient waiting, lover's unfaithfulness and sulking, separation and anxiety in love, eloping and separation from parents. This is more than a mere imaginative or conventional scheme. It shows experience and observation of nature and its impact on human life, creatively reconstructed at a cultural level.[26]

Humans cannot think of themselves as living, except in community. They are born in a community; they become human by relating to others and sharing a culture that shapes them and the way they relate to others and the world. The earth is the living basis or support of their lives together; it gives the air, water and food necessary for life. One cannot think of the human community except in the context of community with the world. This common relatedness is expressed in various ways by different religions. Hinduism speaks of the ideal of *lokasamgraha* or world-maintenance, for which each person is responsible. This is shown by the ritual feeding of gods, ancestors, guests and the animal world before eating.[27] Buddhism stresses the inter-relatedness of all beings and the attitude of compassion.[28] For Christianity, not only is the love of the other the new law, but Christ mediates both the original creation and the reconciliation of all things (Eph. 1:3-14). For primal and popular religions, the whole universe is linked in an ongoing stream of life. Human life is homologous with the life of the earth and its varying seasons. A broad community that includes not only other human beings, but also the universe, seems to be the context of human life.[29] This cosmic solidarity finds expression in social solidarity in tribal communities. Nirmal Minz has described it:

> Let us consider six ingredients in tribal social, economic, political and cultural life in our country. These are (1) Equality of men and women in society, (2) Dignity of manual labour in earning one's livelihood, (3) Community ownership of means of production, (4) Produce to be used for the common

good and not for individual benefit, (5) Consensus in decision-making processes in Society and (6) Facing life with song and dance.[30]

## LOVE AND WISDOM

In this context of community, we reach out to others and the world not only through knowledge, but also through our emotions, particularly through love—that is, in a fully human way. The primary relationship is one of experience, of being with. At this level, there is also a way of knowing that is intuitive, experiential. Rational knowledge that abstracts and objectifies the thing known is at a second level and must lead back to experience, not be absolutized. This might look like a philosophical perspective. But, as a matter of fact, religious traditions tend to stress knowledge or love as the principal means of liberation. The Hindu tradition, for example, speaks of *jnana* and *bhakti margas,* the ways of knowledge and devotion. Oriental religions such as Hinduism and Buddhism are said to stress *gnosis* or knowledge/wisdom, and the Semitic religions stress *agape* or love/service as the path to liberation.[31] In characterizing Oriental traditions as gnostic, one may forget the *bhakti* stream of Hinduism and the compassion of the Buddha, not to speak of the various primal traditions. This dimension of love and compassion finds expression in the spirit of nonviolence toward all forms of life.[32] We have seen that knowledge without love can be violent. Love without knowledge is blind. The need is to integrate both. Aloysius Pieris has spelled this out well.

> Science or knowledge, divorced from love, has become brutal by mating with power.... Both women and nature were reduced to the level of things to be known, tools to be used, machines to be managed and of course, prospective victims of rape. If love without knowledge is blind, knowledge without love is beastly. The lover who is armed with knowledge *empowers* the loved one; the knower who is starved of love *steals power* from the object known. Love enlightened by knowledge invariably turns even *things into persons;* but knowledge untouched by love treats even *persons as things.*[33]

Though some would like to credit Christianity with the merit of promoting modern science and development, the dichotomies that are characteristic of modern science and technology have more to do with Greek culture, in which the gnostic traditions of Indian culture also share, than with Christianity. Today there are efforts to develop a theology of creation as mediating the presence, power and glory of God and of humans as called to care for the earth and to be its stewards.[34] Such a view also offers the foundation of a new ethic that focuses on sustainable development and equitable sharing of the earth's goods.[35]

In theistic traditions that affirm life, God is seen as the source of life. The relationship between God and the world and humanity has been visualized in different ways. Some have divinized the earth as the Great Mother. Others think of a transcendent God who gives life but is cut off from creation. But theistic traditions such as Hinduism and Christianity affirm God as both immanent and transcendent. The

Hindu vision of *advaita* speaks of the deep unity of all being. Though some explanations of it may seem monistic, other traditions speak of a unity in pluralism of which the human becomes the symbol.[36] The world is then seen as the body of God, affirming unity and dependence.[37] The Christian tradition speaks in terms of a community through the mediation of the Word and the Spirit. St. Paul speaks of the world as the body of Christ (Col. 1:15-20). The Bishops of the Philippines, in a special pastoral letter on environmental issues, stress this.

> Our faith tells us that Christ is the center point of human history and creation. All the rich unfolding of the universe and the emergence and flowering of life on Earth are centered on him (Eph. 1:9-10; Col. 1:16-17). The destruction of any part of creation, especially the extinction of species, defaces the image of Christ which is etched in creation.[38]

What all these images point to is a cosmotheandric community that unites God, humans and the universe.[39] The project of God is the sharing of God's life, creative of community. Humans mediate this community. God facilitates this mediation by becoming human. In the process, nature finds conscious awareness and self-expression in humans, who enter into a communion of knowledge and love with each other and with God. The centrality of humans is obvious, but the basic life force is that of God. Humans mediate their self-expression and community in and through nature by the use of technology, however, humans can abuse technology by using it to divide and dominate. Such domination, driven by egoism, shown in self-love and search for power, destroys both nature and community and frustrates God's purpose. Properly used, the cosmos is neither objectified nor deified, but becomes sacramental. It becomes the symbolic mediation of human-human and human-divine encounter.

PART TWO

# RELIGIONS FOR LIBERATION

# 6

# Hinduism and Liberation

Hinduism is popularly thought to be focused on the other world, tolerating injustice and inequality in this one. *Sannyasa* (renunciation) is seen as the ideal for humans. Beliefs in *karma* and rebirth seem to make society immobile. The theory of *karma* explains that what we are undergoing now in this world is the fruit of past actions, good and bad. Such a past is not limited to the present life but also includes former lives. If one acts well in this life, one can improve one's status, at least in a future, and move progressively toward ultimate liberation. Such a cause-effect chain makes people accept their position in the present life with resignation, without seeking to better it. Social change, therefore, is not a desired goal, so Hinduism is considered fatalistic and impervious to winds of change.

It is true that there is an ambiguity at the heart of the dominant classical Hindu tradition. It speaks of four goals and four stages in life. Each person is supposed to go through, in the course of his life, the stages of *brahmacharya* (the student pursuing knowledge and initiated into the traditions of the group), *grihasta* (the householder contributing to the maintenance of life and relationships in the world), *vanaprasta* (the forest-dweller living in retirement, often communicating one's skills to others) and *sannyasa* (the renouncer who wanders around, thinking of and preparing for the afterlife). This fourfold division overlaps somewhat with the four goals in life that each person is supposed to pursue: *dharma* (righteousness, which regulates all human and cosmic activity), *artha* (wealth or well-being), *kama* (love in marriage) and *moksha* (final liberation). Obviously, these four goals cannot be pursued simultaneously. Only *dharma* regulates activity at all stages, even during pursuit of the other three goals. Quite early in the development of tradition, *moksha*, as the ultimate goal in life, took precedence over *artha* and *kama*, so some people go directly from the stage of *brahmacharya* to that of *sannyasa*. This highlighting of ultimate liberation as freedom from life in this world relativizes life here and now. Therefore both commitment to life and its normal processes and an urge to renounce it are part of the tradition.

The goal of salvation/liberation movements in the past, then, was the search, either through personal effort or through divine grace, to escape the cycle of rebirth and attain ultimate liberation. Liberation had no reference to life in this world; that is to say, it had no social, political or economic implications.

This picture of life in Hinduism, however, is not true in practice for the majority of people: the lower castes are not permitted to accede to *sannyasa*. For them, the ideal is more ideological than real. Peasant movements and wars for political and social liberation were not unknown.[1] Some religious movements such as the Bhakti movements in Hinduism and the emergence of Sikhism can be linked to a desire for social liberation. The conversion of outcastes to Islam or Christianity were also efforts, often unsuccessful, of social liberation. In any case, the experience of colonialism and the impact of European civilization that it mediated have challenged the Hindu tradition to change and given birth to movements for liberation.

In the 19th century, as a reaction to the impact of the West and a counterpoint to the efforts of missionaries to propagate Christianity, a movement for religio-cultural reform was led by people like Raja Ram Mohan Roy. There was, on the one hand, an effort to purify religion of superstitions and highlight monotheism. On the other hand, there were campaigns to abolish social practices such as *sati* (the burning of widows on the funeral pyre of their dead husbands) and child marriage and to promote other practices like widow remarriage. These movements slowly provoked a movement for political liberation, though in the beginning the aim was limited to some form of political autonomy. It is at this time that Gandhi burst on the scene.

## MOHANDAS KARAMCHAND GANDHI (1869 - 1948)

Gandhi was born in Porbandar, in western India, in 1869 to a family that had given many prime ministers to the small autonomous princely states in the region.[2] The family was devoutly Hindu. Gandhi also absorbed influences from Jainism, which was quite prevalent in the region. Jainism was founded by Mahavira, an elder contemporary of the Buddha, and its chief tenets included *anekanthavada* (the many-sidedness of truth), *ahimsa* (nonviolence), and practices of self-discipline such as fasting. Early in life, he seems to have realized the value of truthfulness. He also learned from his father the value of love, rather than violence, as a reformative force. He went to London for legal studies (1887-1891) and there, in contacts with the theosophists, he discovered not only the *Bhagavad Gita*, but also the Gospels and the doctrines of other religions such as Buddhism and Islam. On his return to India, he went to South Africa (1891-1914). There he progressively took up the leadership of the Indian community in their fight for equality and freedom and developed the nonviolent technique of struggle that he called *satyagraha* (clinging to truth). He also experimented with the *ashram* as a place of common life where the volunteers who had to engage in *satyagraha* could be trained in life and action based on truth and nonviolence. He translated Ruskin's *Unto This Last* into Gujarati as *Sarvodaya* (the awakening or welfare of all), which will become an image of the ideal society. He also took the vow of *brahmacharya* (chastity), after an early marriage and children, as a symbolic effort to renounce household cares and devote himself fully to the service of the community.[3] In 1908, he wrote *Hind Swaraj* (Indian freedom), in which he criticized the materialistic industrial civilization of the West, contrasting it with the spirituality and simple living of the Indian tradition. He saw the medical and legal professions as particularly exploitative.

With this experience and preparation, he landed in India in 1914. He slowly and progressively took over the leadership of the Indian National Congress and made it a mass movement for total liberation. He further perfected his technique of *satyagraha,* continued his experiments with the *ashrams,* and made effective use of fasting, both as a means of self-discipline and as a political weapon, particularly to force negotiations in tense situations. He introduced the notion of civil disobedience on the principle that no one is obliged to obey unjust laws. He also campaigned for the abolition of untouchability and for inter-religious, particularly Hindu-Muslim, harmony. His march to the sea to make salt, in defiance of a law forbidding it, and his efforts, including fasting, to bring peace among the warring Muslims and Hindus in Calcutta are justifiably famous and symbolic of many similar movements. He sought to promote nationalism and self-reliance through the *swadeshi* movement, advocating among other things the preparation of one's own dress through spinning. The freedom for which he had led the people's struggle came (August 15, 1947) with bloodshed because of the division of the country into Pakistan and India along religious lines. He died a martyr at the hands of a Hindu fanatic (January 30, 1948) as he was on his way to an inter-religious prayer service.

### *A Vision of Integral Liberation*

Gandhi's goal for India can be called integral liberation based on a perspective of spiritual humanism. Gandhi does not talk about 'integral liberation,' but his writings and actions attest to his interest in the total liberation of every human and society.[4] Gandhi speaks of his dream for India in the following words:

> I shall strive for a constitution, which will release India from all thraldom and patronage, and give her, if need be, the right to sin. I shall work for an India, in which the poorest shall feel that it is their country in whose making they have an effective voice; an India in which there shall be no high class and low class of people; an India in which all communities shall live in perfect harmony. There can be no room in such an India for the curse of untouchability or the curse of intoxicating drinks and drugs. Women will enjoy the same rights as men. Since we shall be at peace with all the rest of the world, neither exploiting, nor being exploited, we shall have the smallest army imaginable. All interests not in conflict with the interests of the dumb millions will be scrupulously respected, whether foreign or indigenous . . . This is the India of my dreams.[5]

The immediate goal that Gandhi did achieve was political freedom for India. Gandhi came to believe that freedom from colonialism was the only proper ground on which to construct a new India. He repeated often that no program of action can be imposed on the people; people have to be convinced to take them up freely, or they will neither be in accordance with human dignity nor really effective. Gandhi believed in democracy, but not a huge government apparatus. He spoke of basic democracy, in which each village would be a self-sufficient, autonomous unit, responsible for meeting the basic needs of its people for food, clothing, housing, education and health care.

At the social level, Gandhi was for communal harmony, particularly among Hindus and Muslims, based on mutual tolerance, understanding and collaboration for the well-being of all. He was responsible for bringing women into the national movement and hoped it would liberate them from social and cultural oppression. He was opposed to untouchability and worked constantly for its abolition in theory and practice. He affirmed the untouchables' identity and equality as *harijan*, or children of God. He worked to open the temples to the untouchables and fought everything that sought to set them apart in the name of their caste status, though he did not oppose affirmative action in their favor that offered them educational and job opportunities. He also promoted prohibition of alcoholic drinks, as they destroyed and impoverished poor families.

Economically, he was for promoting equality. He believed in the doctrine of trusteeship, according to which the rich hold what they have not as their own, but as trustees for the welfare of all people. He was also for organizing peasants and laborers in a nonviolent struggle for equal distribution of goods and the ability to look after their own basic needs in a cooperative manner. Though he was not against machines, he was against materialistic industrialization that dehumanized people, enslaved them through mechanization, multiplied their wants, promoted consumerism, destroyed basic village industries, and increased unemployment and the inequality between rich capitalists and poor, exploited workers. For him, the spinning wheel was a symbol of economic self-reliance.

In the realm of culture, Gandhi was nationalistic in spirit, affirming the superiority of Indian cultural traditions to those of the West. He promoted a simple way of life in harmony with nature. He wanted to make education available to all, but education has to be in consonance with the real needs of the people and based on the living experience of the students. He encouraged the education of women and discouraged students from taking part in politics in detriment to their task of research and inquiry.

With regard to persons, he was for self-control and simplicity. He believed in self-discipline through the practice of fasting and prayer. He suggested five rules of self-restraint: *brahmacharya* (celibacy), *satya* (truthfulness), *ahimsa* (love or nonviolence), *asteya* (not stealing) and *aparigraha* (nonpossession).[6] He thought that violence brought out the animal in humans.

In the field of religion, though he himself was rooted in Hinduism, he developed a religious perspective that was deeply moral. From this point of view, he saw a convergence among religions and propagated inter-religious harmony, believers encouraging each other in the pursuit of truth through nonviolent action. He held inter-religious prayer meetings, where passages from different scriptures were read and people prayed together for peace and fellowship. For him, religion was not mysticism, but promoted practical moral behavior. That is why he saw the intimate relation between religion and politics and saw his own political actions as steps in a spiritual quest.

One can see that Gandhi had an integral vision of being human in community that guided his actions. What are the kind of religious perspectives on which Gandhi based his integral spiritual humanism?

Though Gandhi nourished himself from various religious sources, he remained loyal to his roots as a Hindu. Hinduism is not an organized, institutionalized religion, so Gandhi was able to develop his own brand of Hinduism, interpreting traditional Hindu perspectives in his own way.

### The Goal of Life: Truth

Given the Vaishnavite background of his family, he called God Ram, though he claimed that, for him, it did not refer to any historical incarnation. The ideal society for which he was working in the world was *Ramrajya*, or the Kingdom of Ram, which can be considered the equivalent of the Kingdom of God. But *Ramrajya* was the object of eschatological hope for many Hindus, and in this way he immediately tapped into their religious resources in support of his socio-political projects.

Ideologically, God was, for him, truth. The Sanskrit word for truth is *satya*, which includes the term *sat*, which also means 'being.' So *satya* is really what simply *is*. It embraces the whole of being. At the same time, the term 'truth' has a moral tone to it. To search for truth is to be truthful. It is from this word that we also have *satyagraha*. In other words, truth stands for being—the universe or society—as it ought to be according to its nature. If human actions are not in accord with it, then these actions have to be opposed so that truth can be. We can do this only by 'clinging to truth.' To follow truth or to be truthful is simply to *be*. Here 'being' has not only an ontological, but a moral significance, with consequences for our actions individually and as a group.

To attain truth or realize God is the goal of man's life. But God is realized concretely in the world, particularly in other people. Service to others becomes a way to God.[7]

Gandhi believed very deeply in the unity of all things in God. He used to say that his whole spirituality could be summarized in the first verse of the *Isa Upanishad*, which says, "Behold everything in the form of God." This basic affirmation, which is also at the root of the Indian tradition of *advaita*, or nonduality, led Gandhi to respect all forms of life and acknowledge the equality of all human beings, without distinction of caste, race or economic condition. This helped him find God, particularly in the human and the poor. "The best and the most understandable place where He can be worshipped is a living creature. The service of the distressed, the crippled and the helpless among living things constitutes worship of God."[8] This is also the basis for his conviction of the fundamental unity of all religions.

> I do believe that there is only one religion in the world, but I also believe that although it is one mighty tree, it has many branches. . . . And even as all the

branches take their sap from one source, even so all religions derive their
essence from one fountain-source . . . (God) is invisible and indefinable and,
one might literally say that He has as many names as there are human beings
on earth. No matter by what name we describe Him, He is the same without
a second and if we are all children of the same Creator, naturally there cannot be any caste among us. We are one brotherhood and sisterhood, and there
cannot be any distinction of high and low amongst us.[9]

Gandhi's quest for inter-religious harmony and his drive to remove untouchability
were not just political tactics; they were religious imperatives.

### The Way of Nonviolence

Gandhi was only too aware of the many obstacles to realizing this fundamental
unity and equality. He attributed the inequalities and injustices to human selfishness
and desire, though he never spoke much about these negative elements in life and
society. However, he felt called to struggle for truth and his chosen way of struggle
was nonviolence. Though the formulation is negative, it really means love. If the
source of injustice in the world is human selfishness, it can be overcome only
through helping people change. Change cannot be imposed; it can only be induced.
The best way of inducing it is through love. Love is not a passive quality, but active,
manifested in effort and struggle. While Gandhi was concerned that the persons one
is trying to change should not be hurt, he was not for passivity in the face of evil.
Evil has to be resisted actively. But through techniques like non-cooperation, one
seeks to awaken the other to a new consciousness and bring him or her to a dialogue. Dialogue provides an opportunity for persuasion, conviction and change.
Once people change, then they can change the structures.[10] *Ahimsa*, then, is not a
negative, passive attitude but a force for change, the force of truth and love, manifested in action, that is designed to provoke the other to dialogue. In Gandhi's words,

> Without *ahimsa* it is not possible to seek and find Truth. . . . The principle of
> *ahimsa* is hurt by every evil thought, by undue haste, by lying, by hatred, by
> wishing ill to anybody. . . . It is not merely a negative state of harmlessness but
> it is a positive state of love, of doing good even to the evil-doer. But it does
> not mean helping the evil-doer to continue the wrong or tolerating it by pas-
> sive acquiescence. On the contrary, love, the active state of Ahimsa, requires
> you to resist the wrong-doer by dissociating yourself from him even though
> it may offend him or injure him personally.[11]

One cannot really struggle for truth and love in society without practicing truth
and love in one's own life. Hence the importance of personal preparation. Besides
self-discipline, this preparation also involves a readiness to suffer—that is, to
impose suffering on oneself rather than on the other. "The votary of non-violence
has to cultivate the capacity for sacrifice of the highest type in order to be free from
fear. . . . He who has not overcome all fear cannot practice *ahimsa* to perfection."[12]

Another element of preparation is prayer, in which one listens to God. In difficult moments, Gandhi claimed to hear the still, small voice of God, which helped him to discern. But once he discerned the truth of the situation in this manner, nothing or no one could stop him from pursuing it in a single-minded way.

Gandhi also believed that while truth is absolute, it can be realized progressively only through the partial truths of daily existence. "As long as I have to realize this Absolute Truth, so long must I hold by the relative truth as I have conceived it. That relative truth must meanwhile be my beacon, my shield and buckler."[13]

Life therefore was a continuing journey or search toward truth. One is never sure that one's own perception is absolutely correct, so one is therefore open to change. He called the story of his life "My Experiments with Truth." He was therefore open to dialogue and even to compromise. While the absolute goal remained clear, he did not mind compromises along the way, provided the step taken was in the proper direction. He was understanding and tolerant of human limitations, but this tendency to compromise often upset his followers. A compromise, however, is not mixing truth with falsehood, but limiting one's present objective, hoping to go one more small step the next time.

### Hindu Roots

For his struggle, Gandhi drew inspiration from the *Bhagavad Gita*.[14] Though Gandhi was inspired by the Sermon on the Mount and the nonviolent way of Jesus, these seem to have served him as catalysts to rediscover the riches of his own tradition in the Gita. The Gita is set in the battlefield between the two armies representing the good and evil forces in the world, who happen to be cousins in the epic *Mahabharata*. The chief warrior on the side of good hesitates to engage in this fratricidal warfare, and Krishna, who was believed to be the incarnation of the God Vishnu, exhorts him to fight. Gandhi did not believe in literal incarnation; he thought that every living being is an incarnation. Figures such as Krishna are testimonies to "man's lofty spiritual ambition." They challenge man to self-realization.

> The object of the Gita appears to me to be that of showing the most excellent way to attain self-realization.... *That matchless remedy is renunciation of the fruits of action....* There must be action where there is body.... And yet all religions proclaim that it is possible for man, by treating the body as the temple of God, to attain freedom.... How can the body be made the temple of God? The Gita has answered the question in decisive language: By desireless action; by renouncing the fruits of action; by dedicating all activities to God, i.e., by surrendering oneself to Him body and soul.[15]

The Gita, as it stands, may seem to sound a call for war. But as a matter of fact, the call to selfless action supposes nonviolence, because one cannot be selfless without being nonviolent.[16]

As one can see, Gandhi felt free to reinterpret the tradition of Hinduism to suit his own perspectives. The Hindu tradition, being pluralistic, allows such reinterpretation. Unfortunately, it is more difficult to change the social system. Gandhi may be divinized, and some may follow his spiritual path, but Hindu society continues its oppressions in the caste system. While Gandhi had a broad vision of integral liberation, his vision was not shared by all his followers, especially those of the Congress Party. His leadership was accepted in so far it was useful to liberate the country from colonial oppression. Untouchability was abolished by law, but in practice, many of the oppressions he opposed still continue. Even in the socio-economic field, people do not take his economic theories seriously, even if the liberal theories they follow bring only ecological and social destruction.

## SWAMI AGNIVESH

Swami Agnivesh is a *sannyasi* who belongs to the *Arya Samaj.* Arya Samaj is a reform movement within Hinduism started by Swami Dayanand Sarasvati in 1875. It sought to restore Hinduism to its pristine purity in accordance with the *Vedas,* purifying it from later accretions, superstitions and ritualism. It rejected, for example, the caste system as non-vedic. It fought against idol worship and fatalism. It established an order of sannyasis and many schools to propagate its message. It taught people to question authority. It was also involved in the struggle against British colonialism. The radicality of the message can be gauged from the fact that its founder was poisoned at the age of fifty-nine in 1883. As usually happens, institutionalization and history dims the initial fervor of charisms, and *Arya Samaj* was no exception. However, in recent times a band of young sannyasis attempted a revival and an accompanying ideology termed *vedic socialism* that has animated farmers' movements in Haryana, in North India. Swami Agnivesh belongs to this group of reformers and personally leads a movement for the liberation of five million bonded laborers in the stone quarries, brick kilns, the carpet industry and agriculture.[17]

### True Religion Is Revolutionary

Agnivesh thinks that all religions have a social and religious liberative message in their formative stage but lose this liberative thrust as they become hierarchical and institutional. Religions then become instruments in the hands of the oppressors. In spite of a large number of people in India who claim to be spiritual, poverty, inequality and injustice are rampant. The contemporary social system is primarily responsible for this, but in order to escape their own responsibility, the oppressors

> have completely perverted the powerful *karma* theory and made the toiling and suffering masses believe that for all their miseries and sorrows the *karma* or deeds of their own past lives are responsible. Such a fate is something ordained by the all powerful God and cannot be changed by any mortal. The *karma* philosophy in fact is just the opposite. It places human endeavour above divine dispensation and says that even God cannot deny human beings

the fruits of their actions. The *karma* exhortation in essence is for action for liberation with the assured result of social change.[18]

Agnivesh thinks that the Marxist criticism of all religion as oppressive is inaccurate. Religion also has positive elements and leaders and mystics who have sacrificed their lives in the cause of liberation. He sees a possibility of collaboration between religion and Marxist socialism. Even the atheism of Marxism is not an obstacle, since there are religions, such as Buddhism and Jainism, that are atheistic, though they are based on human compassion. The vedic teaching on *dharma* or moral behavior does not make mention of God. Vyasa, the author of *Mahabharata*, sums up the essence of religion as, "Do not do unto others what you would not have others do unto you."[19] Agnivesh attributes the conflict between Marxism and religions to the machinations of the exploiters and the intellectuals at their service. We have, therefore, to demonstrate that "a true religion and a true revolutionary spirit are not mutually hostile, but complementary," as both arise out of the "perennial human passions and ideals" for freedom and justice.[20]

## Individual and Social Change

The process of change suggested by vedic socialism is two-dimensional. The individual has to be changed through the spiritual training and discipline of the *yoga*, while a society based on the principles of *varna ashram* (social order based on the division of labor) has to be established through revolution. The context of this transformation is the trinitarian structure of the world.

The universe is made up of three elements: *prakriti*, or matter, with its inherent attribute of *sat* or existence; *atma*, or the soul, with its inherent attributes of *sat* and *chit* or existence and consciousness; and *paramatma*, or God, with her inherent attributes of *sat, chit* and *anand*, i.e., *satchidanand* or existence, consciousness and bliss. God creates the universe in order to help the soul attain the third attribute, *anand*, which it lacks. The universe is not an end in itself, but only a means toward blissful emancipation.

The aim of life is "to seek Her, be with Her and in a limited sense, merge into Her."[21] Since She is all-pervasive and formless, She has to be sought, not in *avatars* or incarnations and temples, but in oneself. "The moment the soul empties itself of all its sense perception, God emerges as an indescribable experience, the soul transcending into a realm of peace, absolute peace."[22] The *yoga* is a scientific method of meditation leading us to this experience. As a preparation for this, one has to remove from oneself passion and greed, anger and fear, and replace them with love and compassion, truth and justice. "It is unthinkable to attain truth within, without simultaneously fighting the forces of untruth outside. Therefore the fight against untruth, bondage, an unjust social order based on violence and greed and usurpation become part and parcel of one's spiritual pursuit."[23]

The perspective is that of the universe as one universal family. This family spirit must animate our relationship to nonhuman nature such as trees and flowers, mountains and rivers, animals and birds. A family spirit of "from each according to one's capacity, to each according to one's need" must regulate our economic relationships, moving away from an economy based on greed and multiplicity of wants to a spiritual economy of voluntary poverty and 'small is beautiful.' Vegetarianism and non-alcoholism are part of the vedic way of life.

### Vision of a Vedic Society

Agnivesh outlines the cardinal principles of a vedic society as follows. There is no birthright. No one can claim any right or privilege because of his or her birth into a certain family. Hence caste distinctions based on birth and rights of inheritance of means of production and distribution are ruled out. Secondly, each one's life is regulated through the scheme of four *varnas.*

> The entire education system is geared to the task of producing missionaries as opposed to mercenaries. Every child has to choose one of the three missions: mission to fight against forces of ignorance, *ajyan* (Brahman); mission to fight against forces of injustice, *anyaya* (Kshatriya); or the mission to fight against the forces of inadequacy, *abhava* (Vaishya). Only a person failing to qualify for any of these three missions is designated Shudra and is called upon to serve one of these like an apprentice. There is nothing menial or derogatory in the word Shudra. In fact the vedic injunction is that every one is born a shudra. It is only through action that he or she qualifies for twice-born.[24]

One can grasp the significance of the proposal only if one understands the caste system. As it is practiced today in India, the caste system is a rigid hierarchical ordering of society. Each person is born into a caste. Intermarriage between castes is not permitted. One's caste was determined on the hereditary labor that one was engaged in and could not change. As endogamous groups, there are more than 4,000 castes in India today. These castes are ordered hierarchically according to a general scheme of four *varnas,* which literally means 'colors.' These are *Brahmins* (priests), *Kshatriyas* (warriors), *Vaisyas* (merchants) and *Shudras* (servants). Agnivesh suggests that such a division of labor is a good one, but it should not be determined by birth, but by free choice according to one's talent and training.

Agnivesh thus reinterprets the *varna* theory and says that it "has nothing to do with color, caste or racial superiority." We may note in passing that Gandhi was also in favor of such a revamped *varna* theory.

Similarly, Agnivesh reinterprets the theory of the four *ashramas.* The *vanaprasta* is dedicated to social work, and the *sannyasi* is "a declassed social activist, a moving flame devoted to God and Her creation only."[25] Agnivesh thinks that in a society organized according to the *varnas* and *ashramas* there is no room for private property. There is a collective form of living and sharing, with collective ownership of means of food, water and employment. A person is entitled to a status based on his or her action, talent and aptitude. Agnivesh sees the conflict between the *aryas* and the *dasyus,* of which the vedas speak, not as a racial one between the invaders and the local people, as usually interpreted, but as a struggle between the exploiters and the toiling masses. He quotes a vedic verse:

In order to establish your political supremacy
The toiling masses of the world unite,
And expropriate the expropriators.[26]

and affirms: "God is clearly on the side of the noble, the rational and the toiling people when she says: I give this land, this earth to the toiling people."

As in the case of Gandhi, not all Hindus may agree with the interpretations of Swami Agnivesh, but he represents a group that shows that traditional vedic texts can inspire a socialistic movement for the liberation of bonded laborers.

## E. V. RAMASWAMY (1879 - 1973)

E. V. Ramaswamy, popularly known as *Thanthai Periyar* (Father, the Great One), was born in 1879 in Tamil Nadu, in southeastern India, to a family of merchants. His studies did not proceed beyond elementary school. He had a personal crisis at the age of 25, when he became a religious mendicant for a brief period. Then he threw himself into business and civic leadership with success. In 1919 he abandoned civic leadership and entered politics as a member of the Congress Party, then agitating for independence. He was active in movements for the abolition of untouchability. He left the Congress Party in 1925, since it supported caste discrimination in institutions supported by it. He became keenly aware of the domination of Brahmins in public life and government and joined the Justice Party, which agitated for reservation of places for non-Brahmins in educational institutions, government services and public bodies. He started the "Self-respect Movement" in 1929. The main focus of this movement was opposition to Brahmin domination and the Hindu religion, which was seen as supporting this domination.[27]

In its first conference, one can already note the following themes: abolition of caste discrimination and untouchability; combating superstition and its basis, namely religious beliefs and structures; the liberation and promotion of women; support of the workers; control of abuses linked to marriage celebrations; promoting inter-caste marriages and remarriage of widows; free primary education for all; mobilization of the non-Brahmin young people; and promotion of rationalism, especially through popular media.

In 1932, he went for a tour of Europe that included Russia. On his return, he added 'socialism' to his platform, agitating for causes such as protection of poor farmers from moneylenders, cooperation in ownership and trade in order to do away with middlemen, government responsibility for free public services, and so forth.

In 1934, when there was an attempt to impose Hindi as a compulsory subject in all the schools, he saw this as north Indian domination and in 1937 launched the slogan: "Tamil Nadu for the Tamils." In 1944 he launched the *Dravida Kazhagam* (the fellowship of the Dravidians). This led to the reaffirmation by the Tamils of their separate racial, linguistic and cultural identity, as different from the *Aryans* (Brahmins) coming from the north. The secular tradition of ancient Tamil culture was highlighted against the superstitious Hinduism of the *Aryans.*

Periyar refused to enter politics. He kept his movement a social one. Though he was aware of the need for political and economic reform, he thought that priority should be given to social reform. He saw the caste system as the greatest evil and the root of all other evils. He thought that Brahmin domination in every sphere of life was the clear expression of it. He felt that Hindu religion justified Brahmin domination and the caste system. He accused the Brahmins of using the superstitions of Hindu religion to exploit the people. So his quest for social reform led him to an attack on Hindu religion. According to him, Hinduism propagated superstitious beliefs in astrology, fate and rebirth; it was founded on myths that cannot be proved; it supported the caste system and Brahmin domination; it favored many unjust social practices such as discrimination against women; it preached an otherworldly, alienating spirituality focused on heaven-hell, rituals and pilgrimages, which only allowed the priestly caste of the Brahmins to exploit the others more systematically. Besides rationalistic propaganda against superstition, his attack took symbolic forms such as breaking and insulting images of Hindu gods.

## A Denial of God

In his later years, Periyar denied God. At a training session in 1967, he made the crowd repeat after him: "There is no God. There is no God at all. Only a fool will talk about God. One who propagates belief in God is a scoundrel. One who worships God is an uncivilized person."[28] Not only his enemies, but even many of his disciples, consider Periyar an atheist.

Periyar's attack on Hinduism and Hindu gods is no secret, but Periyar himself maintained that people could worship

> a God who is formless,
>      who creates all humans as equals,
>      who is ethical,
>      whom one can worship without any great expense,
>      who does not give place to superstition.[29]

Periyar has also said that he was not an atheist, but a philanthropist, and that his reaction against religion was not meant to hurt anyone but abolish the caste system. Periyar was also very positive toward the teachings of the Buddha, Jesus and Mohammed, though he was critical of Buddhism, Christianity and Islam for following similar superstitious and socially unjust practices.[30] With reason, a recent student of Periyar maintains that he was not an atheist but a counter-cultural prophet who denied false gods and alienating and exploitative religions, while promoting a basic humanism and a rational approach to reality and life.[31] Periyar's denial of God was not a systematic, philosophical affirmation but a practical reaction to social abuses perpetrated in the name of God and religion. Periyar's denial of God should be understood in the context of his profound affirmation of the human. He had no need of a God who would be against or depreciate or deny the human. But he had no problems with a God who affirms the human, who stands for equality and ethics, justice and fellowship.

*A Secular Tradition*

In the context of Tamil Ghat, Periyar could be placed in the line of a succession of prophets spanning over two millennia who had affirmed a basic humanism and, in its name, either prescinded from or criticized alienating religion.[32] In this tradition one could count the early secular poetry on love and war (before and after the common era); the ethical maxims of Tiruvalluvar (3rd century C.E.) that deal with the pursuit of love, wealth and righteousness;[33] the poems of the *Siddhas* (self-realized people—from the 7th century C.E.) who strongly criticized caste distinctions, rituals and dogmas and abuses of established religion, while emphasizing purity of character and mystic piety, with an interest in medicine and alchemy that safeguard and prolong life; and various Bhakti poets (from the 6th to the 20th centuries C.E.) who promoted a devotional path of love and compassion to all creatures and sought to transcend religious barriers.[34] One could call this a 'secular humanism': 'secular' in the sense of 'a-religious' or transcending religious differences, not 'anti-religious.'

A couple of examples from the *siddha* tradition can illustrate this secular tradition. *Tirumular* (7th century C.E.) sings:

If the body is destroyed, soul is destroyed;
and one will not attain true powerful knowledge.
Having acquired the skill to foster the body,
I cherish the body, and I foster the soul.

Another *siddha* poet, *Civavakkiyar* (before the 10th century C.E.), sings:

What are temples? What are bathing tanks?
Fools who worship in temples and tanks!
Temples are in the mind. Tanks are in the mind.
You say that Siva is in bricks and granite,
in the red-rubbed lingam, in copper and brass!
If you could learn to know yourself first,
the God in the temple will dance and sing within you.[35]

Though Periyar himself was overtly anti-religious and anti-theistic, his secular humanistic message found ready ears in Tamil Nadu, thanks to this millennial tradition, even if his hearers did not follow his anti-religious stand. It was also seen as affirming a Tamil, Dravidian identity different from a north Indian, Aryan (Brahmin) identity.[36]

*A Negative Theology*

I think that Periyar is a good example of negative theology. Religion has both prophetic and alienating elements. Periyar focuses on the alienating elements, especially in the religious system as it is lived as creed, cult and code. It is his opposition to religion that leads him to oppose God, as God is conceived by that religion. He is not so much denying God as opposing an anti-humanistic God. Just as the Buddha, he does not elaborate a discourse on God, but concentrates instead on urging social-ethical behavior. His opposition to God is therefore counter-cultural, not absolute. It seems that Periyar himself perceived his stand in this manner.[37] The contextual nature of his opposition is further illustrated by a story. Ambedkar invited Periyar to become a Buddhist, since the Buddha does not talk about God but advocates a way of life. Periyar replied that if he were to become a Buddhist, then he would not be free to criticize Hinduism and reform it from within.[38] Therefore his opposition to religion and God was not absolute and ideological, but counter-cultural within the context of Hinduism as it was being lived by the people.

One of the functions of a theology of liberation is to be critical of religious elements that alienate people from life in this world and legitimate inequality and injustice. Periyar's discourse is a good example of such a negative theology, but one nourished by a positive affirmation of a secular humanism demanding social equality and justice. Periyar's humanistic legacy has been betrayed by other movements that claim the inspiration of Periyar but are more interested in political power than social reform. Periyar was wise not to compromise his social activism by entering party politics, though he animated many nonviolent social movements. Periyar's quest for social equality and justice have an unmistakable mark in the awareness of the Tamil people.

# 7

# Buddhism and Liberation

Buddhism is normally considered a world-denying religion. The ideal Buddhist is the monk who renounces the world and pursues *nirvana*, or emptiness. Economics and politics would not normally interest him. He spends his time in meditation, living a simple life with needs reduced to a minimum, dependent on the generosity of lay people.

But this image of a quiet, peace-loving way of life is challenged by pictures of Vietnamese monks burning themselves in public squares in support of the fight for freedom and liberation, or by the phenomenon of monks taking an active part in politics and development in Sri Lanka. Thailand has an International Society for Engaged Buddhism, and Buddhist activists have gone to prison in defense of their demand for justice.

In the Buddhist tradition, Buddha is seen as the compassionate one and, in the Mahayana tradition, he is honored as the Bodhisattva who forgoes his own liberation to assure the liberation of all. One always looks back to King Ashoka (of India in the fourth century before the common era) as the first ideal Buddhist emperor who not only actively promoted inter-religious harmony and peace, but through various social services, roads, and hospices catered to the poor and the needy. As an informed commentator notes: "Dharma detachment is from ego, not from the world."[1]

When one considers all this, one wonders whether the image of Buddhism as world-denying is a misapprehension made current by people looking at it from the outside, without fully understanding it. It conforms to the stereotype of the spiritual but inactive East, in contrast to which the West feels active and dynamic, even if it is in the pursuit of material well-being.

As a matter of fact, a look around the Buddhist world today shows us many eminent figures leading movements for social transformation, nourished by their Buddhist roots. We shall have a closer look at three such leaders, their activity and their teaching.

## THE SARVODAYA SRAMADANA MOVEMENT

'Sarvodaya Sramadana' means 'universal awakening through the gift of labor.' The movement was founded by A. T. Ariyaratna, a Buddhist schoolteacher. In 1958, he helped organize a holiday work camp for the students of Nalanda College, Colombo. The aim was to help the students "to understand and experience the true state of affairs that prevailed in the rural and poor urban areas . . . (and) to develop a love for their people and utilize the education they received to find ways of building a more just and happier life for them."[2]

Encouraged by the success of the very first work camp, similar camps were organized for briefer or longer periods by other schools. In 1968, Ariyaratna launched the Hundred Villages Development Scheme. Since then, the movement has grown to reach thousands of villages. More than a thousand camps are conducted each year, with many thousand participants.

The focus of the movement slowly shifted from students to villagers, the students serving as volunteers to help organize and animate the villagers. The organization provided expert know-how, facilitated contact with government and other agencies, and offered training programs, but the initiative was taken by the people themselves, who often invited the volunteers to help them. Starting in 1972, a more systematic effort was made to train monks so that instead of being merely ritual functionaries they could become involved in such village development projects.

### Sarvodaya or the Awakening of All

The goal of the development program was local, self-help, self-reliant projects in which the villagers could be collectively involved. In the process, the villagers not only discover their power and creativity but also build themselves as a community. This is presented as different from and an alternative to the industry- and export-oriented, ecologically destructive and internationally dependent government programs, whose benefits go to the elite and do not trickle down to the poor. But these do not seem to have been actively opposed, and the government seems to consider the village development program as complementary to its own and is supportive of it. Sarvodaya is also presented as an alternative to the prevailing capitalist and socialist models. "The contradictions [of both socialist and capitalist models] emanate from their inability to understand the twin or dual character of development, i.e., it involves both the individual and the group, and it must satisfy both economic and spiritual needs."[3]

The sarvodaya process consists of four stages: understanding the problem, including the needs and resources available; building village organizations; establishing village services; and initiating development activities. The goal of this process is to meet ten basic needs of the people: a clean and beautiful environment; a safe and adequate supply of water; basic requirements of clothing; a regular balanced diet; a simple abode; basic health care services; transportation and communications facilities; fuel; continuing education for all; and cultural and spiritual development. The holistic nature of the goal is evident.[4]

My purpose, however, is not to describe the project elaborately, but to see what inspiration it draws from religious resources, especially Buddhism. The original inspiration for the camps seems to have come from the Quakers.[5] The ideological framework owes much to Gandhi, who was Hindu. People of other religions participate in the work camps, since the theory and practices such as meditation are not aggressively denominational. But there is no doubt that the Buddhist tradition has been the main source of religious ideology. There is a special program to train Buddhist monks as animators of the sarvodaya movement. The monks function as instructors to raise awareness, using the life and teachings of the Buddha as well as the *jataka* tales, which are legends surrounding the life of the Buddha. The activities of the work camp are centered around the village temple as a meeting-place and include the participation of monks in chanting prayers and processions.

### Buddhist Roots

The main goal of the program is *sarvodaya,* the awakening of all. This clearly refers to the awakening experience of the Buddha. The awakening is not to some mystical vision, but to one's own reality, resources and power, individually and collectively. Such awakening can have various stages: personal, village, national and international. What happens is that one discovers the interconnectedness of all beings. This relates to one of the basic doctrines of Buddhism, namely "dependent co-arising" (*paticca samuppada*). We shall come back to this doctrine in the next section. The goal is clearly perceived as human/religious: it is not religion that is used to support development; community development helps people realize goals that are essentially religious.

Buddha summarized his teaching in the four noble truths:

1. There is suffering (in life and in the world).
2. Desire or craving is the cause of the suffering.
3. Craving can be overcome.
4. For that we have to follow the eight-fold path, namely right understanding, right intention, right speech, right action, right livelihood, right effort, right mindfulness, and right concentration.

The originality of Ariyaratna was to apply these noble truths to the situation of a village, thus socializing Buddha's teaching.

1. There is a decadent village, characterized by conflict, oppression, disease, harsh speech, poverty and stagnation.
2. The cause of such decadence is egoism, ill-will, disunity, ignorance, possessiveness and competition.
3. These evils can be overcome through selflessness, love, equality, pleasant speech, cooperation, sharing, and constructive activity.
4. The path is spiritual development, cultural development, education, economic development, unity, organizational development, and health.[6]

One moves toward sarvodaya through *shramadana,* the gift or sharing of effort or labor. *Dana* is no longer seen merely as giving of alms; it is giving one's labor to the community, working together. In this manner, the awakened community is built up. The stages through which this community awakening is achieved are described in terms of moving through the four *Brahma viharas* (heavenly abodes):

1. *Metta:* loving kindness—respect for all life. One focuses on someone, wishing that this person is free from fear, greed, sorrow or causes of suffering. This develops our capacity for love and makes us patient.

2. *Karuna:* compassionate action to remove all constraints that prevent the awakening of human personalities to the fullest. One identifies with the sufferings of others and their pain as one's own.

3. *Mudithat:* learning to experience the dispassionate, altruistic joy that one gets when involved in such compassionate action. One can also experience the joy, the gifts and the power of others as one's own. This is the reverse side of compassion.

4. *Upekha:* equanimity or development of psychologically balanced personalities. This comes out of a deep experience of interconnectedness so that one does not feel alone, but feels supported and part of a whole.[7]

While these "heavenly abodes" refer to the experiential level, at the practical level, the Dharma specifies four principles of practical behavior:

1. *Dana* is mutual gift.

2. *Priyavacana* is pleasant speech promoting mutual respect.

3. *Samanatmatha* is social equality that does not discriminate on the basis of caste or class.

4. *Arthachariya* is constructive work, symbolized by the work camps.[8]

### Praxis in Community

The focus of the movement, in contrast to individualism, is on community. This community is experienced in "family gatherings" every morning and evening, in which all those involved in the project discuss problems and possibilities, share and plan together. This unity is further strengthened by meditating together. The process is as follows. They collect their thoughts through *anapanasati* (breath meditation). The energy thus gathered is disseminated for the good of all beings through *metta* (meditation of loving kindness). Then comes *prarthana* (conscious willing), whereby "the purified thought-force is directed toward the goal of a morally righteous and materially contented society." An invocation frequently chanted in sarvodaya gatherings goes

May there be rain enough.
May there be prosperity.
May the whole world be happy.
May the rulers be righteous.[9]

Such focus on the community, however, does not ignore the weak and the needy. Sarvodaya goes with *antyodaya,* i.e., the awakening of the lowliest and the lost.

Such attention to the last and the least is not seen in a conflictual mode. As Ariyaratna explains:

> If the motivating force in the mind is *metta* or respect for all lives then a human being who accepts this principle has to necessarily translate this thought into concrete action called '*karuna.*' We are helping a landless cultivator to liberate himself from the bondage imposed on him by unscrupulous landowners not because we hate the landowner but because we love or respect the life of the poor landless cultivator. . . . We are not prepared to concede revolutionary monopoly only to those who base all their social actions on organized hatred. We have based our revolutionary approach on loving kindness and the organization of compassionate action.[10]

This approach to social action is further exemplified by two options made by the sarvodaya movement. While it is deeply committed to politics in the sense of making the people aware of their rights, increasing their participation in making decisions that concern them and implementing them, it refuses to get involved in either party politics based on particular political ideologies or the search for political power. Sarvodaya is also committed to dynamic nonviolence.

> When human beings are organized, made conscious of their own rights, they can become instruments of active revolution. The revolution Sarvodaya believes in transforms society not by the transference of political, economic, or social power from one party, class, or group to another. It means in the full Sarvodaya sense the transfer of all such power to the people.[11]

Though the focus of the program is village development, it has also resulted in the transformation of the religious institution. The monk becomes an animator of a social movement, instead of merely a ritual specialist. The Mahayana ideal of the *Bodhisattva* seems to be finding a place in the Hinayana tradition of Sri Lanka.[12] The village temple is not merely a place of worship, but a base for community activity. There is also a reconceptualization of traditional doctrines such as the "Four Noble Truths." Even the doctrine of *karma* is being reinterpreted as a call to responsible action, rather than a fatalistic acceptance of predestination.[13]

*Criticisms*

While no one has faulted Ariyaratna for his retrieval and reinterpretation of Buddhism as the religious inspiration for the Sarvodaya Sramadana movement, voices have been raised against some of the movement's political and economic policies: too close a collaboration with the government; dependence on foreign funds; more emphasis on development than on liberation; focus on personal and social conversion instead of on change of unjust structures, etc. These criticisms concern the way the movement has developed and are also probably attendant on its success and the acclaim it has received nationally and internationally. But I think that the inspiration Ariyaratna has drawn from the Buddhist tradition can support a more revolutionary ideology. In other words, I would make a distinction between the liberation perspectives based on Buddhism and the practical policies followed by the Sarvo-daya Sramadana movement.

## BHIKKHU BUDDHADASA (1906 - 1993)

Bhikkhu Buddhadasa was born as Ngeuam Panich in 1906 at Pum Riang, into a small merchant family in southern Thailand.[14] The three primary influences in his childhood were his mother, the Wat (temple) and nature. He had to leave secondary school when his father died, to help look after the family shop. He was an avid reader and became familiar with new currents in Buddhism in Thailand. He became a monk at the age of twenty, after the initial experience of the traditional Rains Retreat, when most young Thai men become monks for a three-month period during the rainy season. He soon became a popular teacher and preacher. Though he went to Bangkok for some higher study, he was not tempted to enter into the ranks of the institutional Sangha. This freedom of spirit enabled him to rediscover the roots of Buddhism from the basic Pali texts, but in his own manner and his own rhythm. It also made it possible for him to be critical of tradition and interpret it for modern times. In 1932, he founded the Suan Mokkh (the Garden of Liberation) monastery. He started a journal, *Buddha-Sasana*, in collaboration with his brother, trying to present basic Buddhist truths in a new, readable way, relevant to modern times. His ideas began to attract attention, and he drew disciples and admirers. He was invited to give conferences in Bangkok and elsewhere. As the number of Thai and international visitors increased, a spiritual theater and International Dhamma Hermitage were built, along with lodgings that can accommodate 800 people at any given time. More than 1,000 trainees receive special instruction each year, not counting the thousands who follow the monthly meditation courses. Buddhadasa died on July 8, 1993, leaving a voluminous body of writings, mostly in the form of lectures. Though a Theravadin, he also drew inspiration from the Mahayana tradition. Donald K. Swearer, who was a student of Buddhadasa for many years, comments: "History may well judge him as the most seminal Theravada thinker since Buddhagosha, and may evaluate Buddhadasa's role within the Buddhist tradition to be on a par with such great Indian Buddhist thinkers as Nagarjuna with whom he has been compared."[15]

The year that Buddhadasa founded his monastery was the year Thailand became a constitutional monarchy. During the period of his mature teaching, Thailand was going through political turmoil. It housed American air bases during the Vietnam war and was becoming the tourist paradise of American soldiers and, later, of others, bringing with it evils such as prostitution and child abuse. The army dominated the government, excluding real participation by the people. The country was being pushed into a liberal, capitalistic economic path, leading to the disruption of the traditional economy, impoverishing the villagers, bringing in rapid urbanization with its attendant problems, increasing inequality and political oppression. The youth were restive and attracted to alternate models, including Communism. It is in this context that Buddhadasa boldly affirms the need for morality and religious spirit in

public life, maintaining that Buddhist tradition offers a socio-political model—
*Dhammic Socialism*—that is a viable alternative to both liberal capitalistic democracy and Communism. He shows that Buddhism is neither world-denying nor focused only on making merit.

## Dhammic Socialism

The main teachings of Buddhadasa have been summarized by Swearer. Though it may not be fully understood at the first reading, it will become more clear as the exposition proceeds.

> The individual is not-self. As such s/he is part of an ongoing, conditioning process devoid of absolute self-nature, a process to which words can only point. This process functions according to universal principles we call nature. It is the true, normative, and moral condition of things. To be a not-self therefore, is to be void of self, and, hence, to be part of the normal, interdependent co-arising matrix of all things, and to live according to the natural moral law in a fellowship voluntarily restrained by other-regarding concerns.[16]

Dhamma refers to nature, reality, or the order of the universe as it is and as it functions. Buddhadasa says: "Dhamma means Nature, which can be distinguished in four aspects: Nature itself, the Law of Nature, the Duty of living things according to Natural Law, and the results that follow from performing the duty according to Natural Law."[17]

Everything in the universe, from the molecule to the solar system, the plant and the animal world, and the whole universe constitute interdependent systems. The good of the system has primacy over that of the individual parts. Or, to be more accurate, the good of the system is also the good of its parts. From another point of view, the good of the part is also the good of the system, provided it conforms to the order of the whole. This is socialism. It is inherent to nature. "The entire universe is a socialist system. Countless numbers of stars in the sky exist together in a socialist system. Because they follow a socialist system they can survive. Our small universe with its sun and planets including the earth is a socialist system. Consequently they do not collide."[18] So one can speak of Dhammic Socialism; that is, nature itself is socialistic.

Unlike material objects or animals, a human being does not spontaneously and automatically conform to the system. S/he is hindered by egoism and selfishness. When s/he voluntarily conforms to the order of nature, she conforms to Dhamma. In theistic systems, this will be understood as conforming to the will of God.

This socialistic vision is based on traditional Buddhist doctrine. I shall mention some of them. First of all, there is the idea of the not-self, with no ego at the center of personality. What we call ego is simply a network of relationships, which is why Buddhism says that the ego is 'empty.' Emptiness does not mean nothingness; it is simply the denial of the ego.

In the most fundamental sense, "emptiness" simply means empty of attachment to me-and-mine. The mind will simply be a mind in its natural state, free of attachment and ignorance because it has seen the emptiness of all things. . . . Emptiness here does not mean nothingness. Rather, it means that everything which ought to exist exists: everything which is useful can be used. . . . When we learn how to free ourselves from suffering, we can say that our actions are in accord with nature or absolute truth. That is emptiness or nibbana.[19]

To deny the ego, therefore, is to affirm the totality of the network and oneself as related to it. There is no self, but there is nature—Dhamma. I think this view of emptiness is a new interpretation of tradition.

### Reality as Interdependent

Reality, nature, or Dhamma is therefore not made up of a collection of individual egos but a network of interdependence. In Buddhist tradition, the doctrine of co-dependent origination seeks to explain the genesis of sorrow. The traditional causal chain is as follows: ignorance, disposition, consciousness, individuality, senses, contact, feeling, attachment, clinging, becoming, rebirth and finally old age and death, tribulation, grief, sorrow, distress and despair.[20] In this way, we see how sorrow is linked back to ignorance. Sorrow is said to arise co-dependently with all these causes. Buddhadasa's originality consists in taking this scheme of network at the level of causality and applying it to the level of reality, so that what we perceive as things or individual beings in this world are interdependent on another in such a way that nothing can be said to be a being in itself. "Understanding of dependent co-origination, when it develops correctly and completely, leads to clearly seeing that there is no real self."[21] The denial of the ego goes together with the affirmation of the reality of the totality. Buddhadasa even says: "Whatever it may be called— God, Dhamma, Tao, the laws of Nature—it is all the same thing."[22]

The problem is that people are ignorant of this interdependence and behave as if they were individuals. They are led to this false perception through ignorance, which leads to attachment. People can identify themselves not only with their ego, but with any of its five aggregates: the physical body, feeling, perception, thinking, and consciousness.[23]

One could then paraphrase the Four Noble Truths: suffering results from the feeling of me-and-mine; the cause of suffering is me-and-mine; the cessation of suffering is the cessation of me-and-mine; the Noble Eightfold Path is the method for eliminating me-and-mine. To eliminate the feeling of me-and-mine is to become aware of one's socialistic nature.

The Noble Eightfold Path can be summarized in three practices: wisdom (right understanding and right intent), moral behavior (right speech, right action and right livelihood), and insight or concentration (right effort, right mindfulness and right concentration).[24] Buddhadasa indicates that this path can be followed in the course of ordinary life in the world. Buddhism is not merely for those who abandon the world. The practice of concentration, on the contrary, may tend to focus too much on the ego.

A Buddhist, therefore, does not run away from the world; he is present in it and acts in a different way. "In becoming involved in things, we must do so mindfully, and our actions must not be motivated by craving." This is true even of monks.

> Buddhist monks are wanderers, not hermits. That is to say, they wander about in order to be involved with people who live in the world, rather than living in the forest cut off from social contact.... Buddhist monks, with the Buddha as their head, are always involved in society in order to teach people about the true nature of the world, to overcome suffering and avoid choking to death on the bones of life. Buddhism wants people neither to escape from the world, nor to be defeated by it, but to live in the world victoriously.[25]

Buddhism, therefore, advocates not a flight from, but living well in, a world that is experienced as socialistic or interdependent. "If we hold fast to Buddhism we shall have a socialist disposition in our very being. We shall see our fellow humans as friends in suffering—in birth, old age, sickness and death—and, hence, we cannot abandon them."[26] This is the ideal of compassion.

### Renunciation and Sharing

According to Swearer, Dhammic Socialism "can be interpreted in terms of three fundamental principles: the good of the whole, restraint and generosity, respect and loving-kindness."[27] As Buddhadasa himself expressed it:

> Solving social problems is dependent on living in a socially moral way; acting in the best interest of the entire community by living according to nature's laws; avoiding the consumption of goods beyond our simple needs; sharing all that is not essential for us to have with others, even if we consider ourselves poor; giving generously of our wealth if we are well-to-do.[28]

True development is not in increasing, but in reducing one's needs. Buddhadasa presents the Sangha as a model community. To practice socialism is not to take more than one's fair share of goods. A monk is allowed only three pieces of cloth for his robe. If he has anything extra, it goes to the Sangha. He has a single bowl for his food. If he gets more, he cannot hoard it, but has to give it away.[29] In Buddhist tradition, a rich person's status is determined by the number of alms-houses he has established. There is no restriction on production. By making use of modern technology, one can produce much, provided the production is not hoarded for personal profit but is distributed to the needy.[30] Villagers in Thailand recite the following verse when they go out to plant.

> Food for a hungry bird is our merit;
> Food for a hungry person—our charity.

Limited consumption therefore does not mean limited production, if one is concerned not only about one's own needs, but about the needs of society. This is a concrete way of showing compassion. It is from this point of view that Buddhadasa recalls the Bodhisattva, "who not only helps others, but sacrifices himself, even his own life, for others."[31] I note in passing that the Bodhisattva ideal is part of the Mahayana tradition.

### Between Capitalism and Communism

From the point of view of Dhammic Socialism, Buddhadasa is very critical of both capitalism and Communism. Capitalism is individualistic, selfish and greedy. Hoarding of goods produces economic and social inequality. A market economy also creates consumeristic demands that go beyond basic needs.[32] Communism, on the other hand, divides the community into classes and thrives on anger and hatred, which work against the peace and harmony of nature. The confrontation between capitalism and Communism threatens mutual global destruction.[33]

Buddhadasa is also critical of liberal democracy, which upholds the ideal of freedom.

> Upholding the personal freedom of individuals who are ruled by *kilesa* (defilement) goes against the fundamental meaning of politics which is concerned with the good of the whole. A political system that does not focus on society as a whole is an immoral system. Freedom in the religious or dhammic sense is important to keep in mind here because it means, in the most fundamental sense, to be free from defilements.[34]

Governance must be moral and focus on the community rather than on the individual. It is from this point of view that Buddhadasa speaks about "dictatorial socialism." If government is according to the Dhamma, it will have to and can limit—by force, if necessary—selfishness and abuses of freedom.

> A truly socialistic government would embody the characteristics of *dhamma*. It would not allow for class distinctions based on wealth. Nor would it permit anyone to accumulate private wealth at the expense of others. Because it would set limits on "freedom" as such, it could be called "dictatorial"; but, it also maintains a harmonious balance that brings about wellbeing in the community, and so extends the socialism of nature to the basis of a political system.[35]

In this context, Buddhadasa evokes the Buddhist tradition of the ideal ruler, who is supposed to be adorned by the following ten virtues: generosity, morality, liberality, uprightness, gentleness, self-restraint, non-anger, non-hurtfulness, forbearance, and non-opposition or freedom from guilt. "If such a king was a dictator, he would be like Asoka whose 'dictatorial' rule was to promote the common good and to abolish the evil of private, selfish interest."[36]

The goal of Dhammic Socialism can only be peace and harmony,[37] turning the world into the Realm of Buddha Maitreya, where there is no dissatisfaction and suffering.[38]

Buddhadasa feels that all religions are socialistic. The founders of all religions wanted people to live according to socialist principles and act in the interests of society as a whole. The real problems of the modern world are not hunger, illiteracy and illness. These are only symptoms of a more fundamental problem, which is the lack of religion and moral principle. Selfish people lack compassion.

Buddhadasa has credit for evolving a theory of Buddhist socialism, not as an amalgam of Buddhist religion with a socialist ideology coming from elsewhere, but emerging from specifically Buddhist categories. Some may find his practical suggestions rather idealistic, but he is a religious teacher, not a politician—an innovative one, close to earthly reality and seeking to be relevant. He is only "trying to *provoke* a right understanding which will transform people's lives and inspire them to build a better and more humane world."[39]

Buddhadasa has not only inspired many social activists such as Sulak Sivaraksa[40] in his own country, but is also the inspiration behind the *International Society of Engaged Buddhism.*

## THICH NHAT HANH

Thich Nhat Hanh is a Buddhist monk from Vietnam. He was very much involved in the peace movement in Vietnam during the war and had to go into exile. He now lives with a community in Plum Village in the southwest of France. He is a zen master, scholar, and poet, the author of numerous books. While Ariyaratna and Buddhadasa are in the Theravada or Hinayana tradition of Buddhism, Thich Nhat Hanh is from the Mahayana tradition. The Mahayana tradition speaks of the role of Bodhisattvas in the world—realized persons who continue to live and work in the world for the liberation of others, moved by compassion at their sufferings. The *mindfulness* at the basis of Nhat Hanh's teaching is not flight from the world into the practice of meditation, seeking inner peace, but an effort to live consciously in the present. Usually our mind is distracted by prejudices, emotions, attachments. The practice of mindfulness helps us see the world and people as they are and live and work with understanding and commitment. As Nhat Hanh says:

Practicing Buddhist meditation is not a way of avoiding society or family life. The correct practice of mindfulness can help us bring peace, joy, and release both to ourselves and to our family and friends as well. Those who practice mindful living will inevitably transform themselves and their way of life. They will live a more simple life and will have more time to enjoy themselves, their friends, and their mutual environment. They will have more time to offer joy to others and to alleviate their suffering. And when the time comes, they will die in peace.[41]

### Solidarity with Reality

Experiencing the world as it is is to realize that everything in it is interdependent and relative. We would not then divide people into good and bad. We would not too easily set up enemies that we have to fight. We would realize that we too are in some way responsible for what happens to our world and to others, and that we can do something to change it, right where we are. We would try to acquire peace in ourselves so that we can radiate it to others. Part of a poem by Nhat Hanh, entitled "Please Call Me by My True Names," reads as follows:

> I am the frog swimming happily
> in the clear water of a pond,
> and I am also the grass-snake who,
> approaching in silence, feeds itself on the frog.

After invoking similar pairs like a twelve-year-old girl and the sea pirate who rapes her, a prisoner of a labor camp and a member of the politburo, and so on, Nhat Hanh concludes:

> Please call me by my true names,
> so I can wake up,
> and so the door of my heart can be left open,
> the door of compassion.[42]

One can feel the deep solidarity of the Bodhisattva with the world as it is, animated by compassion and anxious to bring peace, without judgment, but based on truth. One can also see a glimpse of the interdependence of the universe. We are mutually involved with and responsible for each other. We go looking for enemies outside ourselves, forgetting that those enemies are also part of us, linked to us in many ways.

Nhat Hanh's views on poverty and justice can be summarized in the following brief comment: "If you have compassion, you cannot be rich.... You can be rich only when you can bear the sight of suffering. If you cannot bear that, you have to give your possessions away."[43]

### The Order of Interbeing

In February 1966, Nhat Hanh founded the Order of Interbeing, ordaining its first six members, three men and three women, board members of the School of Youth for Social Service. New members were allowed to join after 1981, and in 1993 there were more than 150 members in the core community, with thousands more as associate members. Membership is open to monks, nuns and lay people. The first six members were busy helping war victims, organizing demonstrations, printing and distributing books and leaflets, managing social service projects and organizing an underground for draft resisters, but they renewed themselves every week with a day of mindfulness.

The term 'Interbeing' spells out the goals of the order. It involves being in touch with reality, with every thing that is, with which we are interconnected. This is done in continuation of the task of the Buddha and the Bodhisattvas promoting enlightenment. True enlightenment does not get caught up in ideas, but transforms life in ourselves and in others. This brings liberation, not in some distant future, but here and now. "There is no way to liberation. Liberation is the way."[44] The Order of Interbeing is guided by fourteen precepts. They are worth quoting in full, since they picture very succinctly the experience and path of liberation. They lose their simple force when they are paraphrased or re-expressed.

1. Do not be idolatrous about or bound to any doctrine, theory, or ideology, even Buddhist ones. Buddhist systems of thought are guiding means; they are not absolute truth.

2. Do not think the knowledge you presently possess is changeless, absolute truth. Avoid being narrow-minded and bound to present views. Learn and practice nonattachment from views in order to be open to receive others' viewpoints. Truth is found in life and not merely in conceptual knowledge. Be ready to learn throughout your entire life and to observe reality in yourself and in the world at all times.

3. Do not force others, including children, by any means whatsoever, to adopt your views, whether by authority, threat, money, propaganda, or even education. However, through compassionate dialogue, help others renounce fanaticism and narrowness.

4. Do not avoid contact with suffering or close your eyes before suffering. Do not lose awareness of the existence of suffering in the life of the world. Find ways to be with those who are suffering, including personal contact, visits, images, and sounds. By such means, awaken yourself and others to the reality of suffering in the world.

5. Do not accumulate wealth while millions are hungry. Do not take as the aim of your life fame, profit, wealth, or sensual pleasure. Live simply and share time, energy, and material resources with those who are in need.

6. Do not maintain anger or hatred. Learn to penetrate and transform them when they are still seeds in your consciousness. As soon as they arise, turn your attention to your breath in order to see and understand the nature of your anger and hatred and the nature of the persons who have caused your anger and hatred.

7. Do not lose yourself in dispersion and in your surroundings. Practice mindful breathing to come back to what is happening in the present moment. Be in touch with what is wondrous, refreshing, and healing both inside and around you. Plant seeds of joy, peace, and understanding in yourself in order to facilitate the work of transformation in the depths of your consciousness.

8. Do not utter words that can create discord and cause the community to break. Make every effort to reconcile and resolve all conflicts, however small.

9. Do not say untruthful things for the sake of personal interest or to impress people. Do not utter words that cause division and hatred. Do not spread news that you do not know to be certain. Do not criticize or condemn things of which you are not sure. Always speak truthfully and constructively. Have the courage to speak out about situations of injustice, even when doing so may threaten your own safety.

10. Do not use Buddhist community for personal gain or profit, or transform your community into a political party. A religious community, however, should take a clear stand against oppression and injustice and should strive to change the situation without engaging in partisan conflicts.

11. Do not live with a vocation that is harmful to humans and nature. Do not invest in companies that deprive others of their chance to live. Select a vocation that helps realize your ideal of compassion.

12. Do not kill. Do not let others kill. Find whatever means possible to protect life and prevent war.

13. Possess nothing that should belong to others. Respect the property of others, but prevent others from profiting from human suffering or the suffering of other species on Earth.

14. Do not mistreat your body. Learn to handle it with respect. Do not look on your body as only an instrument. Preserve vital energies (sexual, breath, spirit) for the realization of the Way. (For brothers and sisters who are not monks or nuns:) Sexual expression should not take place without love and commitment. In sexual relationships, be aware of future suffering that may be caused. To preserve the happiness of others, respect the rights and commitments of others. Be fully aware of the responsibility of bringing new lives into the world. Meditate on the world into which you are bringing new beings.[45]

## The Mahayana Tradition

There is also another set of "Five Wonderful Precepts" that concern more concrete behavior, related especially to the avoidance or removal of suffering.[46] The members have to recite these precepts ritually in community once every two weeks. They project a vision and a praxis of holistic liberation. One can say that they represent a conscious living of the Bodhisattva ideal. We can recall here the fourfold vow of the Bodhisattva in the *Mahayana* tradition. "Living beings are innumerable: I vow to save them all. Illusive desires and lusts are inexhaustible: I vow to extinguish them all. Gates to dharma are numberless: I vow to learn and master them all. The way of enlightenment is peerless: I vow to realize it."

Paradoxically, such an ideal can lead someone to the supreme sacrifice as radical witness and challenge. Cao Ngoc Phuong chronicles such a sacrifice of a young girl from a noble family, who was an associate of the Order of Interbeing. She chose to take her own life in the temple as a concrete way of drawing people's attention to the pursuit of peace and prosperity for all. It had a positive impact on the peace movement.[47] There were similar sacrifices of Buddhist monks during the war for independence in Vietnam.

# 8

# Confucianism and Liberation

A survey on the inspiration that Asian religions provide for projects for liberation cannot be complete without considering the contribution of the Confucian tradition. It has animated and still animates in an unacknowledged manner the vast populations of East Asia that are inspired by the greater Chinese cultural tradition. China, Taiwan, Korea, Japan, Singapore and ethnic Chinese populations in Thailand, Malaysia, Singapore, Indonesia and the Philippines account for one-fourth of the world's population.

But there are three sorts of problems in considering the Confucian tradition. Some would question whether Confucianism is a religion in the usual sense. Secondly, like every religio-cultural tradition, Confucianism has been used by political powers to legitimize their own domination and oppression. As every charism develops into rigid institutional structures, Confucianism too may have become a body of rigid principles and rituals, very different from the original wisdom of Confucius. Some of its traditional perspectives have been strongly criticized by the Communists in China as an obstacle to their revolutionary perspectives. Finally, while the Confucian tradition may, at least partly, be responsible for the economic miracle of East Asia, it is difficult to identify liberation movements inspired by Confucianism. Therefore I cannot follow the method I have used in talking about the other religions. However, there has been some reflection among students of Chinese tradition on the 'liberation potential' of Confucianism. I am basing the following exposition on these few contributions. I think that this is very necessary, since the Confucian tradition confirms and strengthens many of the perspectives of other Asia religions. In any case, one cannot speak of Asian ways to liberation without a serious consideration of Confucianism.

## AN ABSOLUTE: HEAVEN/WAY

I think that the question whether Confucianism is a religious or cultural tradition is an academic question arising out of a narrow definition of religion. If religion is a priori defined as involving belief in a transcendent personal God, then

Buddhism and Confucianism will not qualify as religions. But if religion stands for ultimate perspectives that guide individual and social human behavior, then these have played the role of religion in the societies guided by them. What distinguishes them from culture or ideology is a certain ultimate and absolute character attributed to their perspectives on the human and cosmic world. With regard to Confucianism, Confucius himself does speak about Heaven as an ultimate principle.

> I have heard thus from Confucius, "life and death are the decree of Heaven; wealth and honour depend on Heaven..." (Analects 12:5).

> Confucius said, "I neither complain against Heaven, nor do I blame human beings. I study the things of this world, but my understanding penetrates the things beyond this world. It is Heaven that knows me" (Analects 14:37).

> Confucius said, "The four seasons run their course and all things come into being. Does Heaven say anything?" (Analects 17:19)[1]

It is true that Confucius did not speculate on the nature of "Heaven." But Heaven was for him the basis of *Tao*, or nature, which is the governing structure, law, or principle of the universe. Aloysius B. Chang presents this very perspective as a liberation from superstition and unbelief and, at the same time, affirmation of responsibility for oneself.

> Confucian liberation, then, is concerned with superstitious religious practices and directs humans towards stages of development. It is characterized by the following qualities: 1. Freedom from any unknown power, which may be personified in the form of an anthropomorphic deity or a deified historical person. 2. Ability to take one's own responsibility in all of one's life situations. 3. Freedom to go with the flow of life within oneself, with other human beings and with the entire universe.[2]

The universe is not a rigid mechanical structure. It is dynamic. Its dynamism is governed by the two opposing principles of the *yang* (initiation) and the *yin* (completion). They complement each other. Life and death, growth and decline are inherent to nature. But the Confucian insight is that what we call natural is also moral. It is the *way* that things ought to be done. While natural things and even animals follow the course of nature, humans alone can deviate from the course of nature; hence the need to exhort them to conform to nature.

It is in this context that Confucius speaks of the Mandate of Heaven. Heaven sets up the natural flow of the universe. This flow has to be respected. Confucius does not ask the question "Why?" This is the way things are. This is the way they ought to be. To be in harmony with the *way* is to be happy, free of tension and disorder. To be in disharmony with it is to be in tension and unhappy. Wing-Tsit Chan writes:

> Up to the time of Confucius, the Supreme Power was called *Ti* (the Lord) or *Shang-ti* (the Lord on high) and was understood in an anthropomorphic

sense. Confucius never spoke of *Ti*. Instead he often spoke of *T'ien* (Heaven). To be sure, his Heaven is purposive and is the master of all things. He repeatedly referred to the *T'ien-ming*, the Mandate, will, or order of Heaven. However, with him Heaven is no longer the greatest of all spiritual beings who rules in a personal manner but a Supreme Being who only reigns, leaving his Moral Law to operate by itself. This is the Way, according to which civilization should develop and men should behave.[3]

What is important here is to realize that, for Confucius, nature is not just natural, but also moral. 'What is' is 'what ought to be.' Nature therefore is also the *Way*. Being is also a 'Way of being.'[4] The ideal of life is to be in harmony with the 'Way' things are and ought to be. Deviations from the 'Way' are possible. But the 'Way' offers the basis for prophetic and liberative action, as we shall see below.

## KINGS AND SCHOLARS

Two kinds of persons are particularly connected with the 'Way' in human society. Kings are charged with maintaining the 'Way' in the universe. If they do not, they lose the authority to govern. Scholars have devoted themselves to understanding the 'Way' through the study of nature and humanity. They are therefore in a position to advise and, when necessary, challenge the kings. These perspectives offer the possibility for liberative action in society.

In *The Book of History*, there are many instances where a king or nobleman feels obliged to go to war with another in order to liberate people from tyranny. An example of an oath taken by one such liberator is illustrative.

> The King (T'ang) said, "Come here, all of you, and listen to me carefully. It is not that a small man like me dare to make a rebellion; but it is because the imperial court of Hsia has committed plenty of crimes and therefore Heaven orders me to destroy him.... Now you will say again, 'But what are the crimes of the imperial court of Hsia?' The King of Hsia wilfully exhausted the labor of the people and wilfully injured the national power of the State and all the people are wilfully negligent and unwilling to cooperate."[5]

In other similar oaths, among the crimes of kings that deserve punishment, the following are listed: being cruel to the people, condemning and killing officials, abandoning uncles, being surrounded by evil men, doing evil in the cities, and so forth.

Similar abuses of their authority by kings also provoked the prophetic intervention of the officials, who were learned men. Analyzing the role of the Confucian tradition in Korea, Sung-Hae Kim gives many examples of scholar-officials who protested injustices by sending memorials to the king. Here is a memorial written by an official called Yulogk in 1582.

> I am very much ashamed to ask your majesty to diminish the amount of gifts which people have to send to the palace. It seems to be contrary to the duty of local administrator who is to serve your majesty along with the people.

However, I am keenly aware of the fact that protecting the people is the most urgent work. Loving the people is, in fact, loving your majesty, and so I will willingly receive whatever penalty that I have to endure. It will be easier for me to die in hunger in between the hole of the rock than to watch people dying in silence.[6]

A part of a poem written by another scholar named Dasan (1762-1836) affirms the fundamental equality of all human beings.

> People only know the joy of riding the cart,
> but are ignorant of the suffering
> of the people who carry the cart.
> Carrying the cart, they climb up the steep mountain,
> They go up as fast as steers . . .
> Their shoulders are wounded under the pressure of the cart.
> Their feet are full of blood by the roots of the rocks.
> They themselves are sick,
> but they carry the cart for nobility.
> They work just like donkeys.
> You who carry the cart, I who ride in the cart,
> both of us are originally one people,
> we all have received equality from Heaven.[7]

Here we have examples of intellectuals/officials who considered their loyalty to the moral law and the welfare of the people greater than their loyalty to the king, who is also subject to the moral law. In this manner, the scholar-officials could play a prophetic role in society, opposing even the king, when necessary.

Some commentators suggest that the very institution of scholar-officials is a relativization of social class.[8] Learning is really open to anyone who has the talent. It is not limited to a particular group of people in terms of birth or privilege. They were closely connected to the ruling class, yet were sufficiently independent to be critical of their rulers. They were in this way the "social conscience" of the community.[9] They prided themselves on their fidelity to the principles of 'Heaven.' They were ready to give their lives for them.

## THE WAY AND ITS VIRTUES

Let us now look a little more closely at the main outline of what we have been referring to as the *Way* or moral law. Unlike the western discourse on human rights, the Confucian tradition does not talk about the individual, but about the human person in community. To be human is to be related in multiple ways to the community, therefore there is no abstract consideration of human nature as such. A human is considered in the very act in which it relates to the others. Still, one can look at the different elements that make up this whole: the human person, the different relationships that link that person to the others, and the ritual through which such relationship is expressed. Looking at any of these in an isolated manner will lead to a misunderstanding of all three.

A human is characterized by the virtue of *jan,* which has been translated as 'humaneness,' the manifestation of ideal human nature as it manifests itself in dealing with others. Rather than attempting to describe it in my own words, let us hear Confucius himself describe it.

> Fan Ch'ih asked about humaneness. The Master said: "It is to love others" (Analects 12:22).

> Tzu-chang asked Confucius about humaneness. Confucius said: "He who could put five things into practice everywhere under Heaven would be humane." Tzu-chang begged to ask what they were and he replied: "Courtesy, generosity, good faith, diligence and kindness. If you behave with courtesy, then you will not be insulted; if you are generous, then you will win the multitude; if you are of good faith, then other men will put their trust in you; if you are diligent, then you will have success; and if you are kind, then you will be able to command others" (Analects 17:6).[10]

> Jan Yung asked about humaneness. The Master said: "When you are away from home, behave as if receiving an important guest. Employ the people as if you were officiating at a great sacrifice. Do not do to others what you would not like yourself" (Analects 12:2).

> The Master said: "Now the humane man, wishing himself to be established, sees that others are established, and wishing himself to be successful, sees that others are successful. To be able to take one's feelings as a guide may be called the art of humaneness" (Analects 6:28).[11]

One can see that though the context here is dealing with others, the focus is really on oneself and one's own well-being. But at the same time there is the recognition that one cannot really be happy in isolation. One can be happy only when everybody else is happy. The golden rule comes in handy, in both its positive and negative formulations: "Love others" and "Do not do to others what you would not like to be done to you." This is so different from the individualistic ideals of contemporary commercial-liberal culture, where one's happiness seems to depend on one's capacity to dominate and exploit others. The relationship to the other is not adversarial, but cooperative. The function of the king is to create conditions in which such mutual relationships can be lived in harmony.

Such an ideal community is possible only among people who are not slaves to ignorance and their own passions and desires. Hence Confucius insisted, first of all, on the importance of learning. He himself was a great lover of learning and teaching and taught that learning must be possible for all.[12] Learning consists of five steps. "Study it extensively, inquire into it accurately, think over it carefully, sift it clearly, and practice it earnestly."[13]

Such a process of learning requires self-discipline. Learning is not only from books. "A gentleman, who when he eats, avoids seeking to satisfy his appetite to the full and, when he is at home, avoids seeking comfort, who is diligent in deed and cautious in word, and who associates with those who possess the Way and is rectified by them, may be said to be fond of learning" (Analects 1:4).[14]

Sincerity is essential for a learner. To be sincere is to be authentic, true to oneself.

> Sincerity is the Way to Heaven. To think how to be sincere is the way of man. He who is sincere is one who puts upon what is right without effort and apprehends without thinking. He is naturally and easily in harmony with the Way. Such a man is a sage. He who tries to be sincere is one who sees the good and holds fast to it.[15]

To achieve such sincerity, one has to liberate oneself from inordinate desires and passions. Human nature is good, since it participates in the nature of Heaven. But human beings also participate in animality, and so they become selfish and full of inordinate desires. These must be controlled and mastered. As Confucius has said, "To master oneself and to return to propriety is humanity" (Analects 12:1).[16]

Confucius declared that only at the age of seventy was he able to master all his desires so as to be able to act in harmony with Heaven and with his own nature. "At fifty I knew the Mandate of Heaven. . . . At seventy I could follow my heart's desire without transgressing moral principles" (Analects 2:4).[17]

Confucius may not have explored the social and structural forms that selfish and inordinate desires may take, but these may be implied when he talks about the relationships — not between individuals — but between the people and those who have a social role in the community, such as the king.

## RIGHTS AND RITES

The Confucian tradition lists five kinds of social relationships, first mentioned by Mencius: affinity between father and son, righteousness or duty between ruler and subject, distinction between husband and wife, order between the old and the young, and trust between friends.[18] These relationships can be seen and lived one-sidedly as domination of one pole by the other, but they are in reality reciprocal. If the son honors the father, the father has to care for the son. As the people obey the king, the king protects the people to enable them to follow their own pursuits peacefully. Reciprocity in conjugal relationship is characterized by respect. Reciprocity, therefore, not power, governs these relationships. Reciprocity assumes the integrity of the other party. So we have a community based on mutual trust with a common concern for the welfare of each and all.[19]

Such interaction between humans is governed by *li*, or ritual. Ritual simply lays down the manner in which one is expected to behave in a particular situation. Following ritual, a person grows into a social role, and the social role in turn shapes the person and his or her character.

In a well-learned ceremony, each person adheres to a specific pattern so that the gestures are in harmonious coordination. A series of gestures flow smoothly and effortlessly. It is neither mechanical nor automatic. There is spontaneity and vitality because participants are involved with utter seriousness and sincerity.... Both parties are present to each other and mutual respect is conveyed in the act. It demonstrates the sacred dimension in the profane.[20]

Ritual is the appropriate way to behave in each circumstance. One is not obliged to it by external sanctions; one experiences it as connatural. It expresses creativity rather than power. It transmits culture and socializes a person. It promotes harmony rather than competition. Where there is reciprocity and respect, the individual does not lose his or her uniqueness. Rather his or her individuality is accepted, respected and integrated. That is why there is no uniformity, but harmony.

Li works through spontaneous coordination rooted in reverent dignity. It is both aesthetic and spiritual. Punishment and its concept cluster of command, threat, regulation, force are coercive. Hence they are not natural, not arising out of the humanness of the person. Since li is congruent with human nature, it can empower the community to reform or correct itself. It is thus transformational.[21]

The psychological force through which such transformation takes place is not coercion, but shame. Shame is both internal and external. It is internal when a person feels that he or she has done something inappropriate, because he or she has internalized what is appropriate. It is external when others exert pressure in various ways on a person to encourage appropriate behavior. The force here is moral and personal, not physical. Thus a community governed by li is internally regulated.

In recent times, li has been contrasted with human rights. The idea of human rights is based on the conception of a person as an autonomous individual. Relations between individuals is governed by a social contract. Human rights protect the individual from abuse by society. Democracy respects the right of every individual, but in practice, democracy can become the tyranny of a majority over a minority. Even such tyranny is mediated by a small group that may take hold of power in various unethical ways, under the veneer of formal democracy. The starting point of li is the human person-in-community. The actual difference in social status between persons in a community is recognized, rather than hidden under the fiction of formal equality. Equity seems more realistic in the real world than equality. Human rights have to be protected by law and sanctions. In a society governed by li, there are various informal and consensual mechanisms to resolve conflicts.

There are no metaphysics of morals guaranteeing a concept of human rights. Rather, it is a market place of morals where what is natural and human is open to negotiation. Behind this is the conception that order is defined from the bottom up. Concrete conditions bring generalizations to varying degrees of appropriateness. The notion of universalizability is rendered problematic.

Whereas the West puts priority on abstract universals, Confucian thought puts priority on the concrete particulars. . . . Human rights do not necessitate human dignity. They merely guarantee a minimum standard of life, not a certain quality of life. To Confucian thought, resorting to law and human rights is dehumanizing and impoverishing human dignity. It signifies a failure of community life.[22]

While human rights takes for granted antagonism between individuals, *li* starts with the idea of harmony between individuals-in-community.

In the real world, rights and rites may be complementary. While rights protect an individual from being abused by a dominant community, only rites can build up a community.[23]

## THE FAMILY TRADITION

In recent times, while the harmonious relationship between the state and the people has collapsed, the Confucian tradition has survived and supported the community through maintaining family solidarity and values. Family is a natural grouping, in comparison to which organizations like 'Basic Communities' look artificial. Perhaps the real teaching of the Confucian tradition is that neither families nor basic communities can bring about equality and justice, equity and harmony, without a moral basis that governs relationships and behavior in society.

A lack in the Confucian tradition is any intermediary body between the state and the family — apart from the prophetic intellectuals — that could constitute the base of any people's movement. But there is evidence to show that at least in Korea, community compact associations "served as the organizational base for popular political movements and uprisings in the nineteenth century."[24]

Universal harmony also includes harmony of the human with the cosmos. The Confucian tradition has a particular role for music in promoting such harmony. Confucius has said, "One is roused by the Songs, established by ritual and perfected by music" (Analects 8:8). Music integrates the humans with cosmic harmonies.[25]

# 9

# Christianity and Liberation

In earlier chapters I presented three theologies of Christian inspiration: the *Min-jung* theology of Korea, the *Dalit* theology of India and the theology of *Struggle* from the Philippines. In that process we have come across many Christian liberation theologians from Asia. Some of them have also figured in the chapters on Asian ecological and feminist movements. But there are many others writing and reflecting who are not directly linked to any of these movements. There is a vast amount of literature, as one can see from the Bibliography. One could make the impossible attempt to summarize all that literature, perhaps thematically. But I think it would be more interesting to follow the method I have used with regard to the other religions and present a few theologians who are significant for some specific contribution they have made to the advance of Asian reflection in the field of liberation. My presentation has no claims to be exhaustive. It does not mean to exclude anyone, either. The theologians I am going to focus on are Aloysius Pieris, George Soares-Prabhu, Sebastian Kappen and M. M. Thomas. The reasons for choosing these will become clear as I present them.

## ALOYSIUS PIERIS (1934 -   )

Pieris is a theologian from Sri Lanka. He is not only a scholar in Buddhism but also has close dialogical and experiential contact with Buddhists[1] and is in touch with many multi-religious groups engaged in the struggle for the liberation of the poor.[2] This is the experiential context of his theological reflection.

The Ecumenical Association of Third World Theologians had its third international conference, held for the first time in Asia, in Sri Lanka in 1979.[3] Pieris gave one of the major papers at this conference.[4] Until then, the Latin American perspective of the poor and their struggle for liberation was rather dominant in the association. Pieris affirmed strongly that the poor people of Asia are also very religious. Theological reflection in Asia must take both these elements—poverty and religiosity—together.

### Religiosity and Poverty

The Asian religions, Buddhism in particular, have seen that the cause of poverty is the craving for material goods that leads some to exploit and impoverish others. This craving is therefore countered by the option to *be* poor, giving up both the desire for and the actual possession of material goods.[5] Pieris suggests that people who opt to be poor in this manner must join hands with those who are condemned to be poor by unjust economic and political structures, in order to struggle together for the liberation of everyone from the craving for material goods and the equitable sharing of goods among all.[6] Thus opting to *be* poor leads to the option *for* the poor in a struggle that leads to the liberation of everyone from imposed poverty. When poverty and religiosity come together in this way, both become liberative. Pieris points to this as the specificity of Asian liberation theology.

Pieris sees a model of such an option in Jesus. In the ongoing struggle in the world between God and Mammon, the latter being the power of unjust and exploitative social structures, Jesus chooses to become poor in the very act of his birth. But his identification and struggle with the poor and the outcasts of his day, expressed in his prophetic challenge to the rich and powerful to be converted, leads him to the cross.

> A Christian is a person who has made an irrevocable option *to follow* Jesus; this option necessarily coincides with the option *to be poor*; but the "option to be poor" becomes a true "following of Jesus" only to the extent that it is also an option *for the poor*.... The (theo)logical force of this argument is derived from two biblical axioms: the irreconcilable antagonism between God and wealth, and the irrevocable covenant between God and the poor, Jesus himself being this covenant.[7]

Not only Christians, but many other believers are following Jesus today in his option to struggle with the poor. This is the spiritual way to which all of us are called.

Pieris contrasts this integral way to other partial options that are also prevalent in Asia. Some people focus on the positive aspects of the religiosity of Asia and choose to be poor, but their option to be poor does not become liberative.[8] Others—the Marxist traditions—reject Asian religiosity as superstitious and alienating. They opt to struggle with the poor. Their struggle will not bring liberation, either, since they are not attacking the root cause of poverty, the craving for material goods and the power and status that go with them.[9] Only when the positive elements of poverty and religiosity join together can they become a force for liberation and justice. People who simply focus on development are bound to fail, since they ignore both the religious force of opted poverty and the structural expressions of desire and craving that impose poverty on the many.[10]

### Option to 'Be' the Poor or to Be 'For' the Poor

According to Pieris, while the Asian religions have correctly identified the root cause of imposed poverty in the world as desire and therefore have counseled an option to be poor, only in the Bible do we find the further liberative step of God opting for the poor and struggling with them for their liberation. Pieris sees Jesus as God's defensive pact with the poor for their liberation. Pieris speaks of the twofold evangelizing role of Christians:

> To experience the solidarity with non-Christians by witnessing to the *spirituality common to all religions* (by practicing the beatitudes) and to reveal their *Christian uniqueness* to proclaim Jesus as the new covenant (by joining the poor against mammon's principalities and powers that create poverty and oppression).[11]

Jesus makes visible and embodies an ongoing struggle between God and Mammon. The poor and the oppressed are the agents of this struggle. God in Jesus is taking their side, so that "the struggle of the poor for their liberation coincides with God's own salvific action."[12] That is why many people of good will from other religions are able to take the option that Jesus took. Thus they follow Jesus in practice much more than those who merely profess a formal ritualistic allegiance to Christianity. This option also leads them to reinterpret their own religious traditions.[13] At the level of such praxis in favor of the poor, believers of different religions come together as basic human communities committed to the defense and promotion of equality and justice for all.[14]

In this perspective, the poor have a messianic role in the history of salvation and liberation, because it is through them that God shapes human history. Quoting from George Soares-Prabhu, Pieris shows how being 'poor' in this sense is a biblical, not a 'Marxist' category.

> Poverty in the Bible is indeed primarily a sociological category but it is not to be defined in purely economic, much less in Marxist, terms (non-ownership of the means of production). Biblical poverty has a broader sociological and even a *religious meaning.* The poor in the Bible are an oppressed group in conflict, but it is doubtful whether their conflict can be usefully described as a class struggle. Factors other than the need to control the means of production or to secure economic betterment enter into it, and give it a different colour. The poor in the Bible aspire after a free, fraternal, and non-exploitative community which does indeed call to mind the classless society of Karl Marx. But the Bible goes beyond Marx's classless society in its affirmation of a *religious basis for social justice.* The "new heavens and the new earth" will be "full of the knowledge of the Lord as the waters cover the sea" (Isa. 11:9; 65:25); and in the New Jerusalem God Himself will dwell with humankind and they will be His people and He will be with them (Rev. 21:3-4).[15]

Thus we come back to the merging of poverty and religiosity in the Asian theology of liberation.

I think that Pieris's assertion that while all Asian religions promote the option to *be* poor, the option *for* the poor is something specifically Christian, needs to be qualified. This may be true if Christianity is contrasted with Buddhism. But Hin dus believe that God 'descends' (*avatara*) to the earth in oppressive situations to liberate the oppressed and re-establish justice (*dharma*).

## GEORGE SOARES-PRABHU (1929 - 1995)

Soares-Prabhu was an Indian exegete who wrote extensively about the liberation perspectives in the Bible. He was in touch with and inspired many action groups. Before his untimely death in July 1995, he was planning to write a book on the *Dharma* of Jesus. Fortunately he has left behind him a series of articles that give a clear outline of his thought. *Dharma* is a complex term, meaning the right order of things, duty, righteousness, justice, and norms for behavior.

### God as 'Abba'

The *dharma*, which Jesus both practiced and preached, has its origin in his experience of God.[16] Jesus experienced God as *abba*—unconditionally loving parent (Mt. 11:25; Mk. 14:36; Jn. 11:41). This experience liberated him from all that usually conditions people: their fears and constraints, doubts and compulsions. The world is dominated by *Mammon* (personal bondage) and *Satan* (structured evil). People are slaves to consumerism, eroticism and the pursuit of power, through which they seek to make up for the absence of real love in their lives. That is why God's love brings freedom. Jesus was driven by the Spirit to share this experience of a loving God. It is this personal experience that gave Jesus an authority that ordinary teachers, though they may be learned, do not have.[17] This authority enabled him to challenge the restrictions and formalisms imposed by the Jewish tradition. The law of the sabbath (Mk. 2:27), the rules of purity (Mk. 7:15), and the exclusion of women (Jn. 4:4-42; Lk. 7:36-50; Mk. 14:3-11), children (Mt, 19:13-15), publicans and sinners (Mt. 9:11-13), were radically questioned by him.

The freedom of Jesus, born of God's love for him, found fulfillment in his love or passionate concern for people. He synthesized the love of God (Dt. 6:4-5) and the love of neighbor (Lv. 19:18) into a new commandment (Mt. 22:34-40), where the second is seen, not as a consequence, but as an explanation of the first: to love God means concretely to love the other.[18]

The love of God in us (1 Jn. 4:4; Mt. 5:43-48), reaching out to others, does not allow any distinctions based on caste, race, gender or class. It must be unconditional and embrace all. It has no limits, except death (Jn. 15:13). It includes even 'enemies' (Lk. 6:32-36).

### Love Leading to Justice

The love of God/Jesus responds effectively to the real needs of the people. Thus justice emerges out of love. Jesus' proclamation of the Reign of God offered a vision of a new society. The proclamation of the Reign of God is nothing but the revelation of God's unconditional love. The response required is to open our hearts to this love and express it in loving our neighbor. It is this circuit of love that is at the origin of the new society envisioned by Jesus.

> When the revelation of God's love (the Kingdom) meets its appropriate response in man's trusting acceptance of this love (repentance), there begins a mighty movement of personal and societal liberation which sweeps through human history. The movement brings *freedom* inasmuch as it liberates each individual from the inadequacies and obsessions that shackle him. It fosters *fellowship*, because it empowers free individuals to exercise their concern for each other in genuine community. And it leads to *justice*, because it impels every true community to adopt the just social structures which alone make freedom and fellowship possible. . . . The vision of Jesus summons us, then, to a ceaseless struggle against the demonic structures of unfreedom (psychological and sociological) erected by mammon; and to a ceaseless creativity that will produce in every age new blueprints for a society ever more consonant with the Gospel vision of man. Lying on the horizons of human history and yet part of it, offered to us as a gift yet confronting us as a challenge, Jesus' vision of a new society stands before us as an unfinished task, summoning us to permanent revolution.[19]

In his own life, Jesus engaged in this struggle. His miracles were not isolated acts of compassion but indications of a subversion of 'satanic' structures.[20] He lived a life of solidarity with the poor and of conflict with those who oppress them.[21]

He lived the life of an itinerant religious medicant (Lk. 9:58; 8:1-2). He associated with the outcasts, touching lepers (Mk. 1:40-42) and dining with the tax collectors and sinners, the ritually unclean and socially ostracized (Lk. 15:2; Mk. 2:16).[22] Such solidarity led him into conflict with the theological (scribes—Mk. 2:1-3:6), religious (chief priests—Mk. 11:15-19) and political (Herod—Lk. 13:31-33) establishments. This conflict ended at the cross.[23] But the cross was followed by the resurrection, made present in an experience of the living Jesus, and grounds our hope. This mystery of the living Jesus can be grasped only through praxis, because Jesus is essentially the way. "We understand Jesus and his *dharma* when we begin to practice it."[24]

> To the extent that we are prepared to live by the values of Jesus and commit ourselves to the building up of the community of freedom and fellowship that he envisioned, to that extent spiritual poverty (anti-consumerism) will flourish and oppressive poverty (destitution) will vanish from our lives.[25]

## SEBASTIAN KAPPEN (1924 - 1993)

Sebastian Kappen was born in Kerala, in the southwest part of India, in 1924. He entered the Society of Jesus and completed his doctoral studies in Rome with a thesis on "Praxis and Religious Alienation According to the Economic and Philosophical Manuscripts of Marx." Back in India, he worked closely with many action groups, inspiring them with his reflections. For some time he was also associated with Marxist movements, but later he was disillusioned with doctrinaire Marxism and closer to small groups of people who called themselves 'unattached socialists.' Though he was critical of the church, he was deeply attached to Jesus and explored the liberative and humanizing potential of his life and teachings.[26] Later he also studied the dissenting religious movements in Indian tradition, such as Buddhism and the Bhakti. His reflection focused increasingly on the importance of cultural transformation for integral liberation.[27] He has also written books on Marxism and socialism.[28] In this brief presentation, I would like to focus on his reflections on culture.

### Revolution and Culture

In his book *Jesus and Freedom*, Kappen explored the revolutionary message of Jesus in the economic, political, social, religious and personal spheres of human life in community. His later reflection in *Jesus and Cultural Revolution* considers the contribution of the Jesus tradition to the revolution of consciousness required for the restructuring of Indian society through a new, humane and humanizing culture. Kappen defines culture as "the organic whole of ideas, beliefs, values, and goals which condition the thinking and acting of a community or people."[29] Cultures find embodiment in social institutions. Cultures can be in crisis when the development of culture and social institutions has been unequal. Culture may have grown through new awareness, and the social institutions may be inadequate to bear the new consciousness and its values. Or social institutions may have changed through the influence of colonialism or new technologies, and these may demand a change in value systems. But the most important cause of crisis in culture is its class character. The dominant class normally imposes its vision and values as universally valid upon a whole society. The oppressed classes internalize this culture. But when the oppressed begin to become aware of their oppression and seek liberation, then they begin to challenge the existing culture and to develop a counter-culture. The agents of this transformation are prophetic individuals who evoke the vision of a new society as an object of hope and launch dissenting counter-cultural communities as bearers of this hope.[30] Where such a project of hope fails to take off for some reason, it may seek compensatory outlets. "Chief among these are vertical escape into an illusory heaven above, inscape into one's own isolated self, orgiastic cults issuing in a paroxysm of emotion, and nostalgia for death and dissolution."[31]

Kappen sees such a prophet of a counter-culture in Jesus. He also sees similar prophets in the Buddha and in the Saints of the Bhakti (devotion) tradition in India.

At the time of Jesus, the people in Palestine were suffering under a twofold cultural oppression: forced hellenization by the colonizers and Judaism in decline, where cult, law and apocalypticism had supplanted prophecy. Thanks to his profound experience of the liberating and creative God, Jesus proclaimed a new vision of society that he called the 'Reign of God.' Kappen lists the points of rupture that this new vision effected in the existing value system.[32] In a society that saw riches as a sign of divine favor, he opted for the poor. Against those who put their trust in political power, he chose the weak, who were strong in the power of love. He preferred the simple wisdom of the common people to the sterile erudition of the Scribes and Pharisees. In a male-dominated society, he associated freely with women. He held up children as the heirs of the Reign of God in a community that set much store on age. He challenged the elaborate rules of purity and associated with those considered impure and marginalized, advocating purity of heart and intention. Jesus also founded a prophetic movement, but unfortunately it has not preserved fully the prophetic elan, losing its eschatological consciousness, becoming institutionalized and inculturated in a middle-class community—though prophetic individuals and movements have surfaced from time to time.

## Counter-culture in Indian Tradition

In Indian tradition, the Buddha appears as a counter-cultural force challenging the ritualism and hierarchical domination of the Brahmins. Avoiding metaphysical subtleties, he preaches the way of detachment from craving and universal compassion. His eightfold path is a radical critique of contemporary religion and society. His way is open to everyone, unlike the way of *gnosis*, which is limited to an elite.[33] After the Buddha, we have a series of Bhaktas—people who follow the way of love and devotion—who criticize the ritual and hierarchical structures of Brahminism and advocate the simple way of love accessible to all, irrespective of caste or social status.[34]

## Culture: Traditional and Modern

With the background of these Jesuan and Indian counter-cultural traditions, Kappen looks at the contemporary culture of India and suggests the possible counter-cultural elements we can draw from them today.[35] India is under the impact of two cultural forces: traditional feudal culture and modern capitalistic bourgeois culture. While they oppose each other in some respects, they also strengthen each other in subtle ways.

Traditional culture is centred upon the notion of ritual purity, hierarchical organization of society, the importance of kinship relations, the prevalence of group loyalty, respect for authority, and the magico-religious view of the world. In contrast, bourgeois culture stresses rationality, private interest, individualism, competition, consumerism, monetization of human relations, the rule of quantity over quality, and the cult of efficiency.[36]

One can easily see that these two sets of values are in conflict. Still, the culture has not reached a point of crisis, because these two streams also mingle and strengthen each other. Thus traditional values are integrated within bourgeois institutions. The collectivism of the joint family and the caste adapts itself to the collectivism of capitalist production. Loyalty to the feudal lord is replaced by loyalty to capitalists, politicians and government officials. The hierarchy of status and function takes over from the hierarchy of caste. The caste division of labor finds the capitalist division of production convenient. The capitalist vision of society brings with it its own contradiction, in-so-far as its dreams are realizable only by the rich and powerful few. This brings about unrest among the young, particularly students and the poor, both rural and urban. But cultural, political and hegemonic (interiorized) control keep dampening revolutionary enthusiasm. Kappen concludes:

> Neither tradition nor modernity can lead to the free and full development of the individual. We have to go beyond them in our search for a humane and humanizing culture. But 'going beyond' does not mean discarding them in their entirety. Tradition contains positive elements such as closeness to nature, the sense of belonging to a community, rootedness in the past, and the concreteness of social relations. But these values could not reach full flowering within the framework of caste and obsolete ideologies. Nor may we consider modernity an evil pure and simple. It has brought freedom from magic and superstition; it has emancipated the individual from the stranglehold of the group and extended his lived universe to global proportions. But all this could find only distorted expression under the limiting conditions of capitalism. Only in a genuinely socialist society can the elements of truth in tradition and modernity be realized.... Therefore what the country needs today more than anything else is a cultural revolution.[37]

### Jesus as Counter-cultural

Asking himself what Jesus can offer in order to promote this cultural revolution, Kappen acknowledges that, in spite of the shadows cast by the dogma, cult and institutions of the church, the Good News of Jesus has managed to reach out to many leaders of modern reform movements in India.[38] But its influence has been limited to the elite and has not animated a creative movement of the people. Kappen finds that Jesus can help the Indian people change in the following areas.[39] A cyclical view of history kills enthusiasm for the future; it could be replaced by a creative view that challenges us to make our own history. Then we will not need to run away from history, but will see our own efforts crowned by the gift of God in a 'new world.' A cosmic religiosity that makes us conform to 'nature' can give place to ethics that give value to human initiative and effort animated by love and compassion. Instead of a focus on the individual lost in the cosmic unity of the *Brahman,* we could discover ourselves as persons called to a new community of love and fellowship. Freedom in the Spirit can cast away fear of every kind: fear of pollution, of violence, of spirits, and of the law.

From the Indian tradition, we could learn to experience God as in us, energizing us, rather than dominating us from 'above.' A fully integrated person, rooted in the inner self, freed from every outside compulsion, has always been a highly prized Indian ideal. India also has a keen sense of harmony with nature considered as mother rather than an object to be manipulated and dominated.[40] "Jesuan prophecy must appropriate this sense of oneness and wholeness, while India must make her own the Galilean's dream of the Total Man."[41]

Values, however, cannot change society unless they are embodied and promoted by communities of peoples. Such a community in India today will be open to all believers and people of good will, immersed in the poor masses of India, following the law of love rather than rules and regulations, and making alive traditional symbols such as the Eucharist in an open table-fellowship with the poor and the outcaste, in the manner of Jesus.[42]

Such communities must engage in cultural as well as political action, "aimed at subverting the cultural hegemony of the ruling classes and restoring to the common man the right to think his own thoughts and frame his own scale of values."[43] They will be critical of both the traditional divisive culture of caste and the modern exploitative culture of capitalism.[44] Criticism will have to be complemented by creative activity, giving bodily and sensuous shape to the deepest meaning of life.[45] In this manner, such communities will be manifestations of Jesus in person for the people of today.[46]

## M. M. THOMAS (1916 -    )

Madathiparambil Mammen Thomas was born in 1916 in Kerala, in the southwest of India, into a Mar Thoma Christian Family.[47] From youth, he was involved in social, development, and political activities and in church organizations of animation. In the early forties, his request to join the Communist Party was rejected. He became associate director of the Christian Institute for the Study of Religion and Society at Bangalore in 1957; he was the director from 1962 to 1976. Active in the ecumenical movement at various levels, he was made chairman of the Working Committee on Church and Society of the World Council of Churches in 1961. He served as chairman of the Central Committee of the World Council of Churches in 1968. He became active in politics again in 1975, when Indira Gandhi declared a state of emergency in India. He also briefly served as governor of one of the northeast Indian states, resigning that post because of policy differences with the central government.

M. M. Thomas has written widely on the relation between church and society, carrying on a dialogue with scholars and activists in India and abroad. His interest and involvement in social and political change in India lead him to theological reflection.[48] He has a positive view of the many socio-political liberation movements and religious reform movements in India and Asia. He sees them as a quest for fuller and richer human life, consisting of four elements: the search for freedom as opportunity for creativity; the search for identity for selfhood; the search for new forms of community; and the search for historical vocation. Examining both religious and secular movements in India, he says, "Though from different angles, one from the social and one from the spiritual, both types of neo-Hindus are dealing with the question of the relation between man's ultimate

spiritual destiny and the regeneration of human society in modern Indian
·history."[49]

But due to human sin, these movements also have destructive elements. Power
can be abused without moral control, and the search for liberation can become a
merely human project, resulting in self-righteous pride. However, underlying these
liberation movements there is also a quest for meaning and self-transcendence.[50]

### Christ and Reform Movements in India

Looking at these movements, especially those of India, as a Christian, Thomas
sees the impact of Christ on them. He demonstrated this in his study *The Acknowledged Christ of the Indian Renaissance.*[51] Christ is not merely a hidden, mysterious
presence, as implied in R. Panikkar's *The Unknown Christ of Hinduism.* Christ is
known and is consciously responded to in the reform movements. This leads
Thomas to a broad vision of the presence of Christ in history.

> Christ is present and active in the world today, engaged in a continuous dia-
> logue with men and nations, affirming His kingly rule over them through the
> power of His Law and His Love. The history of His deeds between His res-
> urrection and His coming again in glory holds all other histories within its
> context and control. So the mission of the Church is not to save itself from
> the revolutions of our time but to discern the promise and judgement of Christ
> in them and to witness to His Kingdom in it, waiting for the day of its final
> consummation.[52]

Such a broad, cosmic vision leads him to a certain number of theoretical and practical conclusions.

### Salvation as Humanization

For Thomas, salvation in Christ and humanization are closely related. Salvation
is "the spiritual inwardness of true humanization," and "humanization is inherent
in the message of salvation in Christ."[53] Salvation could be defined as "humanization in a total and eschatological sense."[54] This salvation as humanization is nothing else but the final incorporation of man into Christ's glorified humanity. This is
not a mysterious process, but involves free and creative human action in history.
"Man's transcendence over the structures of society makes restructuring of social
institutions a moral responsibility given to him by God. Social *dharma* or justice is
a dynamic ever-growing concept because of the creativeness of human freedom."[55]

The salvific presence of Christ in human history is not limited to the church but
can be found in all movements for human liberation. It is mediated by various religious and secular ideologies, without being identified with any one of them. This
means that the impact of Christ in history takes on a secular character.[56] The term
'secular' here means worldly, human and historical, but is not identified with any
particular religion, including Christianity.

The cross and the resurrection of Christ are a constant challenge to every liberation movement. This challenge is of two kinds, corresponding to the twofold nature of the deformation of sin in human action. Liberation movements tend to be vitiated by a selfish quest for power that can become oppressive of others. Liberation movements can also become self-righteous, relying purely on human resources to achieve total liberation.

> Creativeness may tempt man to elevate himself as Creator. Self-discovery leads to self-centeredness expressing itself both in the self-seeking of man for power and interests resulting in exploitation and in the endless frustrating search for moral self-justification resulting in ideological fanaticism. The revolution which seeks justice and community may lead to a new ruthless tyranny or the disorder of anarchy. The sense of history and historical purpose and historical vocation may lead nations, classes and races to set themselves up as Providence itself or as the New Messiah to save mankind and bring history to fulfillment.[57]

Christ is a constant reminder of human vulnerability due to sin, with the consequent need for redemption, and of the fact that total liberation is ultimately a gift of God, though it demands human creative action in history. It is from this perspective that Thomas is critical of both Gandhi and Marxism. Gandhi, upholding human moral power, may tend to become self-righteous. The Marxists, engaging in class conflict, may tend to rely too much on political power without moral control.[58]

### Dialogue and Prophecy

It is in this context that Thomas sees the mission of the church as one of dialogue and prophecy. In order to be credible, the Christian must get involved in the world and history, seeking to promote full humanity and participating in the available social and political movements, because this is the common ground for dialogue.

> Common humanity and the self-transcendence within it, more especially the common response to the problems of humanization of existence in the modern world, rather than any common religiosity, or a common sense of the Divine, is the most fruitful point of entry for a meeting of faiths at spiritual depths in our time.[59]

However, the Christian keeps proclaiming Christ as the final answer to the quests of all peoples, through whatever movements, toward full humanity. We have seen in the previous paragraph how Christ fulfills what is lacking in current ideologies, religious and secular. But recognizing the presence and action of Christ in other religions, he has to learn to dialogue with them, giving as well as receiving.

> Christ transcends Christianity, non-Christian religions and Secularism; and judges and redeems their adherents if they are open to Him within their own religious or non-religious setting. . . . The Church's witness to Christ consists

in entering into partnership with men of other religions and secular faiths in the struggle for a secular *koinonia,* learning from them at some points, and correcting them at others, and at the same time pointing to Jesus Christ as the source, criterion and goal of the new humanity they seek.[60]

Since religions and secular ideologies are relativized in this manner, Thomas talks of the need for a creative, Christ-centered syncretism "which would enable Christians to be open to interpenetration at cultural and religious levels, but with Jesus Christ as the principle of discrimination and coherence."[61]

### Christ and the Secular

I think that the two significant elements in the theology of M. M. Thomas are the affirmation of the human and the secular as positive—though open to fulfillment in the risen humanity of Christ—and liberation as an inter-religious, inter-ideological project—though in the horizon of Christ who transcends, while assuming, them. He also highlights the historical impact of the Christ of the Gospels in contemporary religious and secular liberation movements.

# 10

# Islam and Liberation

It would not be surprising if many readers think that Islam and liberation do not go well together. Some would characterize Islam as fundamentalist. Others would think of Muslims imposing the Islamic law (*sharia*) on everyone in countries with a Muslim majority. Still others would think of Islam as violent, putting to death adulterers and blasphemers and cutting off the arms of thieves. All these people tend to look at Islam as a monolith and to form their opinions regarding it from the mass media. While Islam, like every religious tradition, has its drawbacks, at least in practice, Islam has inspired many leaders who have fought for liberation in word and deed. As with other religions, my exploration will focus not on an abstract analysis of Islamic doctrine and tradition, looking for liberative elements in them, but on the writings of Muslims who have inspired and guided movements of liberation in Islamic societies in the 20th century.

Contemporary Islamic liberation movements have their roots in the experience of oppression of Muslim peoples in the colonial and post-colonial periods. The Muslim peoples lost their visible social identity and power under various colonial regimes before the second world war. As the various peoples achieved independence, they were often governed by small groups of westernized, secularized elites, thus continuing the religio-cultural oppression, without much meaningful political participation. On the other hand, various Marxist-socialist movements offered revolutionary but materialistic, atheistic alternatives. In opposition to these socio-political forces, there were some leading Muslim believers in every country who thought that the Islamic tradition—particularly the Qur'an and the Sunna (oral traditions)—offer a blueprint for an integrated and liberated way of life. This belief led them to a deeper study of the sources of Islam and the projection of possible socio-political models for the present and the future. These searches and models are critical of the prevailing powers, whether of the right or left. For this reason, both these forces seek to suppress these movements and deck themselves with a cloak of legitimacy by sponsoring a superficial islamization as part of their own socio-political programs. Suppression, of course, makes these groups more radical and sometimes also more fundamentalist. It depends on one's point of view whether one considers these movements fundamentalist, revivalist or resurgent![1]

Though leaders of such resurgent movements have risen up everywhere in the Islamic world, I shall limit my attention to three examples from Asia. As I mentioned above, I am taking leaders who not only speculated, but were active in promoting their ideas and ideals, their influence sometimes extending far beyond the borders of their own countries. One of them paid for his activism with his life.

## MAWLANA SAYYID ABUL A'LA MAWDUDI (1903-1979)

Mawlana Mawdudi was born in Aurangabad, India, on November 25, 1903.[2] On his father's side, his ancestry is traced back to the Prophet Mohammed. His family had a long line of spiritual leaders in the Sufi orders. He draws his Islamic roots and fervor, moral uprightness and regard for righteousness from his family tradition and education. When he reached the university, he had to discontinue his studies because of the illness and death of his father, but he continued his education on his own, reading and reflecting. He turned to journalism for a living and was appointed editor of the *Taj* at the age of seventeen and later of *al-Jamia* at the age of twenty. This launched his writing career, and he became a prolific writer. His writings were translated into many languages, and his influence extended beyond the borders of the subcontinent. Charles J. Adams says of him, "Today Mawdudi must rank among the most popular and respected authors in the Islamic domains, if indeed he is not the single most widely read writer among Muslims at the present time. His writings give strong expression to the themes basic to the present-day Islamic resurgence."[3]

Mawdudi undertook a study of Islamic tradition in the context of contemporary western worldviews, writing an extensive commentary in Urdu on the Qur'an. He could not ignore the Indian movement for independence, but he was against nationalism. His image of community was the *umma*, which transcended cultural and national boundaries, united by its common submission to God. He was also afraid of a democratic India in which the Hindus would be a majority and the Muslims would lose their significance. His answer to the problematic situation was the founding of a group—the *Jama'at-i-Islami*—meant to be a gathering of people rooted in Islamic values to provide leadership in creating an Islamic society. When India was divided into two countries in 1947, he migrated to Pakistan. There he devoted himself to the task of promoting the creation of an Islamic society. The *Jama'at* became a political party, but Mawdudi was less and less successful in imposing his ideas on the country. Mawdudi was basically a moral-religious leader. Clear and strong in his ideology, he could be intolerant of other views. He was a constant critic. He was not a compromising politician, though he was ready for a progressive realization of his ideals. He died in 1979.

### *The Supremacy of God*

For Mawdudi, the Islamic tradition, especially the Qur'an and the Sunna, provided a complete and adequate way of life. The tradition, of course, needs to be interpreted for contemporary times. The affirmation of the *Tawhid*, of the unity of

God as creator and master of everything and of human life and society, is the basic principle of the Islamic vision of society. God is sovereign, to which every other sovereignty is subject. Thus, while he accepted democracy, he did not accept the sovereignty of the people. The human being is only a vice-regent of God in the world, so people are to submit to and follow God's directives regarding their lives and society.

God has manifested God's will through the prophets. The prophets have mediated God's directives to every people in the world. Mohammed is, of course, the last and greatest of these. Submission to God's directives—*Islam*—is the purpose of human life. Everyone who submits to God belongs to the community of the *umma*, which therefore extends far beyond Muslim borders. The whole universe is governed by this ongoing divine-human dialogue. Mawdudi describes its focus:

> Islam desires, above all, that people should commit themselves entirely to God's Truth and that they should serve and worship only God. Similarly, it desires that the law of God should become the law by which people lead their lives. It demands, too, that injustice be eradicated, that those evils be wiped out which incur God's anger and that those virtues and social values be fostered which are liked by God.[4]

But, as a matter of fact, there is an ongoing conflict between the forces of Islam and those of *Jaihiliya. Jaihiliya* stands for all the worldviews and systems of thought, belief and action that deny God's sovereignty and the authority of Divine guidance.[5] *Jaihiliya* can be total or partial. A recognition of God as creator can go with other false beliefs. It can also take the form of exaggerated spirituality or world renunciation or mystical flights with monistic or pantheistic overtones. Mawdudi is particularly concerned with Muslims compromising with the prevailing *Jaihiliya* of the age in the name of promoting Islam: excessive concern for material interests may disregard the true moral spirit of Islam, or values, principles and modes of conduct are taken over from non-Islamic societies but an Islamic facade is maintained, even using Islamic terminology.

### The Role of Conflict: Jihad

Islamic revival involves analysis of the situation, to discover the form of the *Jaihiliya* present and the weaknesses of Islam. This should be followed by the development of a strategy to bring about change. This strategy will have a threefold thrust. First of all comes information and education. The vision and principles of Islam must be interpreted in the context of the contemporary situation and expressed in a manner intelligible to all. Secondly, there must be an effort to build up the moral fiber of the people, getting them involved in the project for reconstruction. This process is known as *Ijtihad. Ijtihad* at the intellectual level must be accompanied by *Jihad* (struggle) at the practical level.[6] The term *Jihad* is often popularly understood as a fundamentalist struggle leading to indiscriminate violence. Mawdudi explains:

*Jihad* is but another name for the attempt to establish the Divine Order; the Qur'an therefore declares it to be a touchstone of belief. In other words, people who have faith in their hearts will neither succumb to domination by an evil system, nor begrudge giving their wealth and even their lives in the struggle to establish Islam.[7]

*Jihad* is primarily a moral struggle within the Islamic community oriented to reform. The reform focuses both on personal and social change.

In the area of social life, the programme emphasizes resort to public pressure to prevent people from being subjected to injustice; creating a sense of hygiene and cleanliness and fostering co-operation among people so as to ensure healthy conditions of living; drawing up lists of orphans and widows, of the crippled and the incapacitated people, and of poor students and arranging for their financial assistance; and catering for the health requirements of people, especially the poor. Clearly, inspired by Islamic ideals, the objective is to foster the religious, moral, social and material welfare of the people and to move towards creating the social conditions which are conducive to the total transformation of human life.[8]

But more important than social change is personal change. After a critical study of the French, Russian and Turkish revolutions, Mawdudi concluded that if people are not changed with regard to their outlook, goals, motivations, and personality, mere changing of the socio-economic and political framework will not help.[9] Education, not the use of force, a gradual, not a "revolutionary" process, can bring about the desired changes.

*Jihad*, then, is not primarily directed against non-Muslims, unless they oppose the efforts of Muslims to establish an Islamic social order. Mawdudi insisted that both the ends and the means ought to be commendable. Ends do not justify the means.[10] Mawdudi also said that the use of force must be limited to the unavoidable and morally justifiable minimum. Materialistic or political/religious expansionistic goals do not justify *Jihad*. It is interesting to note that the first time Mawdudi was thrown into prison by the Pakistani government was when he declared publicly in a mosque in Peshawar that the invasion of Kashmir by Pakistani forces did not fulfill the conditions of an Islamic *Jihad*.[11]

### The Role of Leadership

According to Mawdudi's analysis, leadership in society is responsible for its social deterioration or betterment. He began one of his lectures:

The objective of the Islamic movement, in this world, is revolution in leadership. A leadership that has rebelled against God and His guidance and is responsible for the suffering of mankind has to be replaced by a leadership that is God-conscious, righteous and committed to following Divine guidance. . . . [12] If power and leadership are vested in God-fearing people, society moves along the right lines, and even the wicked have to follow certain rules. Good flourishes, and evils, if not altogether eradicated, are contained.[13]

He therefore saw the training of good leaders and their taking responsibility for society as a basic requirement of reform. His *Jama' at-i Islami* was precisely a means of training such leaders. The participation of such leaders in political activity then becomes almost a necessity. This is probably the reason why the *Jama' at* became a political party in Pakistan. He was careful, however, to separate the identity of these social leaders from the *Ulama*, the traditional religious leadership in the Muslim community. He was even critical of them, though he collaborated with them for achieving particular political ends. His hopes that good people will automatically rise to leadership positions in a democratic polity were repeatedly belied, as the common people were concerned with more down-to-earth things, once their vague aspirations for an Islamic society were enshrined in the Constitution.

## Theo-democracy

This insistence on the role of leadership does not make Mawdudi forget that it is the Muslim as such—that is, every Muslim—who is a vice-regent of God.

The right to rule belongs to the whole community of believers. There is no reservation or special prerogative in favour of any particular individual, family, clan or class. Such a society cannot tolerate class divisions, and it will not permit disabilities for citizens on the basis of birth, social status, or profession. . . . Neither is there any room for the dictatorship of one individual or a group of persons. The ruler in an Islamic state is only one caliph or vicegerent of God among an entire community of caliphs . . . (and) he is answerable both to them on the one hand and to God on the other.[14]

A practical consequence of this is that everyone has the right to be consulted in every decision that concerns them, even though the actual manner of such consultation has to be worked out in practice.

All administrative matters and all questions about which no explicit injunction is to be found in the *shariah* are settled by the consensus among the Muslims. Every Muslim who is capable and qualified to give a sound opinion on matters of Islamic law, is entitled to interpret the law of God when such interpretation becomes necessary. In this sense the Islamic polity is democratic.[15]

Mawdudi characterizes this as *theo-democracy*. It is based on the loyalty of all to divine guidance. But it is not a theocracy, because no one, particularly not the *Ulamas* or the religious leadership (the 'priesthood'), can claim to be the special interpreter of this divine guidance. It is based on the sovereignty of God, not of the people. The people have only a limited sovereignty in so far as they listen to God and can delegate or depose their rulers.

One of the consequences of this view is that only Muslims can be full citizens of an Islamic state. Non-Muslims who agree to be loyal and obedient to the Islamic state are allowed to live among them, but they have no right to participate in government or hold positions of authority and leadership. Theo-democracy is an exclusive ideological society, based on a sense of divine vocation.[16]

We can understand, then, that in Islamic society there is no separation between religion and other aspects of life. The law of God—the *shariah*—is all-embracing, though there are many areas in modern life that need a re-interpretation and application of the legal tradition as handed down by the Qur'an and the Sunna (practice) of the Prophet.[17] He relativizes, however, the prescriptions dealing with the externals of life as compared to interior attitudes.[18] He has no use for secularism, which he interprets as a separation between religion and the state, or religionlessness. It is from this point of view that he looks at the other models of societies, particularly the western liberal and Marxist models. For him, western society has no sense of direction. While he appreciates its scientific discoveries and sees them as the common property of humanity, western society makes religion a private affair and builds a society without or independent of religion. Marxism is judged more severely as being atheistic. He contrasts these with an Islamic society, where Islam provides the sense of direction needed through divine guidance. He recognizes the existence of basic human qualities everywhere, but Islam "builds a higher system of morality by virtue of which mankind can realize its greatest potential." In addition, Islam "has been entrusted with the mission to spread good in the world and prevent evil . . . (so that) no power in the world can stand against it."[19] We see here a messianic intensity and commitment.

It is this commitment that leads him from being a mere ideologue to active politics, when he finds that he can try to build up an Islamic society in Pakistan. His experience must have shown him the distance between a moral/spiritual vision and practical political action, with its art of compromise. The ideological clarity of his vision seems to have made him an intolerant person and led to successive splits in the party, but his lack of success as a politician takes away nothing from the intensity and inspiring character of his vision.

## DR. ALI SHARIATI (1933 - 1977)

Dr. Ali Shariati was born on November 23, 1933, in Mazinan, near Mashhad, Iran. His domestic environment was intensely religious.[20] He began his life as a teacher in 1952. Even before he received his B.A. from the University of Mashhad in 1959, he joined the National Resistance Movement after the installation of the Shah as king by a 1953 coup. He was arrested and harassed along with his father and fourteen other members of the NRM by the SAVAK, the secret police of the Shah. Unfettered by such harassment, he helped his father found the Center for the Propagation of Islamic Principles in Mashhad and became a leading teacher there. In 1960, he went to Paris for doctoral studies, during which he not only studied many western ideologies and movements but also became involved in the Algerian liberation front, coming into close contact with Frantz Fanon, whom he introduced to the Iranian youth through translations. He also helped found an organization called the Liberation Movement of Iran in 1960 and a second National Front abroad in 1962, on whose behalf he edited a widely read Persian journal called *Free Iran.* On his return to Iran, after securing doctorates in sociology and the history of religions in 1964, he was arrested and thrown into prison. Released after six months, he was unable to find a proper job and took to teaching in school again. After a brief spell of teaching at the University of Mashhad, he was forced to quit his job and returned to Tehran, where he established the famous Husseineh Ershad religious center. He offered guidance to the youth of Iran through free lectures, classes and distribution of books. His lectures and books found a ready and large market. In 1973, the SAVAK closed down the Husseineh Ershad center and, unable to lay hands on him, arrested his father. He surrendered to the police, but was not able to secure the release of his father. He was kept and tortured in prison for eighteen months. Under international pressure, he was released in 1975. Unable to lecture or publish under tight surveillance, he escaped to England in 1977 and, after only three weeks of freedom, died under mysterious circumstances in June 1977, popularly believed to have been martyred by the SAVAK.

Dr. Ali Shariati was a prolific lecturer and writer, and his published works have been collected in more than thirty-five volumes. Some major themes keep recurring, and I shall devote my attention to these. Ali Shariati has been described as the ideologue of Iran's Islamic revolution, but his influence extends far beyond the borders of Iran. Introducing one of his books, John L. Esposito writes:

> Shariati preached what may be termed a liberation theology, which combined a reinterpretation of Islamic belief with modern sociopolitical thought. His Islamic ideology was for the liberation of Iranians, as individuals and as a community, from political oppression and cultural assimilation. It emphasized national identity/unity and socio-economic justice.[21]

In order to situate Shariati's thoughts, it is important to understand the context in which he was writing. Iran was under the power of the Shah, who was perceived as a puppet of the western powers, seeking to impose western values and outlook on the people. People experienced this as colonial oppression. On the world scene, western liberal capitalism was opposed by other ideologies such as Marxism and existentialism. All these ideologies were perceived as basically materialistic and atheistic, and rejected. The Islamic tradition is seen as an alternative that is not only viable, but imperative for Muslims. Hence an effort is made to rediscover Islam and make it a revolutionary force.

### Islam and True Humanism

In this effort at rediscovery, Islam is seen not only as an alternative to modern ideologies but as representing true humanism that has been kept enslaved by various forces throughout history and is now seeking to free itself. Such a perspective of history is interesting, because it shows the special value that a true believer bestows on Islam.

> True humanism is a collection of the divine values in man that constitute his moral and religious cultural heritage. Modern ideologies, in denying religion, are unable to account for these values.... Poor man—always searching for deliverance and finding only disaster. In his flight from the oppression of the powerful and the slave-masters, he turned to the great religions and followed the prophets, and so endured the struggles and martyrdoms only to be captured by the Magi, Caliphs, Brahmans, and most terrible of all, the dark and deadly tumult of the Medieval Church.... Generations struggled and sacrificed to bring about a Renaissance, to mobilize humanity to pursue science and liberation, so that it might be freed from what had been inflicted upon it in the name of religion....
>
> Humanity arrived at liberalism, and took democracy in place of theocracy as its key to liberation. It was snared by a crude capitalism, in which democracy proved as much a delusion as theocracy. Liberalism proved an arena in which the only freedom was for horsemen, vying with one another in raids and plundering.... The desire for equality, for liberation from this dizzying whirl of personal avarice, so horrifyingly accelerated by the machine, led humanity into a revolt that resulted in Communism. This Communism however, simply represents the same fanatical and frightening power as the Medieval Church, only without God....
>
> But the spirit never dies.... It seeks a third road between this one to the tavern and that to the temple, a third road which it is the mission of the Third World to set out upon.... Islam will play a major role in this new life and movement. In the first place, with its pure *tauhid*, it offers a profound spiritual interpretation of the universe, one that is as noble and idealistic as it is logical and intelligible. In the second place, through the philosophy of the creation of Adam, Islam reveals in its humanism the conception of a free, independent, noble essence, but one that is as fully attuned to earthly reality as it is divine and idealistic.[22]

Shariati comes back in various ways to this specificity of Islam as compared to other religions and cultures. He accepts the existence of various prophets but points out a basic difference between the prophets of the religions of the Book and others. While others, such as Confucius, Buddha, and Zoroaster usually come from the noble or priestly sections of the people and associate with the secular power in order to further their objectives, Moses, Jesus and Mohammed rise out of the common people and oppose the rich and the powerful.[23] From another point of view, Shariati says:

> An enlightened Muslim . . . should be fully aware of the fact that he has a unique culture which is neither totally spiritual, as is the Indian culture, nor totally mystical, as is the Chinese, not completely philosophical, as is the Greek, and not entirely materialistic and technological, as is the Western cul-

ture. His is a mixture of faith, idealism and spirituality, and yet full of life and energy with a dominant spirit of equality and justice.... Unlike other religions which justify poverty, Islam condemns it.... (Its) elements are based on constant striving (*jihad*) and justice (*'adalat*). Islam pays attention to bread, its eschatology is based on active life in the world, its God respects human dignity and its messenger is armed.[24]

Shariati's attempt to spell out the specificity of Islamic ideology and culture indicates some of the basic principles of his liberation theology as derived from Islam. We can spell out these in a little more detail.

## The God of the Oppressed

Shariati calls the God of Islam the "God of the oppressed, of those who are fighting for their freedom, of the martyrs for the cause of truth and justice."[25] The basic root of Islam is the *tauhid* or the monotheistic affirmation of One God.[26] But for Shariati, it also represents a worldview that sees the whole world as "constituting a total, harmonious, living and self-aware system,"[27] transcending all dichotomies, guided by the same divine purpose. *Tauhid* is opposed to *shirk*, which means setting something beside God as an object of worship. *Shirk* is idolatry. Shariati, however, gives these principles a sociological content. In the beginning, to the affirmation of one God corresponds a unified society of equality and justice. When this social unity is broken up into differences of classes and groups, polytheism emerges in the sphere of religion. Fighting inequality and injustice in the world is a religious duty, because one is actually fighting polytheism and idolatry.[28] "In fact," says Shariati, "the ruling class has always attempted to establish a polytheistic world-vision in religion, and a materialistic world-vision out of science."[29]

God manifests his divine guidance through the Prophet to the People. The people—the mass, without any distinction of social class—bear the responsibility for their life and destiny. When the people listen to divine guidance, they become the *umma*, a group of people who have come together with a common faith, with the intention of moving toward a common goal. Here the 'mass' acquires, through faith, a dynamism and direction, ideology and commitment.[30]

Man is the representative of God on this earth and also his trustee. This means that he is responsible not only for his own fate, but also has a mission to fulfil the divine purpose for the world. As the representatives and trustees of God, all men are not only equal (in a formal way), but they are brothers, sharing in the same nature. Male and female are of the same nature; they are brothers and sisters.[31] Islam takes seriously both the material and the spiritual nature of the human person. His double nature makes him a dialectical, dynamic being.[32] Islam is not otherworldly or mystical, but is very much concerned with life in this world.

Islam is a realistic religion and loves nature, power, beauty, wealth, affluence, progress, and the fulfillment of all human needs.... Its book, more than being concerned with metaphysics and death, speaks about nature, life, world, society and history. Instead of talking about praying, it talks about struggle.... It invites people to submit themselves to God, and urges revolt against oppression, injustice, ignorance and inequality.[33]

What is specific to man among the whole creation is that, as a spiritual being, he is self-conscious, can make choices and can create. This is what enables him to be God's trustee. With the power of the sciences and love, he can free himself and society from the various structures that oppress him.[34]

### The Context of Conflict

According to Islam, God and Satan are not two powers that are at war with each other in nature. There is only one power in nature: the divine power. It is in man and society that there is a battle between good and evil. Shariati analyzes this as a struggle between the symbolic figures of Cain and Abel. According to the Qur'an, both offer sacrifice to God. Abel's sacrifice alone is accepted and Cain, out of jealousy, murders Abel. Cain was a farmer, and Abel tended animals. Shariati sees this as the emergence of monopoly agricultural production and private property bringing about economic inequality and the domination of power.[35] In the course of history, the Cainian principle appears in three areas: money, power and religion. Shariati has symbolic figures to represent them: Pharaoh as a symbol of power, Croesus as a symbol of riches, and Balaam as the symbol of the clergy, who monopolize religion as a ritual system.[36] These three have always worked together. The unequal and unjust relationship between the powerful few and the powerless, oppressed many represents a basic structure of human society in all ages, though the means and expression of this power relationship may vary from age to age. Slavery, serfdom, feudalism, bourgeoisie, industrial capitalism, and imperialism are only different manifestations of the same basic structure of inequality.[37]

Shariati develops much more in detail the oppressions of contemporary imperialism. There is, of course, economic domination and the effort to make people consumers. As a support to this process, there is an attempt to spread a uniform materialistic culture. The converse of this process is the effort to deprive people of their cultural and religious roots in their own tradition. Shariati feels that to tear people away from their cultural roots is to deprive them of their identity and humanity and thus make them easy objects of exploitation. The West is helped in this by local pseudo-intellectuals who slavishly imitate and propagate little-understood western models. He sees this as a conflict between the West and the East.[38] He points to this process taking place in colonial and post-colonial situations in Africa and Asia.

Colonial powers, particularly at their early stages, under the guise of "attacking fanaticism" fought religion, under the name "condemning reactionism" attacked history, and, using the pretext of "hacking away at superstition and old beliefs," assaulted tradition in order to produce a people without history, without tradition, without culture, without religion, and without any form of identity.[39]

The pity is that this could continue to happen through intermediaries, even after the demise of overt political colonialism. It is further helped by people who project a false image of religion as mainly ritual.[40] He also points to leaders who are reacting to such oppression and affirming their cultural identity, like Frantz Fanon in Algeria, Nyerere in Tanzania, and Nehru in India. Shariati obviously sees the evil effects of cultural westernization in the Iran of the Shah, and criticizing and opposing it is part of his project of liberation. The resurgence of Islam that he proposes is really the recovery of Iran's own historical, cultural and religious resources.[41]

*The Role of Leaders*

It is in this context that Shariati outlines the role of spiritual/intellectual leaders whom he calls "free thinkers" or enlightened persons. Their function is not political leadership, but cultural, bestowing awareness on the masses. I think Shariati tried to be one such, conscientizing the people, particularly the youth, rather than entering politics. The following picture could well be a self-definition, at least as an ideal.

(An enlightened person) is one who is aware of the existing social conflicts and their real causes, who knows the needs of his age and his generation, who accepts responsibility for providing solutions as to how his society can be emancipated, who helps his society to shape and define its collective goals and objectives and, finally, who takes part in mobilizing and educating his static, ignorant society. In a word, a contemporary enlightened person should continue in the path of prophets. His mission is to "guide" and work for justice, his language is compatible with his time, and his proposed solutions conform to cultural values of his society.[42]

The Husseineh Ershad religious center was meant to be a place to train such leaders, and Shariati outlined a detailed program of studies that is a model of what one could call integral education.[43] He also laid out a plan of action for the promotion of Islamic renaissance—"Islamic Protestantism"—offering a critical, revolutionary, aggressive spirit of independent reasoning (*ijtihad*)

An enlightened person has to be a prophet, but unfortunately, prophets are not always welcome, and they often become martyrs. Belonging to the Shia tradition of Islam, with the example of Imam Husayn before him, Shariati was only too sensitive to this dimension of the life of a prophet. Martyrdom is not a tragedy, a death imposed on a hero; it is a death opted for, an act of witness—the only form of testimony to truth possible under the circumstances.[44] Shariati must have been ready when death came knocking at his door.

I would like to conclude this section with an extract from a prayer by Shariati:

O God of the deprived!
Thou who willed

That Thou wouldst grace
The deprived upon the earth,
Those masses who are condemned to weakness
And deprived of life,
Who are the enslaved of history,
The sacrifices of oppression
And the plundering of time,
And who are the wretched upon the earth,
To become the leaders of human beings
And inherit the earth.
Now the time has come
And the deprived upon the earth
Are in anticipation of Thy promise.[45]

## ASGHAR ALI ENGINEER

Engineer, from Bombay, India, is the son of a Bohra Muslim theologian and is a trained theologian. He is involved in human rights movements and efforts to promote harmony among religions. He also works against the use of religion for exploitation and other personal and political interests. In dialogue with Christianity in particular, he has explored the liberative elements in Islam. Unlike Shariati or even Mawdudi, he is more textual in his approach, trying to show from the Qur'an itself perspectives that promote justice and liberation.[46]

### The Prophet and Liberation

The liberative elements in Islam can be traced back to the Prophet himself and his experience. At his time, Mecca was principally a commercial city with some rich merchants but many poor people who depended for their livelihood mainly on their meager earnings from servicing the commercial caravans passing through. The people were ignorant and superstitious, worshiping a multiplicity of gods. Women were oppressed; they could even be buried alive! (Q. 81:8-9). There were many slaves. Against traditional tribal norms, widows and orphans were neglected. There were tribal divisions often leading to conflict. The Prophet himself was from a poor, though noble, family. He was sent by God to liberate the people from their ignorance and oppression. He was not only a teacher, but an activist and fighter. He was forced to flee Mecca when his liberative message was rejected, but he returned with a liberative army to establish justice. Under his inspiration, the Arabs, besides liberating themselves, also sought to liberate people from the oppressive Roman and Sassanid empires.[47] It is from this praxis that the liberative tradition of Islam emerges.

The Qur'an affirms the basic unity of all human beings: "O humankind! we have created you all out of a male and female, and have made you into nations and tribes, so that you recognize one another. Verily, the noblest of you in the sight of God is one who is most righteous (and just)."[48]

Such social unity is based on *tawhid*, or the unity of God. Such a fundamental principle of unity, according to Engineer, is not limited to the racial and ethnic dimension, but also includes the abolition of economic disparity.[49] The two words used in the Qur'an to indicate justice are *'adl* and *qist*. *'Adl* means not only justice, but carries the sense of equalizing and leveling. It is taken as the opposite of *zulm* and *jaur*, wrongdoing and oppression. *Qist* also means equal distribution as well as justice, fairness and equity. Such equal distribution also refers to material resources.[50] This interpretation is confirmed by the Qur'an's attitude to wealth. It says, "It (wealth) may not circulate only among those of you who are rich" (59:7). Again: "And they ask thee what they ought to spend. Say: That which is superfluous" (2:219). This is taken as saying that one need not retain more than is necessary. The Qur'an also discourages ostentatious living as leading to destruction. "And when we would destroy a township, we send commandment to its folk who live at ease, and afterward they commit abomination therein, and so the world (of doom) hath effect for it, and we annihilate it with complete annihilation" (17:16).

The Qur'an's concern for justice is also shown in its attitude in defense of the poor. "Why should you not fight for the cause of Allah and the weak among men and of the women and the children who are saying: Our Lord! bring us forth from out of this town of which the people are oppressors!" (4:75). And again: "And we desired to show favor unto those who were oppressed in the earth, and to make them leaders and make them the inheritors" (28:5). There are also many *hadith*, or traditions of the Prophet, that confirm this: "O Lord, I seek refuge in Thee from poverty, scarcity and indignity." And another: "O Lord I seek refuge in Thee from *kufr* (unbelief) and poverty," thus equating poverty with unbelief.

### Justice in Practice

This attitude to the poor and justice is supported by many positive and negative prescriptions. People are exhorted to be just in their dealings: "O you who believe! Be steadfast witnesses for Allah in equity, and let not hatred of any people seduce you that you deal not justly. Deal justly, that is nearer to piety" (5:8). Extravagance is discouraged: "Look to your adornment at every place of worship and eat and drink, but be not prodigals" (7:31).

The Qur'an levied *zakat*, a form of combined wealth and income tax, on all the faithful. The rate is not specified and could be adjusted according to the need of the situation. It was one of the basic institutions of Islam, together with prayer. The Qur'an says: "And in their wealth the needy and the deprived have due share" (51:19). And again: "Have you observed him who belies religion? It is he who turns away the orphan and does not urge others to feeding of the needy. Woe to those who pray but are heedless in their prayer: who make a show of piety and give no alms to the destitute" (107). The *zakat* was collected in a common treasury and distributed to the needy, the orphans and the widows, to pay off the debts of the indebted, and to free slaves. Land was considered the property of Allah and, through Him, of the people. The Prophet not only forbade sharecropping, but also prohibited retention of land by those who do not cultivate it.[51] The Qur'an was also against usury, which could be taken as a symbol of other forms of exploitation. "O ye who believe! Observe your duty to Allah and give up what remains (due to you) from usury, if you are (in truth) believers. And if you do not, then be warned of war (against you) from Allah and His messenger" (2:278-279).

### The Place of Women in Islam

One of the foci for contemporary liberation movements is the oppression of women. Islam is often accused of discrimination against the rights of women. The Qur'an affirms that with regard to rights and obligations, women are equal to men (2:228). Engineer thinks that the Qur'an gave them a charter of rights never before given to women. The woman was a legal entity in her own right. She could contract marriage or divorce freely. She could inherit and own property. She could have custody of the children. The only point which does not fit in with this charter of liberties is permission for men to marry many women. But the conditions under which this was permitted may not exist any more. Such permission was given for the protection of widows and orphans, so they could be taken care of. Thus the Qur'an says: "And if you fear that you cannot do justice to orphans, marry such women as seem good to you, two, or three, or four, but if you fear that you will not do justice, then (marry) only one of that which your right hands possess" (4:3). Neither polygamy for pleasure nor large harems have Quranic sanction. Even this exception may not be needed any more under modern conditions.

### Attitude to Other Religions

According to Engineer, openness, tolerance and respect for other religions is an important liberative element. The Qur'an says: "For every one of you We appointed a law and a way. And if Allah had pleased He should have made you a single people, but that He might try you in what He gave you. So vie one with another in virtuous deeds" (5:48). Addressing unbelievers, it says: "Unto you your religion and unto me my religion" (2:109). "There is no compulsion in religion" (2:256) seems an unequivocal declaration.

Engineer thinks that religious difference could never be the reason for conflict. The Qur'an always speaks highly of *mujahid* (one who strives, fights for the right cause) (4:95). It is in this context that one should speak of *jihad*. Its only justifications are protecting the interests of the weak and oppressed and the defense of oneself against aggression.[52] The Qur'an says again: "Fight in the way of Allah against those who fight against you, but begin not hostilities. Lo! Allah does not love the aggressors" (53:39).

Liberating the oppressed is not an easy path. The Qur'an calls it the steep uphill road.

And what could make thee conceive what it is, that steep uphill road? (It is) freeing of a human being from bondage or feeding, upon a day of hunger, an orphan near of kin, or of a needy (stranger) lying in the dust and being, withal, of those who attained to faith, and who enjoin upon one another patience in adversity, and enjoin upon one another compassion. Such are they that have attained to the right side (i.e. righteousness) (90:12-18).

## Two Special Questions

Any discussion of Islam and liberation will have to confront the question of *jihad* and the violence connected with it.[53] Though *jihad* means effort and struggle, such struggle does not exclude violence. There are some constants. The only proper goal of *jihad* is not economic, political or territorial gain, but the defense and propagation of the Realm of God, governed by God's law or *shariah*. This divine law is perceived as absolute and universal. Its imposition, therefore, is not seen as oppressive, but natural; this is how things are meant to be. Since Islam does not distinguish between religion and the state, the *jihad* must be considered in the tradition of the just war in Jewish and Christian tradition. It is not a 'holy war' or crusade. While all Muslims would accept the need and legitimacy of *jihad,* there is no agreement among Muslim jurists regarding when it should be waged, how, and who decides to wage it. With regard to 'when?' opinions vary from 'to convert people to Islam' to defense of the Islamic way of life against aggression. Aggression, therefore, could include not only religious persecution but also colonial and other dominations, since Islam does not recognize any distinction between religion and state. War must be inevitable, and must be directed to combatants only. Even since the separation between the religious and secular leadership in Islamic societies, there is always a dispute about who can proclaim a *jihad.* A widely accepted position gives this prerogative to the religious leader, the *imam* or the *lama.* The very disagreement among the jurists shows that the Qur'an is not very clear about it, while not excluding the possibility of war in the pursuit of Islamic goals. Christians who defend the theories of a 'just war' have no reason to be overly critical of the principle of *jihad.*

A second relevant question is Islam's functioning in religiously pluralistic situations. The normal position seems to be the establishment of an Islamic society where Muslims are in a majority, even if the minorities, especially the Jews and the Christians (people of the Book), are granted freedom in the religious sphere. But they are second-class citizens. When Muslims are in a minority, they demand freedom to practice their religion. However, there seems to be some evolution in this area in South and Southeast Asia. There is a group of Indian Muslims who feel that while they must resist idolizing the nation, a secular state that is neutral to all religions and gives freedom of religious belief and practice must be acceptable to Muslims. They should not only tolerate it, but accept and defend it.[54] Besides, if the Muslims believe that the Islamic way of life is natural and rational, then they must be able to promote its wider acceptance through rational argument.[55] In Indonesia, the Muslims seem to be seeking to go one step further. The *pancasila,* or the 'five principles,' namely belief in one God, nationalism, democracy based on consensus, humanitarianism and social justice, provides a common ideological base for the collaboration of all religious believers in the common activities of the nation. Abdurrahman Wahid of Indonesia says:

> Apart from the much-touted "Islamic political theories" offered by scholars and ideologies alike, communities of muslims have developed different frameworks and participated in almost all types of social forms known to history in the past fourteen centuries. . . . Indonesians have shown that Islam could share a common ideology with other beliefs and political persuasions.[56]

What this shows is that Islam is not as monolithic as some of the Muslims, under various socio-cultural and political compulsions, would like to make it.

# 11

# The Cosmic Religions
# and Liberation

We have so far explored the liberative elements in what are usually called the 'great,' or developed, religions. But anyone with some experience of the religious practice of the people knows that it is not the same as what these religions profess or advocate, so we speak of popular religion or religiosity. The 'great' religions often look down upon such popular religions as superstitious and oppressive. One refers to them disparagingly as 'animism,' yet we noted many popular religious elements such as shamanistic practices in Korea and *pasyon* in the Philippines, so we could ask whether popular religions can also help in the process of liberation in some way. This seems all the more urgent as many who are counted among the followers of the 'great' religions may actually engage in popular religious practice.

Though we all speak easily about 'popular religion,' it is difficult to give it an exact definition. 'Popular' could be opposed to 'elite,' 'great' or 'official.' 'Popular' can also refer to something that is widely spread. The religions of the tribal peoples can be considered 'popular,' but one sometimes calls them *primal* religions. There is a 'popular' pole in every religious tradition, which may be variously condemned, tolerated or even encouraged by the 'official' pole. Even the 'elite' may have recourse to 'popular' practices.

## COSMIC AND METACOSMIC RELIGIONS

The distinction of Aloysius Pieris between 'cosmic' and 'metacosmic' religions seems more useful for our discussion.[1] Cosmic religion deals with the cosmic forces that we both need and fear: fire, wind, earth, water, and so on. These are often symbolized as spirits linked to the mysteries of life. One's living relation to these forces is ritualized. In Asia, cosmic religion—except in the case of primal religions—is normally found integrated in metacosmic soteriologies that relate to a 'transphenomenal beyond,' which can be realized here and now through gnosis. Thus we have a twofold level of religious experience. Technology may dominate and desacralize the cosmic forces, destroying at the same time their symbolic power to mediate the mysteries of life. Contemporary ecological movements seek to rediscover this relationship between life and the cosmos. Metacosmic principles will not have any impact on personal and social life unless mediated by cosmic realities. I think that this description, focusing on the religious phenomena itself rather than on the people who practice them, is less judgmental and a better tool of interpretation.

Looking at cosmic religiosity in this manner, one also realizes that it tends to be the same everywhere among all peoples, though under different names and relating to different metacosmic superstructures.

## LIBERATIVE FEATURES OF COSMIC RELIGIOSITY

Aloysius Pieris finds seven liberative features in cosmic religiosity of the poor.[2] Their spirituality is *this worldly.* Their prayers focus on their need for food, work, shelter and meaning in life. They *depend totally on God,* since they have no ready economic and political resources to meet their needs. They *cry* to God *for justice.* The divine that both nurtures the people and punishes their oppressors often has a female form in Asian tradition. Their this-worldliness is *not secular, but cosmic.* Pieris explains the difference in the following way.

> The secular is the non-sacred or the areligious world vitiated by the acquisitiveness-consumerism cycle; the cosmic is a blend of the sacred, the womanly and the earthly, making that vicious cycle physically impossible except when and where the secularizing process (brought by capitalist technocracy) erodes into that world.[3]

In the cosmic religions, women find some space for expression, at least of their oppression. As we have already seen, in chapters 4 and 5 above, feminism goes hand in hand with ecology in Asia. Finally, cosmic religiosity finds ready expression in stories or dramas that narrate God's continuing action among the people.

Looking at various expressions of cosmic or popular religiosity in the context of liberation, one could evoke many messianic movements all across Asia. These are typically movements of peasant groups in revolt against oppressive powers, either local or colonial. They draw inspiration from a religion that draws elements from local popular and other dominant religions present in the area. However, they affirm their identity and difference by the way in which they combine these elements, which offer an alternative way of living and being community. A group called *Samahan* in the Philippines, for instance, believes in Three Persons One God and practices four sacraments (baptism, confirmation, holy orders and matrimony).[4] It has a mass with rituals, prayers and hymns, but one that is celebrated by priestesses. They go on mission performing a two-hour liturgical dance full of religious and patriotic hymns. They believe in spirits and in a voice that guides them. This voice is essentially "an interior experience of a believing community,"[5] not an external physical sound. Similar messianic movements have been active in Korea, as we saw in the chapter on Minjung theology, and in Vietnam.[6]

## COSMIC RELIGIOSITY AND
## CONSCIOUSNESS OF OPPRESSION

Since the cosmic religion of the people is need based and close to the day-to-day life of the people, it is also sensitive to the various oppressions they suffer. The theory of hegemony suggests that people normally interiorize the structures of oppression and accept it unconsciously as inevitable fate. They also may not be aware of the oppressive socio-cultural structures that lie below the surface. That is why one speaks of the need for conscientization.

The narratives of cosmic religiosity, however, demonstrate that while people may be powerless to change the situation of oppression in which they suffer and may not be fully aware of the hidden causes and structures, they not only complain to God about their sufferings in prayer but also protest against the injustice. Rather than mere acceptance, one sees the beginnings of reflection. When there is a real opportunity, they are ready for a liberative struggle, even if their own awareness and reflection may not proceed much deeper than these beginnings. In a mass movement, the leaders and their cadres must be clear about their objectives and methods. When there is trustworthy leadership, the people are normally ready to follow, even without being aware of all the implications. One can see this happening with the masses that followed Gandhi and the crowds that opposed the military might of Marcos in the Philippines. I think the protest literature of popular religiosity prepares the people for such liberative or revolutionary movements.

We saw above how the Minjung in Korea are critical of the powers that be in their popular theater, known as *mudang,* though in their powerlessness, their comments take the form of irony. Similarly, the *pasyon*—the ritual narrative of the passion of Jesus—shows clearly the critical attitude of the people. People, of course, identify with the humble Jesus and the suffering imposed on him by his oppressors. But such an identification with Jesus is also an affirmation of hope, since this Jesus rises again. The usual story of the *pasyon* is a history of salvation that went from creation to the last judgment.[7]

> For popular religiosity suffering is not mere fate but a consequence of a definite stance taken *vis-a-vis* the present system. The drama of the *Pasyon* lies in the figure of Jesus Christ who humbly yet consistently defied current social norms and even at the cost of his own life. . . . The attraction to the suffering and death of Jesus is also to be explained by the promise of future vindication.[8]

In Kerala, India, there is a Dalit caste known as Pulaya, made up of landless agricultural laborers. Their God is known as Pottan and is seen as the flower of divinity. During the annual festival in his honor, there is a narrative of song and dance in a ritual setting, in which Pottan is imagined as coming down to earth in the form of a small Pulaya and affirming his equality with the others. The Pulaya is walking along a narrow band between thorns and thickets in the fields, carrying his child and a pot of toddy on his head. A person of an upper caste comes in the opposite direction and asks him to step aside and make way for him. The Pulaya not only refuses, but bases his refusal on rational argument, questioning the hierarchical distinction between the castes. Here is only a sample of the many arguments.

> When the Chovar rides the elephant
>   we ride the buffalo.
> If so, why quarrel over caste?

> When your body or ours is wounded
>   It is the same blood that gushes out.
> Why then quarrel over the caste?

> We planted a plantain tree in the rubbish heap
> With the fruit thereof you make offering to God.
> Why then distinctions between us?[9]

These arguments may not have transformed the caste system, but they show that the Pulayas are not submitting to it in ignorance and silent acceptance. Unfortunately, mere awareness on the part of the oppressed will not bring about any change without other political and social factors such as a crisis situation, proper, enlightened and trustworthy leadership, a broad-based convergence of interests with consequent collaboration between many sections of society, and a mass mobilization.

One finds similar protests in the popular *bhakti* (devotional) and epic traditions in Hinduism.

## POPULAR RESPONSE TO EVIL

The common people do not indulge in metaphysical speculations about the problem of evil, but they have evolved practical ways of handling evil as they encounter it in daily life in the form of sickness, interpersonal tensions, misfortune and even death. Here I would like to refer to two types of phenomena: spirit-possession and sorcery. The usual reaction to these phenomena is to dismiss them as superstitious and alienating. In the light of recent studies by anthropologists, I would like to suggest that these are culturally conditioned, socially acceptable and symbolic ways of handling social conflict. For example, David Mosse says: "Possession is a socially defined abnormality such that the key to possession is not to be found within the individual but in the ideology with which people think about the world."[10]

Possession and sorcery show that people are not just passive in the face of suffering and injustice; they take culturally appropriate ways of solving social problems. As R. L. Stirrat points out, "What stands out in the Kudagama cosmos is that all relevant beings, both saints and demons, were once human. The world of good and evil is thus a world that is ultimately under human control and the relative balance of good and evil is the result of human choices."[11]

In this sense, the people consider them as liberative gestures. Therefore they will be ready to embrace viable alternatives if they are available. It is not my intention here to explore these phenomena extensively, but only to indicate their possible liberative features.

Phenomena of possession by spirits are common in popular religiosity. There are two kinds of possession. In one type, possession is attributed to ghosts of people who have met an untimely death. These normally point to a person (possessed) who has emotional/psychological problems in an interpersonal or social context. The phenomenon of possession draws the attention of the family and the social group to the situation, not directly, but in its impact on the person possessed. The process of exorcism may lead to subtle social adjustments, not always fully conscious, that result in a solution.

Another type of possession is by gods, goddesses or saints. These normally have a more overtly social role. People possessed in this way feel free to point to a notorious social offender or a problematic social situation in the family or community and demand reparation or adjustment. The 'supernatural' agent is usually listened to, since the community is afraid of cosmic or social catastrophes like a drought, a bad harvest, an epidemic, or social conflict.

Such cases of possession are liberative for women, giving them opportunities to operate on the margins of the official religions that are dominated by male ritual mediators and allowing them to defy the accepted mores of female behavior in society. Kalpana Ram points to this factor.

> Through the mode of spirit possession, in the opposed but dialectically related roles of healer and patient, women play with, mock, utilize and occasionally invert codes of cultural signification which cross-hatch the female body. In doing so, they fashion a modality of resistance and contestation uniquely their own.[12]

The phenomena of sorcery may not seem amenable to a project of liberation; sorcery normally aims at harming someone through the instrumentality of spirits. Here I am focusing on the context in which it is practiced. Gananath Obeyesekere, after studying such phenomena in an area of Sri Lanka, comes to the following conclusions.[13] In almost all cases, a person practices sorcery in retaliation for an actual wrong done to him. He has enough inner control to avoid direct violent retaliation. He is open to a rational solution to the problem, but he has no faith that the police or the judicial system will redress the wrong. In some cases, he has tried legal means without success. No village council or other local body is available to take cognizance of and offer a solution to the problem, so an appeal is made to supernatural agencies.[14] The cultural belief indicates that the supernatural agencies will not act unjustly.

> In general, people who come to sorcery centers labor under a sense of felt injustice, and what they expect of the deity is that "justice be done." If the local institutional structure cannot find means for redressing wrong, then one resorts to supernatural agents to correct wrongs and bring about rightness and justice in the world.[15]

What I wish to underline here is the positive wish to do something effective about protesting injustice in a culturally accepted way. What we are witnessing is social drama. I think one can see in such people a group ready for revolution if an appropriate way is found.

At a popular level, people normally act in symbolic and culturally recognized and acceptable ways. The lack of rational articulation should not lead us to conclude the absence of reflection or intention. Other liberative elements are the affirmation of a divine that is not simply transcendent but involved in the world and concerned for the life and welfare of the people; popular ritual structures that set themselves apart from, and sometimes in opposition to, official ones as independent mediations of the divine; and the predominance of 'lay' people, particularly women, in such contexts. People also cross religious boundaries easily in such situations, pointing to a common human basis for cosmic religiosity.

Such phenomena, like all religious and cultural symbols, can be manipulated and abused by charlatans and people with evil intentions. But this possibility should urge us to discernment, not to a general condemnation or disparagement.

In a secular society where there is no belief in spirits and no appropriate means of protest and redressment, opposition becomes violent and destructive, either of social goods or of the self through drugs. As a reaction, oppression may become more overt and brutal.

## RITUAL AND SOCIAL CHANGE

Religious ritual is the ideal occasion to understand both the possibilities and limits of religion with regard to social change. Rituals are of different kinds. On the one hand we have rites of passage that surround events such as birth, puberty, marriage, and death. There is always a social dimension, and the wider family and friends are involved, but the whole social group does not normally figure in these rituals. On the other hand, there are rituals, such as festivals, in which everyone in a social group is somehow involved. It is about these that I would like to talk.

Victor Turner has suggested that rituals, especially rites of passage, but also more social ones like pilgrimages and spring festivals, went through a particular process that lead from structure through *communitas* to structure. While structure represented the current state of social structures, the *communitas* represented a state of social equality where status differences disappeared. The state of *communitas* may have had a prophetic role, pointing to different possibilities than the one existing, but it did not lead to any real change in social structure. A situation of social equality among pilgrims walking toward a shrine may disappear once the shrine is reached, not even waiting for normal life to resume again. *Communitas* then has a purely ritual role.

A normal village festival does not have even this temporary 'lapse' into equality. It expresses, confirms and even legitimizes in a religious context the existing social structure. The making of decisions, the control of the finances, the roles played during the festival show the existing hierarchical order. When this order is questioned for any reason, the festival becomes the arena for striving toward an equality of social status. This is what happens with the Christian affirmation of the equality of all human beings as children of God. This historical process has been documented with regard to two villages by anthropologists.[16]

In order to avoid needless detail, I shall summarize one of the stories lasting more than a century. In a village there are three major castes and Dalits. Let us call the major castes castes 1, 2 and 3. Similarly, let us call the Dalits Dalit 1 and 2. There are both Hindus and Christians in the village. In the beginning, the priest conforms to the caste order in the village. The headman of the village, belonging to Caste 1, though he is Hindu, has a role in the festival. After some time, Caste 2 improves its economic situation, so they contest the social dominance of Caste 1. To start with, the right of the Hindu headman to participate in a Christian festival is successfully contested. At a second stage, after years of conflict, Castes 1 and 2 share the different roles equally or in alternation. In the meantime, Dalit 1 protests their exclusion. In a changing ideological context, they are supported by the priest. They are temporarily satisfied by being given a special role in a different minor festival. In the course of time, the policy of the church changes and the bishops decide against any special roles for anyone in church festivals. The priest imposes this new rule. In the process, the festival has lost its status as the village festival and becomes the festival of the church (priest).

These changes in the context of the church have not brought about any changes in social order in the context of life in the village. The Dalits who profited by the support of the priest and found a certain equality in the context of the church realize they cannot rely on the church to bring about any real changes in society. Therefore they focus on political means made available in a new democratic order in the country for promoting their status and interests. The process is still going on, no longer in the socio-religious sphere, but in the socio-political one.

The lesson of this story seems to be that religion can be prophetic. It can offer a new vision and inspire new attitudes. But it cannot, on its own, bring about real changes in the socio-political or economic sphere. The people have to take the initiative for that. This can be complex in a multi-religious society where a particular religion does not have the possibility of imposing social order.

## CONCLUSION

While institutional religion may tend to legitimate existing socio-economic and political structures, it also inspires prophecy and proposes a new vision of society, even at a popular level. The poor and the oppressed are not unaware of their oppression or without a desire for change, but religion alone cannot bring about that change. For that, we need clearer social analysis and socio-political mobilization. Religion can help, but people are the agents of their own liberation and transformation.

# PART THREE

# CONCLUSION

# Chapter 12

# Life in Freedom

In the foregoing chapters we have evoked theologies for liberation from the different regions and various religious traditions in Asia. In 1979, at a particular stage in the history of the Ecumenical Association of Third World Theologians, Aloysius Pieris insisted that the reality of Asia is not only its poverty, but also its religiosity.[1] He also showed, as we have seen above, how voluntary poverty is a religious value in Asia and how it is oriented to the abolition of imposed, oppressive poverty. In this manner, he highlighted a positive role for religion in liberation at a time when one tended to see only the alienating aspects of religion.

The role of religions in life and society tends to be ambiguous. In order to be effective and relevant in a particular community, religions have to take particular cultural and institutional forms, but they may end up legitimating and defending cultural and social structures. Sometimes religious identity is used to defend what are perceived as common economic, political or social interests. However, prophets keep arising who, in the name of the ultimate perspectives of religion, challenge both the social and the religious structures. I think the various theologies I have discussed show that all religions have their liberative aspects and prophets who seek to highlight the liberative elements in reinterpreting their religious tradition in a creative and relevant way. Therefore, I think that the relevance of religion for liberation does not need defense.

Asian theologians, including Pieris, have pointed out that Asia is not only religious, but also religiously pluralistic. Such pluralism can be seen as a problem or a source of richness. Many of the theologians I have referred to—Gandhi, Ariyaratna, Buddhadasa, Pieris, and M. M. Thomas—while they reflect from the perspective of their own religions, claim that the social vision they propose and the values they promote can be and are shared by people belonging to other religious traditions. Can religions collaborate in the promotion of that vision and those values?

## LIBERATION AS AN INTER-RELIGIOUS PROJECT

Looking around the world, we see many models relating religion to society in pluri-religious situations.[2] Because of the importance of the state in modern societies in determining and canalizing social relations, such models tend to focus on the relation between religions and the state. There are states that claim to be totally secular or areligious, if not atheistic. Religions are seen as purely personal, even private, affairs.

This perspective is further strengthened when economic and political spheres in modern societies claim total autonomy, governed only by considerations of profit and power. A legal approach replaces a moral one, and enlightened self-interest guides policies and programs. Examples of this situation in Asia would be China and Vietnam. At the other end of the spectrum we have confessional states that claim or have in practice special links to one particular religion as the religion of the majority, whether Christianity, Hinduism, Islam or Buddhism. For example, Nepal is a Hindu kingdom, Thailand is Buddhist, Pakistan is Islamic and the Philippines is Christian. Other religions are tolerated. There may, however, be an ongoing tension between political and religious leaders about the kind of influence that religious leaders actually enjoy in practical orientations and decision making.

In a third kind of socio-political order, we have a separation between the state and religious institutions, but the state claims to be guided by nondenominational religious principles. One speaks of a civil religion. The state does not claim to be totally areligious, as in the first model. We have no such states in Asia. The United States of America would be an example of this.

In the fourth model, the state claims to be positive to all religions, without allying itself to any. In practice, it may try to be particularly sensitive to the minority religious groups, as in India. Some, such as Indonesia, may even claim to base their policies on a consensus of the different religious groups.

It is not my intention to offer an analysis of different political systems with regard to their relations to religious institutions. I have evoked this typology to form a background for what I want to say in regard to the collaboration of religions for liberation and the approach that Christian theology should adopt in a pluri-religious situation.

No religious believer accepts the claims to absolute autonomy made on behalf of cosmic, human and social reality, whether science, economics, culture or politics. Concrete modalities of relationships may be different, according to different historical situations and traditions. People claim the freedom to follow any religion or ideology according to their conscience, so one may resist the legal imposition of a particular religious perspective on other believers. There are problematic situations related to this freedom in some countries where one religion or ideology is predominant—Islam, Christianity, Hinduism or, for that matter, secularist ideologies—but all believers agree that religious or moral perspectives must govern public life. I think this is the basis for any theological reflection in relation to society.

In a situation where believers of different religions share the same economic, political, social and cultural structures and religion is not limited to the private sphere, they must be able to collaborate in the defense and promotion of common human and spiritual values, though each religious group finds motivation and inspiration for such involvement in its own religion.

Common human and spiritual values are not based on some presumed natural law common to all or on some abstract rational philosophy considered universally valid. They should evolve from an ongoing conversation between the different religious groups. There will be consensus on major values. There may be disagreement on others. Even when there is a consensus on values, there may be disagreement about their concrete application and how best to pursue them. Population control and bio-ethics offer examples. There may not be easy solutions, but what is important is that each believer is able to draw on his or her religious resources and tradition and that different religious groups are in an ongoing conversation in fashioning an ever-dynamic consensus. The preferred method is not legal coercion by the majority but tolerance of difference and movement, through persuasion, toward consensus. Such a conversation leading to a convergence or consensus will not be without tensions and difficulties. I think that a basic trust, not only in humanity, but in the ongoing presence and work of God on the part of the believers, would enable them to take the risks necessary in such an ongoing project. This openness does not have to do with what one feels obliged by one's own religious faith to do, but with the respect and tolerance that one owes to other believers.

Such a consensus should normally be the fruit, not of an abstract discussion, but of the concrete common involvement for the promotion and defense of values in daily life, especially when they are threatened. The common commitment would facilitate the emergence of a consensus. Such consensus will constitute the basis of common action programs and liberative projects. Gandhi tried to base his sociopolitical action around such consensus. He often held inter-religious prayer meetings to promote peace and freedom, reading from different scriptures and using songs and prayers from different religious traditions. Inter-religious action programs for the promotion of peace and harmony in tense situations, especially after a conflict sometimes involving religion, are common in India today. The feminist and ecological movements that I have described are based on such an inter-religious consensus. Workers' movements also can lead to common options and actions. The common cosmic base underlying the different metacosmic religions can also facilitate the process.

In religious terms, this means that the various religious traditions agree around a vision of society and a system of values that should guide lives and actions in this world here and now, even though the vision is explained, justified and given ultimate meaning in terms of each religious tradition. For example, let us recall the reaction of various leaders faced with a situation of humanity divided between the rich and the poor and the various oppressions that the poor suffer. Gandhi envisages a just and fraternal society, though he calls it the *Ramrajya* (Kingdom of Ram). He thinks that the reason for the oppression is human selfishness and attachment shown in capitalism and dehumanized science and technology. He suggests personal renunciation and concern for the other as the means to a better human life in community. He sees his liberative action as the pursuit and realization of truth, or God.

Buddhadasa sees the cosmic and human world as a network and egoism as the root of divisions and oppressions. He sees this egoism manifested in contemporary liberal capitalism and suggests compassion and the pursuit of socialism, which he considers as natural or *dhammic.* He reinterprets *nirvana,* not as emptiness, but as egolessness and relatedness.

Ali Shariati sees the idolatry of wealth and power as the obstacle for human and social well-being. He is critical both of secular liberal capitalism and atheistic Marxist socialism. He sees the new society as the *umma* (community) of people obedient to God (Islam).

All of them agree on a vision of a new society as a community of justice and fellowship, in which egoism and consumerism will be absent and the poor and the weak will be specially cared for. They are also committed to work and struggle for such a new community of humans. But each of them bases this vision and commitment on his own religious perspectives and convictions.

These examples also illustrate another important point. Gandhi and Buddhadasa were aware of and open to Christian and other modern perspectives. Both have written about Jesus Christ. Ali Shariati was influenced by European revolutionary traditions. Kappen drew inspiration for his prophetic comments both from the Bible and from the Indian religious tradition. Pieris is in constant dialogue with Buddhism. But each of them was rooted in, developed and reinterpreted his own religious tradition. The model we see operative here is that I, as a Christian theologian, must indeed be open not only to reality but also to the visions and convictions of others belonging to other religious traditions and ideologies, who share with me the same economic, political and socio-cultural context. I must be in constant dialogue with them, but I can only reflect as a Christian, rooted in my own religious tradition, without claiming to evolve an inter-religious or universal theology. This is the only way I can be true to my own identity and roots and at the same time respect the other believer as *other,* without somehow dominating him or her and assuming his or her perspective as an element of my own global vision, pretending to be universal. This is the orientation that governs the following reflections.

I need not elaborate here the fact that this is the authentic way of being a Christian theologian in Asia or, for that matter, elsewhere. When one is open to other believers and is in conversation with them, one is not only sharing one's own perspectives with the other but also being influenced and challenged by the other. Such a challenge may lead me to rethink my own perspectives, to see new aspects of my own tradition that I had not seen before, to reinterpret my tradition, even abandoning perspectives that were taken for granted before, and finally develop my own tradition in new directions by creatively integrating elements from other traditions. Such a process liberates me from the social, cultural and historical conditionings of my own religion—the liberation of faith and theology from the constraints of my own religious institutions.

## TOWARDS AN INTEGRAL LIBERATION

The starting point of theological reflection is experience of life in society. The preceding chapters have made us aware of the reality of Asia: the millions of poor and exploited people, whether peasants or workers or urban slum dwellers; the exploited women and children; the many religious and ethnic minorities who suffer discrimination in one way or another; ongoing conflicts in the name of ethnicity and religion; the Dalits and the socially marginalized of India and other countries; the indigenous people who see their rights and lands violated; the many refugees fleeing from war or oppressive economic conditions; the people living without their political rights and freedoms under authoritarian governments of various types; the earth itself ravished and destroyed. Asia also has pockets of rich people who control the destinies of the others and enjoy power and status.

Before we can reflect fruitfully on the challenges that this experience poses to our faith, we have to understand the phenomena, especially the causes and structures behind it. Certain traditional types of analysis focus mainly on the economic and political dimensions. Asians have insisted that we should take the religious dimension seriously. People have also started to speak about the need for cultural transformation: the change of worldviews and values systems. Religions have usually been accused of stressing only personal conversion. I think that what we need is a framework for an integral analysis of society. I shall suggest one here.

## AN ANALYSIS OF SOCIETY

One can look at social reality in terms of six elements, grouped into three poles: economics-politics, person-society, and culture-religion. One can look at both positive and negative aspects in each element.

*Economics* deals with the production and distribution of goods. Production involves science and technology and their exploitation of the earth and its riches. Distribution involves commerce and banking. Techniques of production and distribution offer the possibility of meeting the basic physical and health needs of a growing population. But capitalism oriented solely to profit leads to unjust accumulation of riches and the pauperization of the many. Economic structures seem to acquire an autonomy of their own, controlled by faceless boards, accountable only to themselves and their markets, not to the wider world of people. Two aspects seem particular causes of concern: the global and uncontested outreach of capitalism today and financial speculation, in which money makes more money.

*Politics* has to do with power relations: Who controls the means of production and the markets? Who dominates whom in society, in terms of social structures? Politics finds expression in the apparatus of the state. Even in democratic societies, the power relations are complex: normally people who have the money also have political control, though it is often exercised indirectly through professional politicians. Dominant groups in power can exploit the people in various more or less open ways. The common good may be sidelined in the complex interplay of group interests.

A *person* is meant to be free and creative. In modern times, one has many opportunities for personal development. Human rights are defined and affirmed in international forums, but in practice, the human person is conditioned in various ways. Egoism and individualism are almost taken for granted. Competition for scarce resources seems to have become a part of life. One is alienated from one's body and nature. People grow up in dysfunctional families without experiencing love and acceptance. There is a difference between the legal and the real availability of human rights. An individualistic defense of rights ignores one's duties toward the others. People fall prey to consumerism. In a secular society, people do not easily find meaning in life. The prevailing anomie leads them to experiment with drugs. People in such circumstances do not seem to be able to relate to others. People are born in families and are meant to be in community.

Yet *society* is experienced as structured and divided. Ethnic, racial and caste divisions fragment social groups. Some groups are dominant and defensive. Others feel excluded and sometimes protest violently. Ethnic and cultural pluralism, instead of being seen as richness, is experienced as a problem. The common good becomes a careful balance of group interests, and solidarity remains an unattainable ideal. With the collapse of the 'socialist' states of the Soviet Union and eastern Europe, talk of social concern or the common good seems to be decreasing. This may be the reason people are seeking—sometimes in a fundamentalistic way—group identities in terms of ethnicity, caste, or religion, pretending that people who share such identities also share common economic and political interests that need to be defended. On the one hand, the possibilities of easy and quick travel and the speed and extent of communications seem to be bringing the people of the world closer together. But this very togetherness seems to be increasing the need for affirming one's identity and difference. The media can promote such division through misinformation or false propaganda.

*Culture* consists of worldviews and systems of values expressed, lived, communicated and celebrated in symbols and rituals. Culture gives meaning to one's world. Language is a special vehicle of culture. Through art and literature, people give expression to their experiences and dreams and mark their human and social identity. Once a human group creates its culture, it is interiorized by succeeding generations. Culture is often unconscious and taken for granted. Every culture is limited; it represents one among many possible creative ways of shaping the world. People, however, under the leadership of creative people, can transform their culture. One's cultural production is conditioned by the geographical, historical and social circumstances of one's life. Correspondingly, one's meaning systems shape one's choices and creativity. Such meaning systems, when they aim at shaping a whole social order, become ideologies. In this manner, culture and society are in an ongoing dialectic, so that one cannot be changed without changing the other. Even under conditions of domination, people hang on to their culture as the source of their human and social identity. Today we see a resurgence of minority and native cultures. Similarly, modern technology—by imposing a superficial instrumental uniformity—seems to be provoking the affirmation of cultural identities before the threat of a faceless homogenization.

*Religion* is that element in culture that is concerned with ultimate meaning. Such meaning comes from the deeper experience of charismatic persons, sometimes also attributed to divine revelation. In its efforts to find expression in life, religion finds embodiment in social and cultural structures. In the process, it might end up legitimating these. The perspectives of the Ultimate, however, keep breaking through, especially in prophetic individuals who challenge existing social, cultural and religious structures. The secularization of society and the privatization of religion is a modern problem. Perhaps we may be moving from social and institutional to experiential and personal religion. Some people find easy security in a fundamentalistic affirmation of religious symbol. Religion can also be used as an easy source of group identity for economic and political ends. Pluralism of religions, as a clash of absolute perspectives, invites to a dialogue, though it may also lead to conflict.

The six elements outlined above can be grouped into three poles. Economics and politics provide the material-social basis of life. People who have the money also control the positions of power. Politics is often seen today as being at the service of economic power. In virtue of their power, they also try to dominate social and cultural dimensions of life. Culture and religion make life meaningful. The people in power always try to corrupt culture and religion and use them to legitimate their position. But artists and prophets cannot always be bought. In the name of worldviews and values, they continue to challenge the inequalities and oppressions. But people in society are masters of, and can be creative agents of, their life, constantly mediating between life and meaning. While economic, political, social and cultural structures seek constantly to condition them, led by charismatic leaders, they can assert their freedom and change the structures that oppress them. They can change economic and political structures, recreate or transform culture, and reinterpret their religion or convert to another one. Because of the mutual involvement and conditioning of the different elements, change will have to take place in all dimensions, though the original impetus may come from one or another source. There are different opinions about which element—economic, political, personal or cultural—is primary. Such a discussion is not very useful. What is relevant to our purpose is the conviction that agents of any real change have to operate at all levels.

## THE POOR

We can understand better the framework of this analysis if we apply it to a concrete problem—for example, the poor. Poverty is, of course, an economic category. People are made poor by economic systems. Some people control the means of production and use them for increasing their own profits, impoverishing others in the process. Politicians seem more interested in protecting economic process than in promoting the common good. The poor are without power to defend their own interests. They do not participate in making decisions that affect them and the community. Egoism and the desire for more material goods, either for enjoyment or as a status symbol, is certainly at the root of the unjust distribution of the wealth produced and of the exploitation of the poor. The poor may be egoists, too. The poor may lack exterior freedom, while both the poor and the rich may lack interior freedom. Economic injustice leads to inequality in society, which may further be strengthened by cultural and religious structures. Poverty often has a racial, caste or gender face. A rational-scientific worldview and a capitalistic ideology, with its system of values, support the existing unjust economic and socio-political structures. An otherworldly or privatized religion may tolerate, if not legitimate, the social system rather than challenge and try to change it.

We see how the elements are interconnected and, so to speak, support each other. An integral and authentic liberation of the poor and the promotion of a just community is not possible without change in all six elements. A merely political revolution changes the masters, not the system. This is true of the so-called democracies. An economic revolution in terms of greater justice is not possible without a political system that is participative and focused on the common good. Structures, while they have a certain autonomy, are made and maintained by people who benefit by them. No change of structures will be permanent or viable unless people are converted to become less egotistic and learn to limit their desires. Structures are social in nature; they can be changed only if the whole social group is involved. This means the creation of community, even if the process of moving toward community includes moments of conflict. The basis for such a project of social change is a new vision of the world and humanity and a new system of values based on it. This is a new culture. This new culture finds inspiration from prophetic currents in religions and ideologies. Such prophecy is normally provoked by the experience of present injustice and oppression. We see how the different elements are mutually involved. Many liberative projects fail because they concentrate only on one or a few of these elements.

A similar integral analysis of the problems of women, ecology, the caste system, or racial discrimination will be an interesting and instructive exercise.

## RELIGION AND THE SOCIAL SCIENCES

In its prophetic role, religion can point to the existing injustice in all of the six dimensions. It can challenge the current worldviews, systems of values and attitudes and offer alternatives. It can criticize the ideology. It can motivate and inspire the agents involved in the work of transformation. It can have a certain direct impact on the meaning system of culture and the motivations of the person. But it cannot, on its own, offer alternatives in the spheres of economics, politics, personal growth or social organization. For this, it will have to depend on the social sciences of economics, politics, psychology and sociology. Even cultures are studied and analyzed by cultural anthropology. Therefore, for the development of any effective program of action for change, it is not enough for the agents to be inspired and motivated by religion. They need to be informed by the other social sciences before they can make concrete options and plan out strategies. But the social sciences are necessarily limited by their particular theoretical frameworks. Pluralism and the need to choose between competing possibilities in these areas are inevitable. This demands a difficult, ongoing dialogue and discernment.

In the remaining pages I shall limit myself to the prophetic voice of religion. In the field of religion, I am speaking as a Christian, though I am keeping in mind the important insights of other religions. A prophet reads an existing situation critically and challenges it to change in the perspective of a particular vision of society. In the Old Testament, the prophets referred back to God's covenant with the people. Israel was called to live as God's people, a free community of equals participating in the life of the community, sharing all that they had, not hoarding anything, committed to God alone, not to any other political or economic power. But Israel went after other gods in the search for power and wealth. The community became divided between the rich and the poor, the exploiters and the exploited. The prophets saw a link between such idolatry and injustice and denounced both. They also condemned a formal ritualistic religious observance without the substance of moral praxis. Jesus came in the tradition of the prophets. In his life, preaching and miracles he evoked the vision of the new society as the Reign of God and called people to conversion. I think that the best way of outlining the task of Christian prophecy today is to look at the present world, outline Jesus' vision of the new society and, in the light of this vision, indicate a possible way of action.

## THE ASIAN SITUATION

Looking at contemporary Asia, the presence of the poor and the oppressed does not need any elaborate demonstration. But looking at the oppressive causes and structures, I would like to suggest the following as needing urgent attention.

Science and technology can be useful instruments for bettering human wellbeing if they are subject to human and social control. The problem is not science and technology as such, but their use by a dominant group in the pursuit of profit and power. Capitalism is the only economic system that seems available today. What makes it problematic is not the system itself, but the way it is used. A liberal ideology justifies the uncontrolled domination and ownership of resources by a small group of people and their unlimited pursuit of profit. The problem is, how we can bring about a social or socially responsible control of the capitalist system. At the economic level, one has to accept limits to growth and the pursuit of profit. But real social control can come only from political will. This can hardly happen unless current political systems are radically changed to permit real participation by the people in making decisions that concern them. Participatory structures can function properly only if people become free of egoism in all its manifestations, especially in terms of the search for power and unlimited consumerism. The exploitation of nature and women are particular instances of this search for power and pleasure to which we are sensitive today. Another element of collective egoism is to find not only elements of identity, but instruments of power and division in ethnicity, culture and religion. Religions themselves need to be liberated from being fundamentalist or alienating, and become relevant and prophetic.

## JESUS' VISION OF A NEW SOCIETY

How does this situation compare with Jesus' vision of a new society? In his proclamation and teaching, praxis and miracles, Jesus uses a multiplicity of symbols and parables to evoke his vision of a new society: a seed that grows into a tree, a harvest, a banquet, various healing and life-giving events, water and food. I think that the most central of all these symbols is the banquet, especially the marriage banquet. A banquet is a symbol of sharing and community, equality and fellowship. It is an experience of love and joy in togetherness. It has to do with food as the symbol of life. The marriage is a further sign of committed love that becomes creative of new life in the community of a family. One finds united here all the central themes of the Reign of God.

Jesus explains one or other aspect of this rich symbolic action in other parables and teachings. He offers life and health through his miracles. He speaks of life-giving water and of food. He gives the new commandment of love and illustrates it as caring for and sharing with the poor, the suffering and the needy. In his table fellowship with the excluded—the publicans and the sinners—he practices what he preaches. He affirms the equality of all by condemning the quest for special places at the dining table. He advises generosity that gives to the needy rather than to those who can reciprocate one's gift. He suggests that our love should reach out to all, without preferences, even to our enemies. In a final gesture, he offers himself as the food and drink of life. He leaves as a memorial for his disciples the eucharistic banquet. He makes it very clear throughout that God is the real source and giver of this life through a multiplicity of mediation and symbols. In love, we share this gift of life with each other and become community. This is an ongoing project in the here and now of history, through which God's reign becomes present and actual. This community is not merely the symbol, but an integration in the community of divine life. If the vine and the branches are symbols of this community, the table fellowship in memory of Christ is its realization.

Jesus, of course, is quite aware that such a community is not a reality in the present. That is why he denounces all that hinders the emergence of this community and calls everyone to conversion. In proclaiming the new commandment to love one another, he is denouncing love of self as the basic evil. This love of self manifests itself in various ways: as love of money and material goods, in which one tends to put one's trust; as love of honor and status that prides itself in its religious observance and social respectability and discriminates against and marginalizes different groups of people such as the publicans, the Samaritans, the common people looked down upon as not keeping the law, the public sinners like the prostitutes, the poor and ignorant Galileans; as love of power, for which one was ready for any kind of compromise. The temptations of Jesus give an indication of what he considered the main obstacles to the Reign of God: egoism, desire for possessions, and love of power. Their religion must have been a constant challenge to God's 'chosen people,' but they had rendered it innocuous and an opportunity to nourish their own pride by making it a list of formalistic observances—purification ceremonies, ostentatious fasts and prayers, undiscerning observance of rules such as the sabbath.

Jesus recognized that because of the various manifestations of self-love and hypocritic formalism in religion, society was actually divided between the rich and the poor; between the powerful and the powerless, whether in the economic, political or the religious sphere; between those who claimed higher social status and those who were marginalized and excluded. In such a situation, Jesus as a prophet made a twofold option. He chose to renounce power, wealth and status. This is seen symbolically in the story of the temptations. He also exercised his prophecy by choosing to be with the poor and looking at the world from their point of view. Between political activists like the Zealots and ritual purists like the Essenes, he chose to be an itinerant preacher proclaiming God's bounteous gift of life through his words and actions and calling people to conversion. By such an invitation to conversion, he refused to demonize anyone, individually or as a group, and proclaimed the boundless mercy of God, not only open to every repentant sinner, but even to one lost sheep. He made a distinction between the sinful structures symbolized by Mammon and Satan and the sinners who are under their power but who are called to change. His prophetic preaching and action were sufficiently threatening that they persuaded the political and religious leaders to do away with him.

## THE REIGN OF GOD AND THE CHURCH

Jesus' vision of a new humanity can be shared by all people. As M. M. Thomas has shown, it has actually inspired many Hindus. The Reign of God, as described by Jesus, is not identified with the church as we experience it. We need to underline this very strongly, because a simple identification of the Reign of God with the church makes the collaboration of all peoples in the building up of the Reign problematic. The church feels called to be the symbol and the servant of the Reign of God, but the Reign of God transcends the church, as it does other religions, and reaches out to all people of good will committed to the building of a new humanity.

For Christians, Jesus was not only in a tradition of the prophets but the symbol and mediation of God's continuing saving presence in history. Thus he assures people of God's concern for them. His miracles symbolize God's saving activity. His resurrection assures his ongoing presence in history. Jesus also assures us of the presence and action of the Spirit, who is powerful and creative. This power and creative action were experienced by the community of Jesus' disciples in various ways. The Spirit is the bond of union between humans and the cosmos, between humans and God. We have a cosmic network animated by the Spirit. This vision of history is full of hope and promise, expressed as the second coming of Christ. God is neither denied, as in secularism, nor objectified as merely transcendent, as in alienating religion. God is with us, present and active, caring for and saving us, but in the process of history, not as a *deus ex machina*. Christ's option for the poor does not mean that he will liberate them in some miraculous way without any effort on their part. It means that he is with them, inspiring and energizing them to struggle for their liberation. This is the source of our hope.

The community of the disciples of Christ continues in the world not to monopolize God's saving action, but as its prophetic symbol and servant. It continues in the world as a counter-cultural community contributing to the emergence of the Reign of God in collaboration with other believers and all people of good will. Like Jesus himself, it follows the way of humility and nonviolence, not substituting itself for God or pretending to be God's unique spokesperson, but proclaiming the good news of God's presence and action in the world and in human history as manifested in the life, death and resurrection of Jesus, trying to discern it in the signs of the times and in peoples' movements and seeking to collaborate with them.

In this humble service to the Reign of God, Christians have in the vision of Jesus a constant challenge to conversion, because the community of Christians has not always been faithful to its prophetic vocation. It has truncated Jesus' vision, not only by the historical and cultural conditions of its existence, but also by its own inadequate response to his call.

## LIBERATIVE ELEMENTS IN ASIAN RELIGIONS

In dialogue with other religions in which it recognizes the presence and activity of God, of God's Word and Spirit, Christianity discovers dimensions of the Reign of God that deepen and enrich its own understanding and experience. It is in this perspective that Christians in Asia look at other religions and the liberative elements in them. As a matter of fact, the Christians in Asia become aware that the modern (recent) liberative tradition in Asia, with people like Gandhi and Buddhadasa, is older than Christian liberation theologies in Asia and elsewhere.

Of the many liberative elements that one could identify in other Asian religions, I think that the following are significant. The Buddhist vision of reality as inter-being helps us see reality as 'socialist,' as Buddhadasa said. We feel this fellowship not only with other people, but with the whole cosmos. We also feel responsible for this world, with which we are called to live in harmony. Ecological movements can particularly benefit from this broad-based vision.

The tension between the *yin* and the *yang*, the male and the female, seems to give a new dynamism to the universe, which is not seen in a hierarchical, static order of things in which the masculine is always dominating, oppressing the feminine. The implications of this vision for contemporary feminist movements are obvious.

In modern culture's urge to dominate and exploit, the option to *be* poor—common to all Asian religions, including Christianity—can constitute the basis of a new spirituality that can lead to a more human and humane life depending on 'being' rather than on 'having' and also sharing and community.

The Asian tradition does not see good and evil as two opposite realities facing each other. Evil is not objectified and demonized. Conflict is not seen as a value in itself. The root of evil is seen in egoism and craving, though they also take structural forms in society. The conflict is interior as well as exterior. The conflict is not absolute, but only a step toward conversion and change. The goal is always a new situation in which such dichotomies are transcended. The option for the poor is not an exclusive option that turns one against the rich but seeks to lead both the poor and the rich to a new, more just society. Such an inclusive view also makes nonviolent means a viable option in conflict.

Technology and the market give priority to impersonal laws and forces. The Asian tradition values humans and their relationships. It takes duties as seriously as rights. Community is as important as the individual. The way of doing things is as important as what one does. Life has not become mechanical, but has a human dimension.

## COMMITTED TO ACTION

Such a broad vision of a new humanity can keep proposing values and provide inspiration and motivation to change. But the religious community—the community of the disciples of Christ, in our case—if it claims to be prophetic, must commit itself to an active search for change. The concrete action that Asian theologians are suggesting for Asian churches—besides developing a theology and spirituality for such action for change—is the formation of prophetic counter-cultural communities that can be symbols, witnesses and servants of the new society of the Reign of God. In Asia, this should be tried at two levels: Basic Human and Basic Christian Communities. A Basic Human Community would coalesce around a concrete project to promote any of the values evoked above. Its geographical situation would probably determine its membership, though it would be in relation with other similar communities elsewhere. Their ongoing action program may also include dialogue at a religious level. Within this wider community, the Christian community and other religious communities will occasionally come together to benefit fully from their own religious resources for motivation and inspiration.

Given the centrality of the banquet as symbolic of Jesus' vision of a new society, I would suggest that the table-fellowship (Eucharist) will have a particular place in bringing the community together. It must, however, become a real banquet, symbolizing and leading to an actual sharing of goods and services. Christians could join other believers in celebrating an *agape.* I think that here, too, a rhythm between Christian and the Human communities in celebrating their fellowship will be helpful. But the celebration itself will be meaningful only if the community, Human and Christian, is actively engaged in promoting just human values in society.

In a world that is divided by oppressive structures, promoting just human values will involve conflict. There may be an occasional big revolution, as happened in the Philippines in 1986. But more often it will be small struggles, local in nature, advancing step by step toward a humane and just society. To be ready for struggle is to be prepared for sacrifices of one's time, money, and comfort.

## A NONVIOLENT STRUGGLE

The struggle, by preference, will be nonviolent. The reasons for this are many. First of all, ends do not justify the means. Our means must be in harmony with the ends. One cannot promote love and community through violence that involves rejection and hatred. Secondly, what one is aiming at is not victory over the other but a change of hearts and structures so that everyone can relate in a new way. Thirdly, while violence immediately provokes the emotions, nonviolence provokes reason and promotes conversation as a means of facilitating change. Finally, the

Asian traditions—Christian, Hindu, Buddhist and Confucian—are largely nonviolent. For a Christian, the way of Christ is the nonviolent way of the cross, which appeals to the heart and conscience of the other.

Nonviolent action is not merely a spiritual option but also an effective strategy. Violent action can bring about change in the realm of politics—wars and revolutions have occasionally overthrown tyrants—but it has never brought about a real change of structures or persons, ideologies or social relations. Education, the use of the media, and symbolic gestures can make nonviolence a moral force. Nonviolence does not mean passivity. It can be active civil disobedience, prophetic protest and mass mobilization. It is not violence against violence in an equation of power, but the force of truth, justice and love against the naked force of economic and political power. It does not merely oppose violence while accepting the terms and goals of the struggle; it offers new structures and relationships as an alternative. When one discusses the use of violence, one tends to discuss in the abstract or about extreme cases. But for the kind of aims we have of building community, nonviolence seems to be the most apt way. Even if the fruits are slow in coming, the struggle itself can be rewarding and transforming for those who are involved in it, because one is actively loving and promoting life.

## THE SPIRITUALITY OF BEING POOR

Engagement in a struggle for justice will not be credible and effective without self-discipline. One point on which all Asian religions agree is that one cannot promote justice without controlling one's egoism and desires. In order to do away with imposed poverty, one must choose to be poor, to control desire, reduce one's needs, limit consumption, and share with others what one has. There must be a growing sense that the world is a gift of God to all peoples, so that what one has, one holds in trusteeship for others. Just as in inter-personal relationships, duties must correspond to rights; ownership of goods should go with a sense of social responsibility.

Given the global nature of today's oppressive structures, the facilities provided by the media and the inter-religious and inter-ideological nature of the struggle, one can talk today of networking for a wider impact.

As Christians, while we struggle for the community of the Reign of God, we know that it is not merely a fruit of human effort but also a gift of God. While it is being shaped in history by our efforts, its full realization may be beyond history. A horizon of hope is in tension with our own expectations and is constantly adding dynamism to our efforts. Our own small, sometime hesitant and inadequate efforts are sustained by the action of the Spirit.

## CONCLUSION: LIFE IN FREEDOM

We have reached the end of a rapid survey of liberation theologies from Asia. Discussing the subtitle of the book, a friend asked me why I had not said "Asian theologies of liberation." While Minjung theology is from and for Korea, some of its insights with regard to the use of popular religiosity and to their own history as salvation history are relevant to liberation movements elsewhere. This is even more so when we consider the liberation theologies I have explored in relation to different religions. The insights of Hinduism, Buddhism and Confucianism, as those of Christianity and Islam, can inspire people everywhere, even if the movements and leaders that gave birth to them are localized in Asia. I think, therefore, that these theologies are a challenge from Asia to the whole world.

Calling these *liberation* theologies shows a bias, because the terminology is one to which Christians are accustomed. We saw that Christians in the Philippines prefer to call their reflection 'the theology of struggle,' focusing more on their current experience than on the future goal. But as we approach the end of our reflection, I feel that the term liberation is really inadequate to describe the goal that the various Asian thinkers and people are pursuing. Liberation is certainly necessary from the many oppressions that we are suffering, but liberation is not merely *from* something, but also *for* something. We Christians call this goal the new human community in which God's sovereignty is acknowledged. Muslims speak of the *umma.* Buddhists evoke the experience of inter-being. Confucians talk of a harmonious universe. Hindus aim at the experience of the oneness of Being. The followers of cosmic religions affirm the network and continuity of life.

Looking at these various images of the goal, I think that *Life* could serve as a common symbol for all, though different people may interpret it differently. While Christianity and Islam focus on human life in community, the other religions evoke life in harmony with the cosmos. The people whom we have encountered in these pages speak of life not in another world, but in this one, though it still remains to be achieved, an object of realistic hope and individual and collective effort, because the injustices that people have done, they can also undo.

To live in harmony, we need to be free. This freedom is not only from the many forces that oppress us, either from the outside through other persons or from within as interiorized worldviews and systems of values. It is also freedom from our own limitations of egoism and desire, both individual and collective. It is significant that the Asian theologians (of all religions) are concerned with both kinds of oppression. When we are liberated from these oppressions from without and from within, we will be free to live authentically, to relate, to create community, and to live in harmony with the whole universe.

To live in freedom is also to live in the Spirit (Rom. 8:21-24), who "blows where She wills" (Jn. 3:8), who helps us transcend ideological, denominational and religious boundaries while making creative use of all our resources in solidarity, dialogue and collaboration.

The goal of all the theologies of liberation from Asia is one and is capable of uniting all peoples in a common quest relevant to their context and motivated and inspired by their respective religions: *life in freedom.*

# Notes

## 1. Minjung Theology of Korea

1. Jung Young Lee, "Minjung Theology: A Critical Introduction," in idem. (ed.), *An Emerging Theology in World Perspective: Commentary on Korean Minjung Theology* (Mystic, CT: Twenty-Third Publications, 1988), pp. 3-4.

2. Cf. Suh Kwang-sun David, "Korean Theological Development in the 1970s," in Commission on Theological Concerns of the Christian Conference of Asia (ed.), *Minjung Theology: People as Subjects of History* (Maryknoll, NY: Orbis Books, 1983), pp. 38-46; George Ogle, "A Missionary's Reflection on Minjung Theology," in Lee, op. cit., pp. 59-74.

3. Suh Nam-dong, "Towards a Theology of *Han*," in *Minjung Theology*, p. 58.

4. Ibid., p. 56.

5. Quoted in Lee, op. cit., p. 1.

6. Cf. *Minjung Theology*, pp. 64-65; Lee, op. cit., pp. 10-11.

7. Lee, op. cit., p. 11.

8. See Hyun Young-hak, "A Theological Look at the Mask Dance in Korea," in *Minjung Theology*, pp. 47-54.

9. Ibid., p. 52.

10. Lee Oo Chung, "Korean Traditional Culture and Feminist Theology," in *The Task of Korean Feminist Theology* (Seoul: Korean Association of Women Theologians, 1983), quoted in Chung Hyun Kyung, *Struggle to Be the Sun Again* (Maryknoll, NY: Orbis Books, 1991), pp. 43-44.

11. Cf. Ahn Byung-mu, "Jesus and the Minjung in the Gospel of Mark," in *Minjung Theology*, pp. 138-154.

12. Cf. Moon Hee-suk Cyris, "An Old Testament Understanding of Minjung," in *Minjung Theology*, pp. 123-137.

13. Cf. Suh Nam-dong, "Historical References for a Theology of Minjung," in *Minjung Theology*, p. 159.

14. *Minjung Theology*, p. 53.

15. Ibid., pp. 167-171.

16. In Japanese Buddhism, the 'western paradise' is called 'Pure Land' and gives its name to one of the Buddhist traditions.

17. *Minjung Theology*, p. 175.

18. Ibid., p. 176.

19. C.S. Song, "Building a Theological Culture of People," in Lee, op. cit., pp. 126-132.

20. Cf. Lee, op. cit., p. 23.

21. Cf. Kim Yong-bock, "Messiah and Minjung: Discerning Messianic Politics over against Political Messianism," in *Minjung Theology*, p. 188; see also Suh Nam-dong, ibid., pp. 170-171.

22. Cf. Choo Chai-yong, "A Brief Sketch of Korean Christian History from the Min-jung Perspective," in *Minjung Theology*, pp.73-79; Kim Yong-bock, "Korean Christianity as a Messianic Movement of the People," ibid., pp. 80-119.

23. *Minjung Theology*, pp. 22-23.

24. Ibid., pp. 77-78.

25. Ibid., pp. 30-31.

26. Kim Yong-bock, ibid., pp. 184-185.

27. Suh Nam-dong, ibid., pp. 162-163.

28. Ibid., p. 186.

29. Quoted in ibid., p. 29.

30. See Kyung, op. cit., pp. 64-66 for further references.

31. Lee, op. cit., p. 12.

32. Cf. ibid., pp. 13-14; *Minjung Theology*, pp. 163-165.

## 2. A Theology of Struggle from the Philippines

1. Mary Rosario Battung et al. (eds.), *Religion and Society: Towards a Theology of Strug-gle. Book I.* (Manila: FIDES, 1988); Francisco F. Claver, *The Stones Will Cry Out* (Maryknoll, NY: Orbis Books, 1978); Niall O'Brien, *Revolution from the Heart* (Quezon City: Claretian, 1987); Rose Marie Cecchini, *Women's Action for Peace and Justice: Christian, Buddhist and Muslim Women Tell Their Story* (Maryknoll Sisters: no date), pp. 17-142; Edicio de la Torre, *Touching Ground, Taking Root* (Manila: Socio-Pastoral Institute, 1986); Mary John Manan-zan, *The Woman Question in the Philippines* (Pasay City: St. Paul, 1991).

2. Cf. Ma. Aida Velasquez, "Ecological Work and the Church in Asia," in Office for Human Development, *Colloquium on the Social Doctrine of the Church in the Context of Asia* (Manila, 1993), pp. 77-86; Loreta B. Ayupan and Teresita G. Oliveros, "Filipino Peasant Women in Defence of Life," in Vandana Shiva (ed.), *Minding Our Lives* (New Delhi: Kali for Women, 1993), pp. 113-120.

3. Cf. Alfeo G. Nudas, *God with Us: The 1986 Philippine Revolution* (Quezon City: Cardinal Bea Institute, 1986). EDSA is the name of the wide avenue in Manila that was the scene of the successful nonviolent confrontation of the people with an advancing army col-umn.

4. Cf. Battung, op. cit., p. ix.

5. For a report, see *Religion and Development in Asia: A Sociological Approach with Christian Reflections* (Manila, 1976).

6. Quoted in Karl M. Gaspar, "Doing Theology (in a situation) of Struggle," in Bat-tung, op. cit., p. 45.

7. Ben Dominguez, "A Theology of Struggle: Towards a Struggle with a Human Face," *Kalinangan* (March, 1986): 24-25.

8. De la Torre, op. cit., p. 156.

9. Cf. Battung, op. cit., p. vi.

10. Cf. ibid., pp. 48-49.

11. Ibid., p. 54.

12. Amado Picardal, quoted in ibid., p. 53.

13. Tranquilino Cabarubias, murdered lay leader, quoted in ibid., pp. 63-64.

14. De la Torre, op. cit., pp. 157-159.

15. Quoted in ibid., p. 159.

16. Pedro Lucero, quoted in Battung, op. cit., p. 57.

17. *Where Are We Going!* (Manila: CFA, 1983), pp. 38-39.

18. Battung, op. cit., pp. 145-146.
19. Melchior Morante, quoted in ibid., p. 52.
20. Quoted in Battung, op.cit., p. 70.
21. De la Torre, op. cit., pp. 205-206.
22. Jeremias Aquino, quoted in Battung, op. cit., p. 66.
23. Ibid., pp. 67-69.
24. Feliciano V. Cariño, "Violence, Class Struggle and Faith," in Battung, op. cit., pp. 121-127.
25. Claver, op. cit., pp. 20-21.
26. Battung, op. cit., pp. 74-75.
27. Brendan Lovett, *Life Before Death: Inculturating Hope* (Quezon City: Claretian, 1986).
28. Brendan Lovett, *On Earth as in Heaven* (Quezon City: Claretian, 1988).
29. Francisco F. Claver, "Cultures in Crisis: Trends in the Church and Society in Asia," in Tarcisius Fernando and Helene O'Sullivan (eds.), *Launching the Second Century: The Future of Catholic Social Thought in Asia* (Hong Kong: Asian Center for the Progress of Peoples, 1993), p. 40.
30. Ruben L. F. Habito, *Total Liberation: Zen Spirituality and the Social Dimension* (Maryknoll, NY: Orbis Books, 1989), p. xvii.
31. De la Torre, op. cit., p. 127.

## 3. Dalit Theology in India

1. For more details on the following paragraphs, see M. Amaladoss, *A Call to Community: The Caste System and Christian Responsibility* (Anand: Gujarat Sahitya Prakash, 1994); Pauline Kolenda, *Caste in Contemporary India: Beyond Organic Solidarity* (Menlo Park, CA: The Benjamin/Cummings Publishing Co., 1972); Andre Beteille (ed.), *Social Inequality* (Hammondsworth: Penguin, 1969); John Maliekal, *Caste in Indian Society* (Bangalore: CSA Publications, 1980).
2. *Rig Veda* X,90:11-12.
3. Cf. James Silverberg (ed.), *Social Mobility in the Caste System in India* (The Hague: Mouton, 1968); M.N. Srinivas, *Social Change in Modern India* (New Delhi: Orient Longman, 1966).
4. Cf. James Freeman, *Untouchable: An Indian Life History* (Stanford, CA: Stanford University Press, 1979); Michael Mahar (ed.), *The Untouchables in Contemporary India* (Tucson: University of Arizona Press, 1972); Robert Deliège, *Les Paraiyars du Tamil Nadu* (Nettetal: Steyler, 1988); Mulkraj Anand and Eleanor Zelliot (eds.), *An Anthology of Dalit Literature* (New Delhi: Gyan, 1992); Arjun Dangle (ed.), *Poisoned Bread* (Bombay: Orient Longman, 1992).
5. Imtiaz Ahmed (ed.), *Caste and Social Stratification among the Muslims* (Delhi: Manohar, 1973); John Thattumkal, *Caste and the Catholic Church in India* (Rome: Lateran University, 1983); Duncan B. Forrester, *Caste and Christianity* (London: Curzon Press, 1980).
6. Cf. P. A. Augustine, *Social Equality in Indian Society: The Elusive Goal* (New Delhi: Concept, 1991).
7. *The Dhammapada*, 393.
8. See Eleanor Zelliot, *From Untouchable to Dalit* (Delhi: Manohar, 1992), p. 5.
9. Ibid.
10. Quoted in Maliekal, op. cit., p. 100.
11. Quoted in Zelliot, op. cit., p. 202.

12. Antony Raj, *Children of a Lesser God (Dalit Christians)* (Madurai: DCLM, 1992).

13. Cf. Ambrose Pinto, *Dalit Christians: A Socio-Economic Survey* (Bangalore: Ashirvad, 1992); Jose Kananaikal, *Christians of Scheduled Caste Origin* (New Delhi: Indian Social Institute, 1983).

14. Amaladoss, op. cit., pp. 48-52.

15. Cf. Ghanshyam Shah, *Social Movements in India* (New Delhi: Sage, 1990), pp. 107-120; Gail Omvedt, *Reinventing Revolution: New Social Movements and the Socialist Tradition in India* (Armonk, NY: M. E. Sharpe, 1993), pp. 47-75.

16. For greater detail and references, see Amaladoss, op. cit., pp. 53-67.

17. Anita Diehl, *Periyar E. V. Ramaswami* (Delhi: B.V. Publications, 1978).

18. Cf. Zelliot, op. cit.

19. Quoted in ibid., pp. 300-301.

20. Cf. R. S. Khare, *The Untouchable as Himself: Ideology, Identity, and Pragmatism among the Lucknow Chamars* (Cambridge: Cambridge University Press, 1984).

21. Ibid., p. 85.

22. Quoted in V. Thomas Samuel, *One Caste, One Religion, One God: A Study of Shree Narayana Guru* (New Delhi: Sterling, 1977), p. 98.

23. Ibid., p. 123.

24. Quoted in Ignatius Jesudasan, *A Gandhian Theology of Liberation* (Maryknoll, NY: Orbis Books, 1984), p. 78.

25. There are many collections, some contributions figuring in more than one collection. M. E. Prabhakar (ed.), *Towards A Dalit Theology* (Delhi: ISPCK, 1989); Arvind P. Nirmal (ed.), *Towards a Common Dalit Ideology* (Madras: Gurukul, n.d.); Xavier Irudayaraj (ed.), *Emerging Dalit Theology* (Madras: Jesuit Theological Secretariat, 1990); James Massey, *Indigenous People: Dalits: Dalit Issues in Today's Theological Debate* (Delhi: ISPCK, 1994).

26. In Massey, op. cit., p. 220.

27. In Prabhakar, op. cit., p. 56.

28. In Massey, op. cit., pp. 220-221.

29. Ibid., pp. 223-230.

30. George Koonthanam, "Yahweh the Defender of the Dalits: A Reflection on Isaiah 3:12-15," *Jeevadhara* 22. (1992): 112-123.

31. A. Mariaselvam, "The Cry of the Dalits: An Interpretation of Psalm 140," *Jeevadhara* 22 (1992): 124-139.

32. In Massey, op. cit., pp. 231-249.

33. "Outside the Gate: Sharing the Insult," *Jeevadhara* 11 (1981): 203-231.

34. George Soares-Prabhu, "The Table Fellowship of Jesus: Its Significance for Dalit Christians in India Today," *Jeevadhara* 22 (1992): 140-159; Amaladoss, op. cit., pp. 110-112.

35. Prabhakar, in Massey, op. cit., pp. 212-213; Amaladoss, op. cit., pp. 128-132.

36. Ambedkar himself thought so. See Maliekal, op. cit., p. 61.

37. In Massey, op. cit., p. 268.

38. Ibid., p. 270.

39. Ibid., p. 274.

40. Cf. Amaladoss, op. cit., pp. 100-140.

### 4. The Awakening of Women in Asia

1. I am making a synthetic narrative here. Detailed reports and testimonies can be seen in the following. Asia Partnership for Human Development, *Awake: Asian Women and the Struggle for Justice* (Sydney, 1985); Gabriele Dietrich, "The World as the Body of God:

Feminist Perspectives on Ecology and Social Justice," *The Journal of Dharma* 18. (1993): 258-284; Mary John Mananzan, *The Woman Question in the Philippines* (Pasay City: St. Paul, 1991); Rose Marie Cecchini, *Women's Action for Peace and Justice: Christian, Buddhist and Muslim Women Tell their Story* (Maryknoll Sisters); Ilina Sen (ed.), *A Space Within the Struggle* (New Delhi: Kali for Women, 1990); Leelamma Devasia and V. V. Devasia (eds.), *Women in India: Equality, Social Justice and Development* (New Delhi: Indian Social Institute, 1990); Jessie Tellis Nayak, "Why This Oppression of Women?" *Jeevadhara* 17 (1987): 9-22; Mary Pillai, "Women against Women?" ibid., pp. 42-50; special issue on "Born of a Woman," *Jeevadhara* 17 (1987): 181-260.

2. Asian Partnership, op. cit., p. 12.

3. Cf. Cecchini, op. cit., for Asia; for India: Gail Omvedt, *Reinventing Revolution* (Armonk, NY: M.E. Sharpe, 1993), pp. 76-99; Ghanshyam Shah, *Social Movements in India* (New Delhi: Sage, 1990), pp. 130-147.

4. Cf. Corona Mary, "People's Theology - A Woman's Perspective," *Jeevadhara* 22 (1992): 214-224.

5. Vandana Shiva, *Staying Alive: Women, Ecology and Survival in India* (New Delhi: Kali for Women, 1988), pp. xvii-xviii.

6. Cf. Gabriele Dietrich, "On Doing Feminist Theology in South Asia," *Kristu Jyoti* 6. (1990): 47.

7. Ibid., p. 37.

8. Aloysius Pieris, "Woman and Religion in Asia: Towards a Buddhist and Christian Appropriation of the Feminist Critique," *Dialogue* 19-20 (1992-1993): 175.

9. Cf. Omvedt, op. cit., p. 221.

10. Cf. Cecchini, op. cit., pp. 108f.

11. Cf. Pieris, op. cit., pp. 149-175.

12. Cf. Paulus Kullu, "Tribal Religion and Culture," *Jeevadhara* 24. (1994): 107.

13. Cf. Dietrich, op. cit., pp. 52-58.

14. Quoted in ibid., pp. 55-56.

15. A. K. Ramanujan, *Speaking of Siva* (Hammondsworth: Penguin, 1973), p. 131.

16. For a good summary of Asian feminist theology, see Chung Hyun Kyung, *Struggle to Be the Sun Again: Introducing Asian Women's Theology* (Maryknoll, NY: Orbis Books, 1991).

17. An Urdu song quoted in Omvedt, op. cit., p. 209.

18. "God as Mother in the Old Testament," *Jeevadhara* 21 (1991): 117.

19. For the general Indian tradition, see John Stratton Hawley and Donna Marie Wulff, *The Divine Consort: Radha and the Goddesses of India* (Delhi: Motilal Banarsidass, 1982).

20. Cf. Subash Anand, "The Lady and the Demon," *Vidyajyoti Journal of Theological Reflection* 50. (1986): 454-468.

21. See Chung, op. cit., pp. 49-50.

22. Pieris, op. cit., pp. 124-129.

23. Cf. Joseph Sebastian, *God as Feminine According to Subramania Bharati Seen in the Light of Christian Tradition* (Rome: Gregorian University, 1994), p. 36.

24. Cf. ibid., pp. 26-34.

25. Cf., for a good summary, Chung, op. cit., pp. 53-73.

26. Cf. Bernie Silva, "The Gospels and Liberation of Asian Women," *Jeevadhara* 17. (1987): 80-95; George Mangatt, "Jesus' Option for Women," *Jeevadhara* 21. (1991): 161-175.

27. Though born in Germany, Gabriele Dietrich is a naturalized Indian citizen with many years of experience in India. She is an Asian theologian.

28. Gabriele Dietrich, "The Blood of a Woman," quoted in *Jeevadhara* 17. (1987): 220-222.

29. Chung, op. cit., pp. 74-84.

30. Corona Mary, "Woman in Creation Story," *Jeevadhara* 21. (1991): 95-106.

31. M. Amaladoss, "Women and the Future of Humanity," *Vidyajyoti Journal of Theological Reflection* 54 (1990): 233-244.

32. Cf. Pieris, op. cit., p. 182.

## 5. In Harmony with the Earth

1. For technical and other details see, for example, S. Sivadas, "A New Gospel on Nature," *Jeevadhara* 21 (1991): 421-432.

2. Cf. Matthew Parakkal, "Environmental Diseases," *Jeevadhara* 21. (1991): 434-452; Mira Shiva, "Environmental Degradation and Subversion of Health," in Vandana Shiva (ed.), *Minding Our Lives* (New Delhi: Kali for Women, 1993), pp. 60-77.

3. See Joseph K. Kurian, "Forests and Environmental Protection," *Jeevadhara* 21 (1991): 453-461; Philip Viegas and Geeta Menon (eds.), *The Impact of Environmental Degradation on People* (New Delhi: Indian Social Institute, 1989), pp. 7-20; Gail Omvedt, *Reinventing Revolution* (New York: M.E. Sharpe, 1993), pp. 127-149.

4. Viegas and Menon, op. cit., pp. 20-36.

5. Vandana Shiva, "The Seed and the Earth: Biotechnology and the Colonisation of Regeneration," in idem., op. cit., pp. 128-143.

6. Omvedt, op. cit., p. 139.

7. Anil Agrawal, quoted in ibid., p. 143. See also idem., "Ecological Destruction and the Emerging Patterns of Poverty and People's Protests in Rural India," *Social Action* 35 (1985): 54-90.

8. Cf. Vandana Shiva, *Staying Alive* (New Delhi: Kali for Women, 1988).

9. Claude Alvares, *Science, Development and Violence* (Delhi: Oxford, 1994), pp. 113-124.

10. Madhav Gadgil and V.D. Vartak, "The Sacred Uses of Nature," in Ramachandra Guha, *Social Ecology* (Delhi: Oxford, 1994), pp. 82-89.

11. Ibid., pp. 56-63.

12. Madhav Gadgil, "Forest Management, Deforestation and People's Impoverishment," *Social Action* 39 (1989): 357-383.

13. See Alice Lukose, "We Work Hard All Night Long and Catch Nothing," *Jeevadhara* 16.(1986): 217-227; Tom Kochery, "Where I Met Jesus," *Jeevadhara* 21 (1991): 185-192.

14. John Kurien and T.R. Thankappan Achari, "Overfishing the Coastal Commons: Causes and Consequences," in Ramachandra Guha (ed.), *Social Ecology* (Delhi: Oxford, 1994), pp. 218-246.

15. Cf. Gabriele Dietrich, "The World as the Body of God: Feminist Perspectives on Ecology and Social Justice," *Journal of Dharma* 18. (1993): 258-284.

16. Enakshi Ganguly Thukral, "Dams: For Whose Development?" in Walter Fernandes and E.G. Thukral (eds.), *Development, Displacement and Rehabilitation* (New Delhi: Indian Social Institute, 1989), pp. 39-61; Loreta B. Ayupan and Teresita G. Oliveros, "Filipino Peasant Women in Defence of Life," in V. Shiva (ed.), *Minding Our Lives*, pp. 113-120.

17. Smithu Kothari, "Ecology vs Development: The Struggle for Survival," *Social Action* 35. (1985): 379-392; Walter Fernandes, "Power and Powerlessness: Development Projects and Displacement of Tribals," ibid., 41 (1991): 243-270.

18. Joseph Velamkunnel, "The Jharkhand Movement: A Response to Tribal Oppression?" *Vidyajyoti Journal of Theological Reflection* 53. (1989): 299-311.

19. Cf. Omvedt, op. cit., pp. 241-244.

20. Cf. ibid., pp. 137-141; M.V. Nadkarni, "Agricultural Policy and Ecology," *Social Action* 43 (1993): 271-280; Avadhoot Nadkarni, "The Green Revolution: Twenty Five Years Later," ibid., pp. 280-294.

21. Cf. Viegas and Menon, op. cit., pp. 20-36, 45-54.

22. Cf. Alvares, op. cit., pp. 136-138, 144f.

23. Cf. Omvedt, op. cit. The whole book is a demonstration how Marxists neglect the new movements of the people.

24. Cf. Alvares, op. cit.; Ashis Nandy, *Science, Hegemony and Violence* (Delhi: Oxford, 1988); Nandy, *Traditions, Tyranny and Utopias* (Delhi: Oxford, 1987); Mahatma Gandhi, *Hind Swaraj* (Ahmedabad: Navajivan, 1982. reprint).

25. Cf. Shiva, *Minding Our Lives*, pp. 138-139.

26. Cf. A.K. Ramanujan, *Poems of Love and War (from the Eight Anthologies and the Ten Long Poems of Classical Tamil)* (New York: Columbia University Press, 1985).

27. M. Amaladoss, "Ecology and Culture," *Jeevadhara* 18. (1988): 51-53.

28. Thich Naht Hanh, *Interbeing* (Berkeley: Parallax Press, 1993).

29. Paulus Kullu, "Tribal Religion and Culture," *Jeevadhara* 24 (1994): 89-109.

30. Nirmal Minz, "Anthropology and the Deprived," *Religion and Society* 32,4. (1985): 3-19.

31. Aloysius Pieris, *Love Meets Wisdom* (Maryknoll, NY: Orbis Books, 1988).

32. Ignatius Jesudasan, *Gandhian Theology of Liberation* (Maryknoll, NY, Orbis Books, 1984) pp. 179-189.

33. Aloysius Pieris, "Woman and Religion in Asia: Towards a Buddhist and Christian Appropriation of the Feminist Critique," *Dialogue* (NS) 19-20 (1992-1993): 181-182.

34. George Therukattil, "Towards a Biblical Eco-Theology," *Jeevadhara* 21 (1991): 465-483; R.J. Raja, "Eco-spirituality in the Psalms," *Vidyajyoti Journal of Theological Reflection* 53 (1989): 637-650; "Eco-spirituality in the Book of Revelation," ibid. 55 (1991): 681-697; "Wisdom Psalms and Environmental Concerns," ibid. 57. (1993): 201-214.

35. S. Arokiasamy, "Ecological Ethics in a Divided World," *Jeevadhara* 21. (1991): 484-494.

36. Antony Kalliath, "Atman, the Locus of Eco-Theology: A New Arena for Indian Theology," *Jeevadhara* 23. (1993): 330-343.

37. Gabriele Dietrich, "The World as the Body of God: Feminist Perspectives on Ecology and Social Justice," *The Journal of Dharma* 18 (1993): 258-284.

38. Bishops of the Philippines, quoted in Sean McDnagh, *The Greening of the Church* (Maryknoll, NY, Orbis Books and London: Geoffrey Chapman, 1990), p. 213.

39. Cf. R. Panikkar, *The Cosmotheandric Experience* (Maryknoll, NY: Orbis Books, 1993); M. Amaladoss, *Towards Fullness* (Bangalore: NBCLC, 1994); Aloysius Pieris, "Woman and Religion in Asia," *Dialogue* (NS) 19-20 (1992-1993): 189-194; Rudolf C. Heredia, "Towards an Ecological Consciousness: Religious, Ethical and Spiritual Perspectives," *Vidyajyoti Journal of Theological Reflection* 55. (1991): 489-504, 569-588.

## 6. Hinduism and Liberation

1. Cf. Ranajit Guha and Gayatri Chakravorty Spivak (eds.), *Selected Subaltern Studies* (Oxford: Oxford University Press, 1988).

2. For the life of Gandhi, see Gandhi, *An Autobiography: The Story of My Experiments with Truth* (Ahmedabad: Navajivan Publishing House, 1945); B.R. Nanda, *Mahatma Gandhi: A Biography* (Boston: Beacon Press, 1958); Ignatius Jesudasan, *A Gandhian Theology of Liberation* (Maryknoll, NY: Orbis Books, 1984).

3. Cf. Jesudasan, op. cit., p. 17.

4. Cf. Gandhi, *Constructive Programme: Its Meaning and Place* (Ahmedabad: Navjivan, 1945). See also Gandhians of Sevagram, *A New Social Order: The Gandhian Alternative* (Varanasi: Sarva Seva Sangh Prakashan, 1991).

5. Quoted in Jesudasan, op. cit., p. 128.

6. Ibid., p. 72.

7. Ibid., p. 73.

8. *Navajivan,* May 5, 1928.

9. Quoted in Jesudasan, op. cit., pp. 77-78 from Mahadev Desai, *The Epic of Travancore* (Ahmedabad: Navajivan, 1937).

10. Cf. J.S. Mathur, *Non-Violence and Social Change* (Ahmedabad: Navajivan, 1977).

11. Gandhi, *From Yerawada Mandir: Ashram Observances* (Ahmedabad: Navajivan, 1957), p. 8.

12. *Harijan,* Sept. 1, 1940.

13. Gandhi, *Autobiography,* Introduction.

14. Gandhi, *The Message of the Gita,* compiled by R.K. Prabhu (Ahmedabad: Navajivan, 1959).

15. Ibid., pp. 9-10.

16. Ibid., p. 32.

17. Swami Agnivesh, "Vedic Socialism," *Seminar 339* (November, 1987): 18-22.

18. Ibid., p. 19.

19. Ibid., p. 20.

20. Ibid.

21. Ibid., p. 21.

22. Ibid.

23. Ibid.

24. Ibid., p. 22.

25. Ibid.

26. Ibid.

27. For Periyar's life and movement, see M. Amaladoss, "Periyar and Liberation in Tamil Nadu," in Paul Puthanangady (ed.), *Towards an Indian Theology of Liberation* (Bangalore: NBCLC, 1986), pp. 184-198; K.M. Balasubramaniam, *Periyar E.V. Ramaswami* (Trichy: Periyar Self-Respect Propaganda, 1973); P.D. Devanandan, *The Dravida Kazhagam* (Bangalore: Christian Institute for the Study of Religion and Society, 1960); Anita Diehl, *Periyar E.V.R.: A Study of the Influence of a Personality in Contemporary South India* (New Delhi: B.I.Publication, 1978).

28. Jerry, *Manitham* (in Tamil)(Madras: Niti Publications, 1994), p. 109.

29. Ibid., p. 113.

30. Ibid., pp. 176-204.

31. Ibid.

32. Cf. Hans-J. Klimkeit, "Indigenous Elements in Modern Tamil Secularism," *Religion and Society* 23, 3. (1976): 77-98.

33. Cf. Tiruvalluvar, *The Kural,* trans. P.S. Sundaram (New Delhi: Penguin Books, 1990).

34. See, for example, A.K. Ramanujan, *Speaking of Siva* (Harmondsworth: Penguin, 1973).

35. These quotations are taken from Klimkeit, op. cit., pp. 91-92. 'Lingam' is a black stone image, considered the phallic symbol of Siva.

36. Cf. Charles A. Ryerson, "Primordial Sentiments in Tamil Nadu: The Cultural Roots

of the Plea for Greater Autonomy," *Religion and Society* 22, 1 (1975): 27-28; idem., "Meaning and Modernization in Tamil Gnat: Tamil Nationalism and Religious Culture," *Religion and Society* 17,4 (1970): 6-21.

37. Cf. Jerry, op. cit., pp. 114-115. See also Anita Diehl, op. cit. Anita Diehl personally interviewed Periyar a number of times before his death.

38. Cf. Jerry, op. cit., p. 192.

## 7. Buddhism and Liberation

1. Joanna Macy, "In Indra's Net: Sarvodaya and Our Mutual Efforts for Peace," in Fred Eppsteiner (ed.), *The Path of Compassion: Writings on Socially Engaged Buddhism* (Berkeley: Parallax Press, 1988), p. 171.

2. Joanna Macy, *Dharma and Development: Religion as Resource in the Sarvodaya Self-Help Movement* (West Hartford, CT: Kumarian Press, 1983), p. 24, quoting from A.T. Ariyaratna, *In Search of Development* (Moratuwa: Sarvodaya Press, 1981), p. 1.

3. Macy, *Dharma and Development*, p. 46.

4. Ibid., p. 35.

5. Robert Bobilin, *Revolution from Below: Buddhist and Christian Movements for Justice in Asia* (Lanham, MD: University Press of America, 1988), p. 25.

6. Macy, *Dharma and Development*, p. 34.

7. Bobilin, op. cit., p. 23; also Macy, "In Indra's Net," pp. 177-178.

8. Macy, *Dharma and Development*, p. 40.

9. Ibid., pp. 77-78.

10. Bobilin, op. cit., p. 24.

11. Ibid., p. 42.

12. The *Mahayana* and the *Hinayana* are two sections of Buddhism. The *Hinayana*, or the 'little vehicle,' claims to be faithful to the teachings of the Buddha and focuses on renunciation of desire and remains agnostic with regard to an Absolute. The *Mahayana*, or the 'great vehicle,' is more devotional, making the Buddha into an incarnation. The mahayanist claim to base their tradition on Buddha's teachings that remained hidden originally, but were revealed later. For example, the Buddhists in Sri Lanka and Thailand follow the *Hinayana* tradition, while the Vietnamese Buddhists follow the *Mahayana* tradition. Popular Buddhism everywhere does not follow these rigorous 'scholastic' distinctions.

13. Macy, *Dharma and Development*, pp. 75-76.

14. For his life, see Donald J. Swearer, *Me and Mine: Selected Essays of Buddhadasa* (Albany, NY: State University of New York Press, 1989), p. 2; Bhikku Santikaro, "Buddhadasa Bhikku: Life and Society through the Natural Eyes of Voidness" (mss), pp. 2-10.

15. Buddhadasa Bhikku, *Dhammic Socialism*, trans. and ed. Donald K. Swearer (Bangkok: Thai Inter-Religious Commission for Development, 1993), p. 14. 'Theravada' is another term for 'Hinayana.' See note 12 above.

16. Swearer, op. cit., p. 6.

17. Quoted in Santikaro, op. cit., p. 17.

18. Bhikku, op. cit., p. 34.

19. Swearer, op. cit., p. 106.

20. Ibid., pp. 115-125.

21. Santikaro, op. cit., p. 21.

22. Bhikku, op. cit., p. 48.

23. Swearer, op. cit., p. 30.

24. Ibid., p. 109.

25. Ibid., p. 83.

26. Bhikku, op. cit., p. 102.

27. Swearer, op. cit., p. 12.

28. Ibid., p. 180.

29. Bhikku, op. cit., p. 56.

30. Ibid., p. 57.

31. Ibid., p. 107.

32. Ibid., pp. 81-85.

33. Ibid., p. 110.

34. Ibid., p. 84.

35. Ibid., p. 90.

36. Ibid., p. 95.

37. Swearer, op. cit., pp. 204-207.

38. Ibid., p. 175.

39. Bhikku, op. cit., p. 40.

40. Some of his works include S. Sivaraksa, *A Socially Engaged Buddhism* (Bangkok: Thai Interreligious Commission for Development, 1988); *Seeds of Peace* (Bangkok: International Network of Engaged Buddhists, 1992); *A Buddhist Vision for Renewing Society* (Bangkok: Thai Interreligious Commission for Development, 1994); Sivaraksa et al. (eds.), *Buddhist Perception for Desirable Societies in the Future* (Bangkok: Thai Interreligious Commission for Development, 1993).

41. Thich Nhat Hanh, *Transformation and Healing* (London: Rider Books, 1993), p. 147.

42. In Eppsteiner (ed.), op. cit., pp. 32-33.

43. Daniel Berrigan / Thich Nhat Hanh, *The Raft Is Not the Shore* (Boston: Beacon Press, 1975), p. 102.

44. Thich Nhat Hanh, *Interbeing: Fourteen Guidelines for Engaged Buddhism* (Berkeley: Parallax Press, 1993), p. 6.

45. Ibid., pp. 17-20. For a commentary, see pp. 20-49.

46. Ibid., pp. 55-59.

47. Cao Ngoc Phuong, "Days and Months," in Eppsteiner (ed.), op. cit., pp. 155-169.

## 8. Confucianism and Liberation

1. Quoted from Aloysius B. Chang, "Liberative Elements in the Confucian Tradition," *Japanese Religions*, p. 27. Chang quotes from *A Source Book in Chinese Philosophy*, trans. and comp. Wing-Tsit Chan (New York: Princeton University Press, 1963).

2. Chang, op. cit., p. 27.

3. Chan, op. cit., p. 16.

4. Cf. Archie J. Bahm, *The Heart of Confucius* (New York: Harper and Row, 1971), pp. 18-25.

5. Chang, op. cit., p. 29. See also pp. 28-31.

6. Quoted in Sung-Hae Kim, "Liberation Through Humanization: With a Focus on Korean Confucianism," *Ching Feng* 33:1-2 (1990): 39.

7. Ibid., p. 30.

8. Ibid., p. 41.

9. Ibid., p. 28.

10. Texts quoted in Raymond Dawson, *Confucius* (Oxford: Oxford University Press, 1981), p. 37.

11. The previous texts are quoted in ibid., p. 40.

12. Ibid., pp. 17-18.

13. Quoted from *The Doctrine of the Mean* by Chang, op. cit., p. 41.

14. Quoted in Dawson, op. cit., p. 10.

15. Quoted from *The Doctrine of the Mean* by Chang, op. cit., p. 41.

16. Cf. ibid., p. 34.

17. Cf. ibid., p. 35.

18. Cf. Kevin Shun-Kai Cheng, "The Social Dimension of Liberation in Early Confucian Tradition," *Ching Feng* 36,2-3 (1993): 70. Quoted from Mencius, 3A4.

19. Ibid., p. 71.

20. Ibid., p. 67.

21. Ibid., p. 70.

22. Ibid., p. 75.

23. Cf. ibid., p. 78.

24. Wm. Theodore de Bary, "The Prophetic Voice in the Confucian Nobleman," *Ching Feng* 33,1-2 (1990): 16.

25. Cf. Dawson, op. cit., pp. 33-36.

## 9. Christianity and Liberation

1. See Aloysius Pieris, *Love Meets Wisdom* (Maryknoll, NY: Orbis Books, 1988).

2. Pieris lists such groups in Sri Lanka in his *An Asian Theology of Liberation* (Maryknoll, NY: Orbis Books, 1988), pp. 57-58. He is closely associated with the Christian Workers' Fellowship.

3. For a report, see Virginia Fabella (ed.), *Asia's Struggle for Full Humanity* (Maryknoll, NY: Orbis Books, 1980).

4. Cf. ibid., pp. 75-95; also reprinted in Pieris, *An Asian Theology,* pp. 69-86.

5. Cf. Pieris, *An Asian Theology,* p. 121.

6. Cf. ibid., p. 20.

7. Ibid., p. 15.

8. Cf. ibid., pp. 93-96.

9. Ibid., pp. 77-78.

10. Ibid., p. 83.

11. Aloysius Pieris, "An Asian Paradigm: Inter-religious Dialogue and Theology of Religions," *The Month* (April, 1993): 133.

12. Cf. Pieris, *An Asian Theology,* p. 120. See also pp. 59-65.

13. See ibid., pp. 96-110; also Pieris, "An Asian Paradigm," p. 132.

14. Cf. Pieris, *An Asian Theology,* pp. 57, 121.

15. George Soares-Prabhu, "Class in the Bible: The Biblical Poor, a Social Class?" *Voices from the Margin: Interpreting the Bible in the Third World,* ed. R.S. Sugirtharajah (Maryknoll, NY Obis Books, 1991) (italics added), quoted in Pieris, ibid., p. 123.

16. Besides the articles cited in the notes below, a summary by Soares-Prabhu in an (so far) unpublished paper on "The Dharma of Jesus" has been helpful in the following rapid exposition.

17. George Soares-Prabhu, "Jesus the Teacher: The Liberative Pedagogy of Jesus of Nazareth," *Jeevadhara* 12 (1982): 432-456.

18. George Soares-Prabhu, "The Synoptic Love-Commandment: The Dimensions of Love in the Teaching of Jesus," *Jeevadhara* 13 (1983): 85-103.

19. George Soares-Prabhu, "The Kingdom of God: Jesus' Vision of a New Society," in D. S. Amalorpavadass (ed.), *The Indian Church in the Struggle for a New Society* (Bangalore: NBCLC, 1981), pp. 601, 607.

20. George Soares-Prabhu, "The Miracles of Jesus: Subversion of a Power Structure?" in S. Kappen (ed.), *Jesus Today* (Madras: AICUF, 1985), pp. 21-29.

21. George Soares-Prabhu, "The Spirituality of Jesus as a Spirituality of Solidarity and Struggle," in J. Vattamattom and others (eds.), *Liberative Struggles in a Violent Society* (Hyderabad: Forum, 1991), pp. 136-161.

22. George Soares-Prabhu, "Jesus and the Poor," in J. Murickan (ed.), *Poverty in India: Challenge and Responses* (Bangalore: Xavier Board, 1988), pp. 261-290; "The Table Fellowship of Jesus: Its Significance for Dalit Christians in India Today," *Jeevadhara* 22 (1992): 140-159.

23. George Soares-Prabhu, "Jesus and Conflict," *The Way* 26 (1986): 14-23.

24. See paper referred to in note 16 above, p. 9.

25. George Soares-Prabhu, "Good News to the Poor: The Social Implications of the Message of Jesus," in D.S. Amalorpavadass (ed.), *The Indian Church in the Struggle for a New Society,* p. 626.

26. Sebastian Kappen, *Jesus and Freedom* (Maryknoll, NY: Orbis Books, 1977).

27. Sebastian Kappen, *Jesus and Cultural Revolution: An Asian Perspective* (Bombay: BUILD, 1983); *Tradition, Modernity, Counterculture: An Asian Perspective* (Bangalore: Vishtar, 1994).

28. Sebastian Kappen, *Marxian Atheism* (1983); *Liberation Theology and Marxism* (1986); *The Future of Socialism and Socialism of the Future* (1992).

29. Kappen, *Jesus and Cultural Revolution,* pp. 9-10.

30. Ibid., pp. 10-13.

31. Ibid., p. 14.

32. Ibid., pp. 18-28.

33. Ibid., pp. 37-42. See also chapter 7 above, on Buddhism.

34. For our purpose here, a mere list of names is not helpful. See Subash Anand, "Mahisa-Mardana: A Myth of Holistic Liberation Theology"; Walter Fernandes, "Bhakti and a Liberation Theology for India"; S. Arulsamy, "Virasaivism as a Liberation Movement," in Paul Puthanangady (ed.), *Towards an Indian Theology of Liberation* (Bangalore: NBCLC, 1986).

35. Kappen, *Jesus and Cultural Revolution,* pp. 46-51. See also his *Tradition, Modernity,* pp. 1-25, 50-59, 94-106.

36. Kappen, *Jesus and Cultural Revolution,* p. 46.

37. Kappen, *Tradition, Modernity,* pp. 24-25.

38. Kappen, *Jesus and Cultural Revolution,* pp. 56-57.

39. Ibid., pp. 58-66.

40. Ibid., pp. 66-70.

41. Ibid., p. 71.

42. Ibid., pp. 72-75.

43. Ibid., p. 76.

44. Kappen, *Tradition, Modernity,* pp. 50-59, 94-106.

45. Ibid., pp. 84-93.

46. Ibid., pp. 76-79.

47. The Mar Thoma Church is a Protestant tradition in the Syrian Orthodox Church. M. M. Thomas has written an autobiography in Malayalam: *Ente Christhava Dharmanveshana Paryadanam* (My Journey in Search of Christian Dharma). For a brief account of his

life, see T. M. Philip, *The Encounter Between Theology and Ideology: An Exploration into the Communicative Theology of M.M. Thomas* (Madras: The Christian Literature Society, 1986), pp. 1-18.

48. M.M. Thomas, *The Christian Response to Asian Revolution* (London: SCM, 1966), p. 7.

49. M.M. Thomas, *Salvation and Humanization* (Madras: Christian Literature Society, 1971), p. 21.

50. See Philip, op. cit., p. 33; M.M. Thomas, *Towards a Theology of Contemporary Ecumenism* (Madras: The Christian Literature Society, 1978), pp. 57-72.

51. M.M. Thomas, *The Acknowledged Christ of the Indian Renaissance* (Madras: The Christian Literature Society, 1970).

52. Thomas, *Contemporary Ecumenism*, p. 77.

53. Thomas, *Salvation and Humanization*, p. 10.

54. Ibid, p. 18.

55. M.M. Thomas, "A Christian View of Society," *Religion and Society* 7. (October-December 1960): 54-55.

56. Cf. M.M. Thomas, *Secular Ideologies and the Secular Meaning of Christ* (Madras: The Christian Literature Society, 1976).

57. Thomas, *Contemporary Ecumenism*, p. 68.

58. Cf. Philip, op. cit., pp. 89-108.

59. M.M. Thomas, *Man and the Universe of Faiths* (Madras: Christian Literature Society, 1975), p. vi.

60. M. M. Thomas, *New Creation in Christ* (Delhi: ISPCK, 1976), pp. 29, 47-48. See also M. M. Thomas, *Man and the Universe of Faiths* (Madras: The Christian Literature Society, 1975).

61. M. M. Thomas, "Christ-Centered Syncretism," *Religion and Society* 25 (March 1979): 31.

### 10. Islam and Liberation

1. Cf. Chandra Muzzaffar, "Islamic Resurgence: A Global View," in idem., *Islamic Resurgence in Malaysia* (Petaling Jaya: Penerbit Fajar Bakti Sdu. Bhd., 1987).

2. For Mawdudi's life, see Khurshid Ahmad and Zafar Ishaq Ansari, "Mawlana Sayyid Abul A'la Mawdudi: An Introduction to His Vision of Islam and Islamic Revival," in idem. (eds.), *Islamic Perspectives: Studies in Honour of Mawlana Sayyid Abul A' la Mawdudi* (Leicester: The Islamic Foundation, 1979), pp. 360-365; and Charles J. Adams, "Mawdudi and the Islamic State," in John L. Esposito (ed.), *Voices of Resurgent Islam* (Oxford: Oxford University Press, 1983), pp. 100-111.

3. Adams, op. cit., p. 99.

4. M. Mawdudi, *The Islamic Movement: Dynamics of Values, Power and Change* (Leicester: Islamic Foundation, 1984), p. 79.

5. Cf. Ahmad and Ansari, op. cit., p. 373.

6. Ibid., p. 376.

7. Mawdudi, op. cit., p. 79.

8. Ahmad and Ansari, op. cit., pp. 379-380.

9. Ibid., p. 380.

10. Ibid., p. 381.

11. Cf. Adams, op. cit., p. 108.

12. Mawdudi, op. cit., p. 71.

13. Ibid., p. 77.

14. Adams, op. cit., p. 110.

15. Ibid., p. 117.

16. Ibid., p. 120.

17. Ibid., pp. 112, 125-127.

18. Mawdudi, op. cit., pp. 133-136.

19. Ibid., p. 99.

20. For the life of Ali Shariati, please see Ali Shariati, *Man and Islam,* trans. Fatollah Marjani (Houston: Filinc, 1981), pp. vii-xviii; Ali Shariati, *What Is to Be Done?: The Enlightened Thinkers and an Islamic Renaissance,* ed. Farhang Rajaee (Houston: IRIS, 1986), xvii-xix; Ali Shariati, *On the Sociology of Islam,* trans. Hamid Algar (Berkeley: Mizan Press, 1979), pp. 11-38.

21. Shariati, *What Is to Be Done?,* pp. xi-xii.

22. Ali Shariati, *Marxism and Other Western Fallacies: An Islamic Critique,* trans. R. Campbell (Berkeley: Mizan Press, 1980), pp. 91-95.

23. Cf. Ali Shariati, *Martyrdom,* trans. Laleh Bakhtiar and Husayn Salih (Tehran: Abu Dharr Foundation, n.d.), pp. 19.

24. Shariati, *What Is to Be Done?,* pp. 22-23.

25. Ibid., pp. 1,71.

26. Ibid., *On the Sociology,* pp. 82-87.

27. Ibid., p. 85.

28. Cf. Shariati, *Man and Islam,* pp. 20-21; *On the Sociology,* p. 33.

29. Shariati, *Man and Islam,* p. 28.

30. Shariati, *On the Sociology,* pp. 119-120.

31. Shariati, *Man and Islam,* pp. 6-7.

32. Shariati, *On the Sociology,* pp. 88-95.

33. Shariati, *What Is to Be done?,* pp. 43-44.

34. Shariati, *Man and Islam,* pp. 48-62.

35. Ibid., p. 18.

36. Ibid., p. 19; *On the Sociology,* p. 115: Ali Shariati, *Hajj,* trans. Somayyah and Yaser (Bedford: FILINC, 1977), pp. 100-103.

37. Shariati, *On the Sociology,* pp. 112-114.

38. Shariati, *Man and Islam,* pp. 113-117.

39. Shariati, *What Is to Be done?,* pp. 30-31.

40. Ibid., p. 35.

41. Shariati, *Man and Islam,* pp. 29-45; 63-81; *What Is to Be Done?* is a blueprint of what needs to be done in terms of courses and programs in a cultural center.

42. Shariati, *What Is to Be done?,* p. 17.

43. Ibid.

44. Cf. Shariati, *Martyrdom.*

45. Ibid., p. 86.

46. Asghar Ali Engineer, *Islam and Liberation Theology: Essays on Liberative Elements in Islam* (New Delhi: Sterling Publishers, 1990) offers a collection of his articles.

47. Ibid., pp. 28-30.

48. Ibid., p. 32.

49. Ibid., p. 88.

50. Ibid., p. 51.

51. Ibid., pp. 26, 85-86.

52. Ibid., p. 7.

53. For a good survey and representative articles from contemporary Iranian Islamic scholars, see Mehdi Abedi and Gary Legenhausen (eds.), *Jihad and Shahadat: Struggle and Martyrdom in Islam* (Houston: IRIS, 1986).

54. Cf. John J. Donohue and John L. Esposito (eds.), *Islam in Transition: Muslim Perspectives* (New York: Oxford University Press, 1982), pp. 169-177.

55. S. 'Abid Husain, in ibid., p. 170.

56. Abdurrahman Wahid, mss., p. 85.

## 11. The Cosmic Religions and Liberation

1. Aloysius Pieris, *An Asian Theology of Liberation* (Maryknoll, NY: Orbis Books, 1988), pp. 71-73.

2. Aloysius Pieris, "An Asian Paradigm: Inter-religious Dialogue and Theology of Religions," *The Month* (April 1993): 131-132.

3. Ibid., p. 132.

4. See Arche Ligo, "Liberation Themes in Philippine Popular Religiosity: A Case Study," *Voices from the Third World* 16. (1993): 122-126.

5. Quoted in ibid. from Vicente Marasigan, *A Banahaw Guru* (Quezon City: Ateneo University Press, 1985), pp. 23-24.

6. Cf. Nguyen Xuan Nghia, "Les mouvements messianiques du delta du Mekong de la fin du 19eme siecle a 1975," *Social Compass* 42 (1995): 317-328.

7. Cf. Reynaldo Ileto, *Pasyon and Revolution* (Quezon City: Ateneo University Press, 1979).

8. Ligo, op. cit., p. 139.

9. Abraham Ayrookuzhiel, "Cinna Pulayan: The Dalit Teacher of Sankaracharya," pp. 7-8.

10. David Mosse, *Caste, Christianity and Hinduism: A Study of Social Organization and Religion in Rural Ramnad* (unpublished D.Phil. thesis, Oxford University, 1986), p. 480.

11. R.L. Stirrat, *Power and Religiosity in a Post-Colonial Setting: Sinhala Catholics in Contemporary Sri Lanka* (Cambridge: Cambridge University Press, 1992), p. 91. Kudagama is a pilgrim center specializing in exorcism.

12. Kalpana Ram, *Mukkuvar Women* (Delhi: Kali for Women, 1992), p. 79. See also pp. 93-105. Mukkuvar are a caste of fisher-people in the south of India.

13. Gananath Obeyesekere, "Sorcery, Premeditated Murder, and the Canalization of Aggression in Sri Lanka," *Ethnology* 14 (1975): 1-24.

14. See also Gilles Tarabout, "Violence et Non-Violence Magiques: La Sorcellerie au Kerala," *Purusartha* 16 (1994): 155-185.

15. Obeyesekere, op. cit., p. 17.

16. David Mosse, op. cit.; Susan Bayly, *Saints, Goddesses and Kings: Muslims and Christians in South Indian Society* (Cambridge: Cambridge University Press, 1989).

## 12. Life in Freedom

1. Cf. Aloysius Pieris, "Towards an Asian Theology of Liberation: Some Religio-Cultural Guidelines," in Virginia Fabella (ed.), *Asia's Struggle for Full Humanity* (Maryknoll, NY: Orbis Books, 1980), pp. 75-95.

2. Cf. M. Amaladoss, "Liberation as an Inter-religious Project," in Felix Wilfred (ed.), *Leave the Temple: Indian Paths to Human Liberation* (Maryknoll, NY: Orbis Books, 1992), pp. 158-174.

# Selected Bibliography
# on Liberation

**Abedi, Mehdi and Gary Legenhausen (eds.)**. *Jihad and Shahadat: Struggle and Martyrdom in Islam*. Houston: IRIS, 1986.

**Abesamis, Carlos H**. *The Mission of Jesus and Good News to the Poor*. Quezon City: Claretian, 1987.

_____. *Where Are We Going! Heaven or New World?* Manila: Communication Foundation for Asia, 1983.

**Abraham, K.C.** "A Theological Response to Ecological Crisis." *Bangalore Theological Forum* 25, 1993: 3-14.

**Agarwal, Satya P**. "Lokasamgraha and Ahimsa in the Bhagavad Gita." *Journal of Dharma* 16, 1991: 255-268.

**Agnes, Sr**. "Facing Conflicts in My Life." *Jeevadhara* 23, 1993: 9-15.

**Agnivesh, Swami**. "Vedic Socialism." *Seminar* 339, 1987:18-22.

**Agrawal, Anil**. "Ecological Destruction and the Emerging Patterns of Poverty and Peoples' Protests in Rural India." *Social Action* 35, 1985: 54-90.

**Ahmad, Khurshid and Zafar Ishaq Ansari (eds.)**. *Islamic Perspectives: Studies in Honour of Mawlana Sayyid Abul A' la Mawdudi*. London: The Islamic Foundation, 1979.

**Akhtar, Shabbir**. *The Final Imperative: An Islamic Theology of Liberation*. London: Bellew Publishing, 1991.

**Aleaz, K.P.** "Vedic-Vedantic Vision in Indian Christian Theology of Nature." *Bangalore Theological Forum* 25, 1993: 25-40.

**Alforque, Benjamin E**. "Biblical Underpinnings of Our Theology of Struggle." *CTC Bulletin* 10,1, 1991: 5-14.

**Alvares, Claude**. *Science, Development and Violence*. Delhi: Oxford University Press, 1994.

**Amaladoss, Michael**. *Becoming Indian: The Process of Inculturation*. Rome: Centre for Indian and International Studies, 1993.

_____. *A Call to Community: The Caste System and Christian Responsibility*. Anand: Gujarat Sahitya Prakash, 1994.

_____. "Ecology and Culture." *Jeevadhara* 18, 1988: 40-54.

_____. "Folk Culture as Counter Culture: The Dalit Experience." *Jeevadhara* 24, 1994: 31-42.

_____. "Periyar and Liberation in Tamil Nadu: Towards an Indian Theology of Liberation." Paul Puthanangady (ed.). Bangalore: National Biblical, Catechetical and Liturgical Centre, 1986.

_____. "Religions and Human Rights." *Walking Together*. Anand: Gujarat Sahitya Prakash, 1992, pp. 140-154.

_____. "Religious Conflict and Spirituality." *Jeevadhara* 23, 1993: 27-35.

_____. *Towards Fullness: Searching for an Integral Spirituality.* Bangalore: National Biblical, Catechetical and Liturgical Centre, 1994.

_____. "Women and the Future of Humanity." *Vidyajyoti Journal of Theological Reflection* 54, 1990: 233-244.

Ambedkar, Bhimrao. *Annihilation of Caste.* New Delhi: Arnold Publishers, 1990.

Ambroise, Yvon. "Culture: Liberating or Alienating?" *Jeevadhara* 22, 1992: 26-32.

_____. "The Ecological Problem in India and Its Consequences." *Jeevadhara* 18, 1988: 5-22.

Anand, Mulkraj and Eleanor Zelliot (eds.). *An Anthology of Dalit Literature.* New Delhi: Gyan, 1992.

Anand, Subash. "Women in Hindu View and Way of Life." *Jeevadhara* 17, 1987: 51-63.

Ananda, Sri. "Religio-Cultural Approach to the Gender Problem in India." *Journal of Dharma* 13, 1989: 351-381.

Anthonysamy, S.J. "The Kingdom of God and Ecology: Ecological Insights in Mk. 1-4." *Bible Bashyam* 19, 1993: 176-187.

Arapura, John G. "Ahimsa in Basic Hindu Scriptures, with Reference to Cosmo-ethics." *Journal of Dharma* 16, 1991: 197-210.

Ariyaratna, A.T. *In Search of Development: The Sarvodaya Shramadana Movement's Efforts to Harmonize Tradition with Change.* Moratuwa: Sarvodaya Press, 1982.

Arokiasamy, S. "Ecological Ethics in a Divided World." *Jeevadhara* 21, 1991: 484-498.

_____. "Human Rights: Collective, Societal and Liberational Perspectives." *Jeevadhara* 21, 1991: 53-62.

_____. "Liberation Ethics of Ecology." *Jeevadhara* 18, 1988: 32-39.

_____. "Sarvodaya through Antyodaya —The Liberation of the Poor in the Contextualization of Morals." *Vidyajyoti Journal of Theological Reflection* 51, 1987: 545-564.

Arokiasamy, S. and G. Gispert-Sauch (eds.). *Liberation in Asia: Theological Perspectives.* Anand: Gujarat Sahitya Prakash, 1987.

Asi, Emmanuel. "Liberation Theology: A Pakistani Perspective." *Logos* 28, 1989: 1-53.

*Awake: Asian Women and the Struggle for Justice.* Sydney: Asia Partnership for Human Development, 1985.

Ayrookuzhiel, A.M. Abraham. "Christian Dalits in Revolt." *Jeevdhara* 23, 1993: 267-273.

_____. "Dalit History and Culture: Its Challenges and Dalit Response." *Bangalore Theological Forum* 21, 1989: 30-48.

_____. "The Ideological Nature of the Emerging Dalit Consciousness." *Religion and Society* 37,3, 1990: 14-23.

_____. "Religion and Culture in Dalits' Struggle for Liberation." *Religion and Society* 33, 1986: 33-44.

Bahm, Archie J. *The Heart of Confucius.* New York: Harper and Row, 1971.

Balasubramaniam, K.M. *Periyar E.V. Ramaswami.* Trichy: Periyar Self-respect Propaganda, 1973.

Balasundaram, F.J. "Dalit Theological Perspectives —Arvind P. Nirmal, A Case Study." *Voices from the Third World* 15, 1992: 74-108.

_____. "Feminist Concerns in Asia: An Ecumenical Christian Perspective." *Bangalore Theological Forum* 23, 1991: 39-75.

Balasuriya, Tissa. "Mary and Human Liberation." *Logos* 29, 1990: 1-192.

Baltazar, Stella. "Mary in the Struggle of Women." *Word and Worship* 24, 1991: 331-341.

Bary, William Theodore de. *East Asian Civilizations: A Dialogue in Five Stages.* Cambridge, MA: Harvard University Press, 1988.

_____. "The Prophetic Voice in the Confucian Nobleman." *Ching Feng* 33, 1990: 3-19.

**Battung, Mary Rosario et al. (eds.)** *Religion and Society: Towards a Theology of Struggle, Book I.* Manila: Fides, 1988.

**Batumalai, S.** "Politics and Religion from a Malaysian Perspective." *CTC-Bulletin* 10,2&3, 1992: 23-29.

**Bayly, Susan.** *Saints, Goddesses and Kings: Muslims and Christians in South Indian Society 1700-1900.* Cambridge: Cambridge University Press, 1989.

**Berrigan, Daniel and Thich Nhat Hanh.** *The Raft Is Not the Shore.* Boston: Beacon Press, 1975.

**Bhatt, Bansidhar.** *Ahimsa in the Early Religious Traditions of India.* Rome: Centre for Indian and Inter-religious Studies, 1994.

**Bobilin, Robert.** *Revolution from Below: Buddhist and Christian Movements for Justice in Asia.* Lanham, MD: University Press of America, 1988.

**Bragt, Jan van.** "Liberative Elements in Pure Land Buddhism." *Inter-Religio* 18, 1990: 44-69.

**Buddhadasa, Bhikku.** *Dhammic Socialism.* Bangkok: Thai Inter-Religious Commission for Development, 1986.

**Carr, Dhyanchand.** *God, Christ and God's People in Asia.* Hong Kong: CCA, 1995.

_____. *Sword of the Spirit: An Activist's Understanding of the Bible.* Geneva: WCC, 1992.

**Caspersz, Paul.** "Asia's Third World Response to Catholic Social Thought." *Vidyajyoti Journal of Theological Reflection* 55, 1991: 561-568; 631-638; 698-705.

_____. "Christian Reflection on Economic Development in Asia. *Vidyajyoti Journal of Theological Reflection* 53, 1989: 579-588, 651-660.

_____. "Empowerment of the Poor in the Political Economy of South Asia." *Vidyajyoti Journal of Theological Reflection* 57, 1993: 471-480.

_____. "The Relationship Between the Catholic Church and the Economic Order." *Vidyajyoti Journal of Theological Reflection* 55, 1991: 177-186.

**Cecchini, Rose Marie.** *Women's Action for Peace and Justice: Christian, Buddhist and Muslim Women Tell Their Story.* Maryknoll Sisters, no date.

**Chan, Wing-Tsit (ed).** *A Sourcebook in Chinese Philosophy.* New York: Princeton University Press, 1963.

**Chang, Aloysius B.** "Liberative Elements in the Confucian Tradition." *Japanese Religions* 16, 1990: 24-42.

**Cheng, Kevin Shun-Kai.** "The Social Dimension of Liberation in Early Confucian Tradition." *Ching Feng* 36, 1993: 61-81.

**Choi, Man Ja.** "The Liberating Function of Feminine Images of God in Traditional Korean Religion." *Ching Feng* 35, 1992: 22-43.

**Chung Hyun Kyung.** *Struggle to Be the Sun Again: Introducing Asian Women's Theology.* Maryknoll, NY: Orbis Books, 1991.

_____. "Patriarchy and Death." *Pacific Journal of Theology* 2,5, 1991: 41-53.

**Cohn-Sherbok, Dan.** *World Religions and Human Liberation.* Maryknoll, NY: Orbis Books, 1992.

***Colloquium on the Social Doctrine of the Church in the Context of Asia.*** Manila: Office of Human Development, 1993.

**Commission on Theological Concerns of the Christian Conference of Asia (ed.).** *Minjung Theology: People as the Subjects of History.* Maryknoll, NY: Orbis Books, 1983.

_____. *Towards the Sovereignty of the People.* Singapore, 1983.

**Coyle, Kathleen.** "Renewing the Face of the Earth." *Asia Journal of Theology* 7, 1993: 114-127.

**Cruz, Hieronymus.** "The Conflict Spirituality of Jesus." *Jeevadhara* 23, 1993: 78-86.

*Culture: A Force for Change*. Manila: Socio-Pastoral Institute, 1988.

**D'Mello, John.** "Mahatma Phule and the Reinterpretation of Culture." *Jeevadhara* 22, 1992: 49-58.

**Dalai Lama.** *Worlds in Harmony: Dialogues on Compassionate Action*. Berkeley: Parallax Press, 1992.

**Dangle, Arjun (ed.).** *Poisoned Bread: Translations from Modern Marathi Dalit Literature*. Bombay: Orient Longman, 1992.

**Das, Somen.** "Religion, Power and Politics from a Theological-ethical Perspective." *CTC-Bulletin* 10,2&3, 1991: 30-34.

**Dawson, Raymond.** *Confucius*. Oxford: Oxford University Press, 1981.

**De la Torre, Edicio.** *Touching Ground, Taking Root: Theological and Political Reflections on the Philippine Struggle*. Manila: Socio-Pastoral Institute, 1986.

**Deliège, Robert.** "A Comparison between Hindu and Christian Paraiyars of South India." *Indian Missiological Review* 12, 1990: 53-64.

_____. *Les Paraiyars du Tamil Nadu*. Studia Instituti Anthropos 42, Nettetal: Steyler Verlag, 1988.

**Desrochers, John.** *Towards a New India*. Bangalore: Centre for Social Action, 1995.

**Devanandan, P.D.** *The Dravida Kazhagam*. Bangalore: Christian Institute for the Study of Religion and Society, 1960.

**Devasia, Leelamma and V.V. Devasia (eds.).** *Women in India: Equality, Social Justice and Development*. New Delhi: Indian Social Institute, 1990.

**Devi, Swarnalata.** "Kavi Jashuva's Reflections on Andhra Christian Dalits." *Religion and Society* 37, 1990: 35-42.

**Diehl, Anita.** *Periyar E.V.R.: A Study of the Influence of a Personality in Contemporary South India*. New Delhi: B.I. Publications, 1994.

**Dietrich, Gabriele.** "On Doing Feminist Theology in South Asia." *Kristu Jyoti* 6, 1990: 26-65.

_____. "Women, Ecology and Culture." *Bangalore Theological Forum* 21, 1989: 1-29.

_____. *Women's Movement in India: Conceptual and Religious Reflections*. Bangalore: Breakthrough Publications, 1988.

_____. "Women's Perspective on Ecology." *Religion and Society* 37,2, 1990: 54-60.

_____. "The World as the Body of God: Feminist Perspectives on Ecology and Social Justice." *Journal of Dharma* 18, 1993: 258-283.

**Dingayan, Luna L.** "Towards a Christology of Struggle." *CTC Bulletin* 10,1, 1991: 15-34.

**Donohue, John J. and John L. Esposito (eds.).** *Islam in Transition: Muslim Perspectives*. New York: Oxford University Press, 1982.

**Drego, Pearl.** "Values, Human Development and Women's Oppression." *Vidyajyoti Journal of Theological Reflection* 51, 1987: 155-167.

**Emmanuel, S.J.** *Church, Politics and War in Sri Lanka*. Jaffna: Centre for Better Society, 1994.

**Engineer, Asghar Ali.** *Ideology and the Oppressed*. Seminar 339, 1987: 26-30.

_____. "Islam, Status of Women and Social Change." *Islam and the Modern Age* 21, 1990: 180-199.

_____. *Islam and Liberation Theology*. Delhi: Sterling Publishers, 1990.

_____. *Islam and Revolution*. Delhi: Ajanta Publications, 1984.

_____. "Mohammad as Liberator." *Jeevadhara* 18, 1988: 189-201.

**Engineer, Asghar Ali (ed.).** *Religion and Liberation*. Delhi: Ajanta Publications, 1989.

**Eppsteiner, Fred (ed.).** *The Path of Compassion: Writings on Socially Engaged Buddhism*. Berkeley: Parallax Press, 1988.

**Erikson, Erik H**. *Gandhi's Truth: On the Origins of Militant Nonviolence*. New York: W.W. Norton, 1969.

**Esposito, John L.** (ed.). *Voices of Resurgent Islam*. New York: Oxford University Press, 1983.

**Exem, A. van**. "Man-Nature-Spirit: A Holistic Approach." *Vidyajyoti Journal of Theological Reflection* 48, 1984: 557-567.

_____. "The Tribe: God's Own People: A Theological Perspective." *Sevartham* 12, 1987: 45-64.

**Fabella, Virginia** (ed.). *Asia's Struggle for Full Humanity*. Maryknoll, NY: Orbis Books, 1980.

**Fabella, V., P. Lee, and D. Kwang-sun Suh** (eds.). *Asian Christian Spirituality: Reclaiming Traditions*. Maryknoll, NY: Orbis Books, 1992.

**Fabella, Virginia and S.A. Lee Park**. *We Dare to Dream: Doing Theology as Asian Women*. Maryknoll, NY: Orbis Books, 1990.

**Falcao, Nelson**. *Theology of Co-operation*. Rome: Urbaniana, 1988.

**Ferm, Deane William**. *Third World Liberation Theologies: A Reader*. Maryknoll, NY: Orbis Books, 1986.

**Fernandes, Walter**. *Inequality: Its Bases and Search for Solutions*. Delhi: Indian Social Institute, 1986.

**Fernandes, Walter** (ed.). *Social Activists and People's Movements*. Delhi: Indian Social Institute, 1985.

**Fernandes, Walter and Enakshi Ganguly Thukral** (eds.). *Development, Displacement and Rehabilitation*. New Delhi:   Indian Social Institute, 1991.

**Fernandez, Eleazar S.** *Towards a Theology of Struggle*. Maryknoll, NY: Orbis Books, 1994.

**Fernando, Tarcisius and Helene O'Sullivan** (eds.). *Launching the Second Century: The Future of Catholic Social Thought in Asia*. Hong Kong: Asian Center for the Progress of Peoples, 1993.

**Forrester, Duncan B.** *Caste and Christianity*. London: Curzon Press, 1980.

**Gadgil, Madhav**. "Forest Management, Deforestation and People's Impoverishment." *Social Action* 39, 1989: 357-383.

**Gajiwala Lobo, Astrid**. "Breaking the Silence: Violence against Women." *Word and Worship* 25, 1992: 33-46.

**Gandhi, M.K.** *All Men Are Brothers*. Calcutta: Orient Longmans, 1966.

_____. *Constructive Programme: Its Meaning and Place*. Ahmedabad: Navajivan, 1945.

_____. *From Yerawada Mandir: Ashram Observances*. Ahmedabad: Navajivan, 1957.

_____. *Hind Swaraj*. Ahmedabab: Navajivan, 1982.

_____. *The Message of Jesus Christ*. Bombay: Bharatiya Vidya Bhavan, 1963.

_____. *The Message of the Gita*. Ahmedabad: Navajivan, 1959.

_____. *The Story of My Experiments with Truth: An Autobiography*. Ahmedabad: Navajivan, 1945.

**Gandhians of Sevagram**. *A New Social Order: The Gandhian Alternative*. Varanasi: Sarva Seva Sangh Prakashan, 1991.

**Gaspar, Karl M.** *A People's Option: To Struggle for Creation*. Quezon City: Claretian, 1990.

**Gauhar, Altaf** (ed.). *The Challenge of Islam*. London: Islamic Council of Europe, 1978.

**George, P.G.** "Ecological Agenda of Wisdom." *Bible Bashyam* 19, 1993: 169-175.

**Gispert-Sauch, G.** "Meditation on the Bank of the Yamuna." *Jeevadhara* 17, 1987: 74-79.

**Gnanadason, Aruna**. "God Knows Why You Women Weep and Weeps with You." *Jeevadhara* 20, 1990: 189-196.

_____. "A Spirituality that Sustains Us in Our Struggles." *Voices from the Third World* 14, 1991: 66-84.

_____. "What do These Women Speak of? Indian Women on a Journey of Faith and Faithfulness." *Voices from the Third World* 16, 1993: 33-47.

**Griffiths, Bede.** "Nature, Technology and the New Society." *Jeevadhara* 18, 1988: 23-31.

**Guha, Ramachandra (ed.).** *Social Ecology.* Delhi: Oxford University Press, 1994.

**Habito, Ruben L.F.** "Lotus Buddhism and Its Liberational Thrust: A Re-reading of the Lotus Sutra by way of Nichiren." *Ching Feng* 35, 1992: 85-112.

_____. *Total Liberation: Zen Spirituality and the Social Dimension.* Maryknoll, NY: Orbis Books, 1989.

**Hanh, Thich Nhat.** *The Heart of Understanding.* Berkeley: Parallax Press, 1988.

_____. *Interbeing.* Berkeley: Parallax Press, 1993.

_____. *The Miracle of Being Awake.* Bangkok: International Network of Engaged Buddhists, 1989.

_____. *Transformation and Healing.* London: Rider, 1993.

**Heredia, Rudolf C.** "Towards an Ecological Consciousness: Religious, Ethical and Spiritual Perspectives." *Vidyajyoti Journal of Theological Reflection* 55, 1991: 489-504, 569-588.

**Ileto, Reynaldo.** *Pasyon and Revolution.* Quezon City: Ateneo University Press, 1979.

**Irudayaraj, Xavier.** *Emerging Dalit Theology.* Madras: Jesuit Theological Secretariat, 1990.

**Iyer, Raghavan (ed.).** *The Moral and Political Writings of M.K. Gandhi.* 3 Vols. Oxford: Clarendon Press, 1987.

**Japhet, S.** "Christian Dalits: A Sociological Study of the Problem of Gaining a New Identity." *Religion and Society* 34, 1987: 59-87.

**Jebaraj, D.** "Paradigms in Dalit Theology." *AETEI Journal* 6,2, 1993: 11-17.

**Jesudasan, Ignatius.** "Gandhian Perspectives on Conflict Spirituality." *Jeevadhara* 23, 1993: 36-43.

_____. *A Gandhian Theology of Liberation.* Maryknoll, NY: Orbis Books, 1984.

**John, Simon.** "Christian Dalits in Kerala." *Religion and Society* 34, 1987: 26-30.

**John, T.K.** "Theology of Liberation and Gandhian Praxis: A Social Spirituality for India." *Vidyajyoti Journal of Theological Reflection* 49, 1985: 502-518.

**John, T.K. (ed.).** *Bread and Breath.* Anand: Gujarat Sahitya Prakash, 1991.

**Kappen, Sebastian.** *The Future of Socialism and the Socialism of the Future.* Bangalore: Vishtar, 1992.

_____. *Jesus and Cultural Revolution: An Asian Perspective.* Bombay: Build Publications, 1983.

_____. *Jesus and Freedom.* Maryknoll, NY: Orbis Books, 1977.

_____. *Liberation Theology and Marxism.* Puntamba: Asha Kendra, 1986.

_____. *Tradition, Modernity, Counterculture: An Asian Perspective.* Bangalore: Visthar, 1994.

**Karakunnel, George.** "Advaita as a Social Programme." *The Living Word* 99, 1993: 71-91.

**Kasuya, Koichi.** "A Catholic Commentary on 'A Theology of the Crown of Thorns': The Buraku Liberation Theology." *The Japan Mission Journal* 47, 1993: 3-17.

**Kattukaran, Paul.** "Earth Alive in Art and Symbolism." *Journal of Dharma* 18, 1993: 71-84.

**Keel, Hee-Sung.** "Zen and Minjung Liberation." *Inter-Religio* 17, 1990: 24-37.

**Khan, Mumtaz Ali.** "Social Conditions of the Scheduled Castes." *Journal of Dharma* 16, 1991: 20-32.

**Kim, Sang Yil.** "Hanism as Liberating Spirituality in Korea." *Voices from the Third World* 14, 1991: 95-106.

**Kim, Sung-Hae.** "God's Creation as Liberation of Minjung." *CTC Bulletin* 9, 1990: 18-21.

_____. "Liberation through Humanization: With a Focus on Korean Confucianism." *Ching Feng* 33, 1990: 20-46.

Kim Yong-Bock. "Justice, Peace and the Integrity of Creation: An Asian Perspective." *Voices from the Third World* 16, 1993: 93-109.

King, Alexander and Bertrand Schneider. *The First Global Revolution: A Report by the Council of the Club of Rome.* Bombay: Orient Longman, 1993.

Kinsley, David R. "Reflections on Ecological Themes in Hinduism." *Journal of Dharma* 16, 1991: 229-245.

Kishwar, Madhu and Ruth Vanita (eds.). *In Search of Answers: Indian Women's Voices from Manushi.* New Delhi: Horizon, 1991.

Klimkeit, Hans-J. "Indigenous Elements in Modern Tamil Secularism." *Religion and Society* 23,3, 1976: 77-98.

Klostermaier, Klaus K. "Bhakti, Ahimsa and Ecology." *Journal of Dharma* 16, 1991: 246-254.

Kochery, Tom. "Where I Met Jesus." *Jeevadhara* 21, 1991: 185-192.

Koonthanam, George. "Israel as a Peoples' Movement for Liberation." *Jeevadhara* 15, 1985: 288-306.

_____. "Yahweh, the Defender of the Dalits: A Reflection on Isaiah 3:12-15." *Jeevadhara* 22, 1992: 112-123.

Kothari, Rajni. "From Religions to Religiosity." *Jeevadhara* 20, 1990: 72-88.

Kothari, Smithu. "Ecology vs Development: The Struggle for Survival." *Social Action* 35, 1985: 379-392.

Kulandai, John. "Spirituality of Conflict." *Jeevadhara* 23, 1993: 48-55.

Kullu, Paulus. "Tribal Religion and Culture." *Jeevadhara* 24, 1994: 89-109.

Kurian, Joseph K. "Forests and Environmental Protection." *Jeevadhara* 21, 1991: 453-461.

Kwon, Jin-Kwan. "Minjung Theology and Its Future Task for People's Movement." *CTC-Bulletin* 10,2&3, 1991: 16-22.

Lai, Whalen. "The Chinese Universe of Moral Discourse." *Ching Feng* 32, 1989: 85-100.

Lakra, C. "Christianity and Tribal Identity." *Religion and Society* 36, 1990: 30-39.

Lee, Agnes Chwen-Jiuan. "The Philosophy of Liberation in Laotzu and Chuang Tzu." *Ching Feng* 33, 1990: 191-204.

Lee, Jung Young (ed.). *An Emerging Theology in World Perspective: Commentary on Korean Minjung Theology.* Mystic, CT: Twenty-Third Publications, 1988.

Lee, Peter K.H. "Tai-Ping and Liberation: Implications for Liberation in the T'ai-P'ing Ching." *Ching Feng* 35, 1992: 65-83.

Ligo, Arche. "Liberation Themes in Philippine Popular Religiosity: A Case Study." *Voices from the Third World* 16,2, 1993: 117-142.

Lobo, Goerge V. "Church's Teaching on Violence." *Jeevadhara* 20, 1990: 461-480.

_____. "Teaching of the Church on Human Rights from an Indian Perspective." *Indian Theological Studies* 28, 1991: 209-233.

Lopez, Melba. "Can Women Be Empowered to Become Agents of Change?" *Vidyajyoti Journal of Theological Reflection* 54, 1990: 29-34.

Lourdusamy, Stan. "Peoples' Movement in India Today and the Mission of the Church." *Jeevadhara* 15, 1985: 259-278.

Lovett, Brendan. *Life Before Death: Inculturating Hope.* Quezon City: Claretian, 1986.

_____. *On Earth as in Heaven.* Quezon City: Claretian, 1988.

Luke, Kuriakose. "Nature in the Perspectives of the Hebrew Bible." *The Living Word* 99, 1993: 167-191.

_____. "Reflections on the Phenomenon of Violence." *Jeevadhara* 20, 1990: 431-454.

**Lukose, Alice.** "We Work Hard All Night and Catch Nothing." *Jeevadhara* 16, 1986: 217-227.

**Macy, Joanna.** *Dharma and Development: Religion as Resource in the Sarvodaya Self-Help Movement.* West Hartford, CT: Kumarian Press, 1983.

**Madtha, William.** "Dalit Theology: Voice of the Oppressed." *Journal of Dharma* 16, 1991: 74-92.

**Mananzan, Mary John.** *Essays on Women.* Manila, 1991.

_____. *The Woman Question in the Philippines.* Pasay City: St. Paul, 1991.

**Mangatt, George.** "Jesus' Option for Sinners." *Bible Bashyam* 18, 1992: 208-220.

_____. "Jesus' Option for Women." *Jeevadhara* 21, 1991: 161-176.

**Manickam, Sundararaj.** "Origin and History of the Christian Dalits in Kerala and Tamil Nadu." *Religion and Society* 34, 1987: 7-25.

**Manimala, Varghese.** "Structural Violence, Human Rights and the Right to Protest." *Jeevadhara* 20, 1990: 481-496.

**Marasigan, Vicente.** *A Banahaw Guru.* Quezon City: Ateneo University Press, 1979.

**Mariaselvam, Abraham.** "Conflict and Spirituality in the Old Testament: Prophets as Paradigms." *Jeevadhara* 23, 1993: 64-77.

_____. "The Cry of the Dalits: An Interpretation of Psalm 140." *Jeevadhara* 22, 1992: 124-139.

**Mary, Philomin.** "Casting the Net on the Right Side." *Jeevadhara* 21, 1991: 193-200.

**Massey, James.** *A Concise History of the Dalits.* Delhi: ISPCK, 1991.

**Massey, James (ed.).** *Indigenous People: Dalits.* Delhi: ISPCK, 1994.

**Mathew, K.V.** "Ecological Perspectives in the Book of the Psalms." *Bible Bashyam* 19, 1993: 159-168.

**Mathew, Philip and Ajit Muricken.** *Religion, Ideology and Counter Culture.* Bangalore: Horizon Books, 1987.

**Mathur, J.S.** *Non-violence and Social Change.* Ahmedabad: Navajivan, 1977.

**Mawdudi, Sayyid Abul A'la.** *The Economic Problems of Man and Its Islamic Solution.* Delhi: Markazi Maktaba Islami, 1966.

_____. *Fundamentals of Islam.* Delhi: Markazi Maktaba Islami, 1980.

_____. *The Islamic Movement: Dynamics of Values, Power and Change.* Leicester: The Islamic Foundation, 1984.

_____. *The Meaning of the Quran.* Delhi: Markazi Maktaba Islami, 1968.

_____. *Towards Understanding Islam.* Delhi: Markazi Maktaba Islami, 1972.

_____. *Witnesses unto Mankind: The Purpose and Duty of the Muslim Ummah.* London: The Islamic Foundation, 1986.

**Menezes, Baptist.** "Response of the Indian Church to Social Issues." *Indian Theological Studies* 28, 1991: 259-290.

**Michael, S.M.** "Tribal Culture and Women's Liberation." *Jeevadhara* 22, 1992: 19-25.

**Mies, Maria and Vandana Shiva.** *Ecofeminism.* New Delhi: Kali for Women, 1993.

**Minz, Nirmal.** "Anthropology and the Deprived." *Religion and Society* 32,4, 1985: 3-19.

_____. "Meaning of Tribal Consciousness." *Religion and Society* 36,2, 1989: 12-23.

_____. "Religion and Culture as Power in the Context of Tribal Aspirations in India." *Religion and Society* 33, 2, 1986: 45-54.

_____. "A Theological Interpretation of the Tribal Reality in India." *Religion and Society* 34,4, 1987: 71-85.

**Munda, Ram Dayal.** "The Bases of Cultural Identity of Chotanagpur." *Religion and Society* 36,2, 1989: 24-29.

_____. "Dispossession and Exploitation of Tribal People Through Communication Manipulation with Special Reference to Jharkhand." *Religion and Society* 39,1, 1992: 32-41.

**Muzzaffar, Chandra**. *Islamic Resurgence in Malaysia*. Petaling Jaya: Penerbit Fajar Bakti, 1987.

**Nanda, B.R**. *Mahatma Gandhi: A Biography*. Boston: Beacon Press, 1958.

**Nandy, Ashis**. *The Intimate Enemy: Loss and Recovery of Self under Colonialism*. Delhi: Oxford University Press, 1983.

_____. "Questions to Indian Liberation Theologians." *Vidyajyoti Journal of Theological Reflection* 51, 1987: 599-600.

_____. *Science, Hegemony and Violence: A Requiem for Modernity*. Delhi: Oxford University Press, 1988.

_____. *Traditions, Tyranny, and Utopias: Essays in the Politics of Awareness*. Delhi: Oxford University Press, 1987.

**Nasr, Seyyed Valli Reza**. *The Vanguard of the Islamic Revolution*. Berkeley: University of California Press, 1994.

**Neraparambil, Lucius**. "An Eco-theology Foreshadowed in the Gospel of John." *Bible Bashyam* 19, 1993: 188-204.

**Nirmal, Arvind, P**. *A Reader in Dalit Theology*. Madras: Gurukul, 1989.

_____. *Towards a Common Dalit Ideology*. Madras: Gurukul, n.d.

**Nudas, Alfeo G**. *God with Us: The 1986 Philippine Revolution*. Manila: Loyola School of Theology, 1986.

**Obeyesekere, Gananath**. "Sorcery, Premeditated Murder, and the Canalization of Aggression in Sri Lanka." *Ethnology* 14, 1975: 1-24.

**O'Brien, Niall**. *Revolution from the Heart*. Quezon City: Claretian Publications, 1987.

**Omvedt, Gail**. *Reinventing Revolution: New Social Movements and the Socialist Tradition in India*. Armonk, NY: M.E. Sharpe, 1993.

_____. *We Will Smash This Prison: Indian Women in Struggle*. London: Zed Publications, 1980.

**Pandharipande, Rajeshwari**. "Spiritual Dimension of Fertility Cult and Power in Women." *Journal of Dharma* 13, 1988: 267-281.

**Panikkar, Raimon**. *The Cosmotheandric Experience*. Maryknoll, NY: Orbis Books, 1993.

**Parakkal, Matthew**. "Environmental Diseases." *Jeevadhara* 21, 1991: 432-452.

**Park, Jae Soon**. "Jesus' Table Community Movement and the Church." *Asia Journal of Theology* 7, 1993: 60-83.

**Pattery, George**. "Satyagraha-Religiousness: A Dialogue Way of Liberation." *Vidyajyoti Journal of Theological Reflection* 55, 1991: 7-22.

**Pearson, Anne**. "Aspects of Hindu Women's *vrat* Tradition as Constitutive for Eco-spirituality. *Journal of Dharma* 18, 1993: 228-236.

**Philip, T.M**. *The Encounter between Theology and Ideology: An Exploration into the Communicative Theology of M.M. Thomas*. Madras: Christian Literature Society, 1986.

**Phonphit, Seri**. "Liberative Elements in Theravada Buddhism in Thailand Today." *Inter-Religio* 18, 1990: 70-78.

**Pieris, Aloysius**. "An Asian Paradigm: Inter-religious Dialogue and Theology of Religions." *The Month*, 26, April 1993:129-134.

_____. *An Asian Theology of Liberation*. Maryknoll, NY: Orbis Books, 1988.

_____. *Love Meets Wisdom: A Christian Experience of Buddhism*. Maryknoll, NY: Orbis Books, 1988.

_____. "Three Inadequacies in the Social Encyclicals." *Vidyajyoti Journal of Theological Reflection* 57, 1993: 73-94.

_____. "Woman and Religion in Asia: Towards a Buddhist and Christian Appropriation of the Feminist Critique." *Dialogue.* NS 19-20, 1992-1993: 119-203.

**Pieris, Aloysius (ed.).** "Buddhism, Social Change and the Marxist Factor." *Dialogue,* NS 12, 1-3, 1985: 1-111.

**Pillai, Mary.** "Cultural Hegemony: Its Traditional Roots and Present Manifestations." *Jeevadhara* 22, 1992: 33-48.

_____. "Grassroot Movements: Utopia or a Sign of Hope for the 1990's." *Jeevadhara* 20, 1990: 29-41.

_____. "Women against Women." *Jeevadhara* 17, 1987: 42-50.

**Pinto, Ambrose.** *Dalit Christians: A Socio-Economic Survey.* Bangalore: Ashirvad, 1992.

**Podimattam, Felix M.** "Violence and Struggle for Justice." *Jeevadhara* 20, 1990: 497-510.

**Prabhakar, M.E.** "Caste in Andhra Churches: A Case Study of Guntur District." *Religion and Society* 34, 1987: 31-51.

_____. "Developing a Common Ideology for Dalits of Christian and Other Faiths." *Religion and Society,* 37,3, 1990: 24-39.

_____ (ed.). *Towards A Dalit Theology.* Delhi: ISPCK, 1989.

**Pushparajan, A.** "Gandhi's Approach to Women's Liberation." *Journal of Dharma* 13, 1988: 39-63.

**Puthanangady, Paul (ed.).** *Towards an Indian Theology of Liberation.* Bangalore: National Biblical, Catechetical and Liturgical Centre, 1986.

**Raj, Antony.** *Children of a Lesser God (Dalit Christians).* Madurai: DCLM Publication, 1992.

_____. "The Dalit Christian Reality in Tamil Nadu." *Jeevadhara* 22, 1992: 95-111.

**Raja, R.J.** "As It Was in the Beginning." *Bible Bashyam* 19, 1993: 210-230.

_____. "Eco-spirituality in the Book of Revelation." *Vidyajyoti Journal of Theological Reflection* 55, 1991: 681-697.

_____. "Eco-Spirituality in the Psalms." *Vidyajyoti Journal of Theological Reflection* 53, 1989: 637-650.

_____. "Wisdom Psalms and Environmental Concerns." *Vidyajyoti Journal of Theological Reflection* 57, 1993: 201-214.

**Ram, Kalpana.** *Mukkuvar Women.* Delhi: Kali for Women, 1992.

**Ranjan, P. Swarnalata.** "Christian Dalit Aspirations as Expressed by Jashuva Kavi in Gabbilam (The Bat)." *Religion and Society,* 34, 1987: 52-58.

**Rao, O.M.** "The Healing of Creation." *Bible Bashyam* 19, 1993: 205-209.

**Rao, S.N.** "The Hindu Perspective on Ecology and Environment." *Kristu Jyoti* 7, 1991: 15-34.

**Rayan, Samuel.** "The Earth Is the Lord's." *Vidyajyoti Journal of Theological Reflection,* 54, 1990: 113-130.

_____. "Theological Perspectives on the Environmental Crisis." *Religion and Society* 37,2, 1990: 18-34.

**Rodrigo, Michael.** "Buddhism and Christianity: Towards the Human Future." *East Asian Pastoral Review* 25, 1988: 133-143.

**Rouner, Leroy S (ed.).** *Human Rights and the World's Religions.* Notre Dame, IN: Notre Dame University Press, 1988.

**Ryerson, Charles A.** "Meaning and Modernization in Tamil Nadu: Tamil Nationalism and Religious Culture." *Religion and Society* 17,4, 1970: 6-21.

_____. "Primordial Sentiments in Tamil Nadu: The Cultural Roots of the Plea for Greater Autonomy." *Religion and Society* 22,1 1975: 22-33.

_____. "Religion, Culture and Power." *Religion and Society,* 33, 1986: 5-26.

**Sabin, Marie.** "The Liberating Experience in Buddhism and Christianity." *Dialogue* 18, 1991: 49-67.

**Sahi, Jyoti.** "Folk Art and Quest for Justice." *Jeevadhara* 24, 1994: 16-30.

_____. *Stepping Stones: Reflections on the Theology of Indian Christian Culture.* Bangalore: Asian Trading Corporation, 1986.

**Scott, David C.** "Keeping Faith with Life: Mother Earth in Popular Religious Traditions." *Journal of Dharma* 18, 1993: 50-70.

_____. "The Social Vision of Basava and Jesus." *Religion and Society* 39,2-3, 1992: 3-7.

_____. "Some Reflections on 'A Theological Response to Ecological Crisis'." *Bangalore Theological Forum* 25, 1993: 15-24.

**The Search for a Spirituality of Liberation.** "Reports from Asia." *Voices from the Third World* 13, 1990: 1-152.

**Sebastian, Joseph.** *God as Feminine: A Dialogue.* Frankfurt: Peter Lang, 1995.

**Sebastian, Mrinalini.** "Oppression, Literature and Differing Points of View." *Journal of Dharma* 16, 1991: 5-19.

**Selvaraj, X.D.** "Social Awakening of the Indian Church." *Caste Culture in Indian Church.* Sebasti L. Raj and G.F. Xavier Raj (eds.), New Delhi: Indian Social Institute, 1993.

_____. "Social Conflicts and Spirituality." *Jeevadhara* 23, 1993: 16-26.

**Sen, Ilina (ed.).** *A Space within the Struggle.* New Delhi: Kali for Women, 1990.

**Shah, Ghanshyam.** *Social Movements in India: A Review of the Literature.* New Delhi: Sage Publications, 1990.

**Shanti, Margaret.** "Towards a Feminist Liberation Theology: Orientations and Perspectives." *Kristu Jyoti* 6, 1990: 72-89.

**Shariati, Ali.** *Hajj.* Bedford: FILINC, 1977.

_____. *Man and Islam.* Houston: Filinc, 1981.

_____. *Martyrdom.* Tehran: Abu Dharr Foundation, n.d.

_____. *Marxism and Other Western Fallacies: An Islamic Critique.* Berkeley: Mizan Press, 1980.

_____. *On the Sociology of Islam.* Berkeley: Mizan Press, 1979.

_____. *What Is to Be Done? The Enlightened Thinkers and an Islamic Renaissance.* Houston: IRIS, 1986.

**Shen, Vincent.** "Confucianism, Science and Technology." *Ching Feng* 32, 1989: 120-137.

**Shiri, Godwin.** "Basava, Casteism and Untouchables." *Religion and Society* 39, 1992: 17-24.

**Shiva, Vandana.** *Staying Alive: Women, Ecology and Survival in India.* New Delhi: Kali for Women, 1988.

**Shiva, Vandana (ed.).** *Minding Our Lives.* Delhi: Kali for Women, 1993.

**Silva, Bernie.** "The Gospels and the Liberation of Asian Women." *Jeevadhara* 17, 1987: 80-95.

**Silva, Lily de.** "Teachings of the Buddha and the Liberation of the Poor." *Dialogue* 15, 1988: 36-55.

**Sivadas, S.** "A New Gospel on Nature." *Jeevadhara* 21, 1991: 421-432.

**Sivaraksa, Sulak.** "Buddhist Ethics and Modern Society." *Ching Feng* 35, 1992: 13-21.

_____. *A Buddhist Vision for Renewing Society.* Bangkok: Thai Inter-Religious Commission for Development, 1994.

_____. *Seeds of Peace: A Buddhist Vision for Renewing Society.* Bangkok: International Network of Engaged Buddhists, 1992.

_____. *A Socially Engaged Buddhism.* Bangkok: Thai Inter-Religious Commission for Development, 1988.

**Sivaraksa, Sulak et al. (eds.).** *Buddhist Perception for Desirable Societies in the Future.* Bangkok: Thai Inter-Religious Commission for Development, 1993.

**Soares-Prabhu, George.** "Anti-greed and Anti-pride: Mark 10:17-27 and 10:35-45 in the Light of Tribal Values." *Jeevadhara* 24, 1994: 130-150.

_____. "The Bible and the Poor." *Poverty in India.* J. Murickan (ed.). Bangalore: Xavier Board, 1988.

_____. "Class in the Bible: The Biblical Poor a Social Class?" *Voices from the Margin: Interpreting the Bible in the Third World.* R.S. Sugirtharajah (ed.). Maryknoll, NY: Orbis Books, 1991.

_____. "Good News to the Poor: The Social Implications of the Message of Jesus." *The Indian Church in the Struggle for a New Society.* D.S. Amalorpavadass (ed.). Bangalore: National Biblical, Catechetical and Liturgical Centre, 1981, pp. 609-626.

_____. "Jesus and Conflict." *The Way* 26, 1986: 14-23.

_____. "Jesus and the Poor." *Poverty in India: Challenges and Responses.* J. Murickan (ed.). Bangalore: Xavier Board, 1988, pp. 261-290.

_____. "Jesus the Teacher: The Liberative Pedagogy of Jesus of Nazareth." *Jeevadhara* 12, 1982: 432-456.

____. "The Kingdom of God: Jesus' Vision of a New Society." *The Indian Church in the Struggle for A New Society.* D.S. Amalorpavadass (ed.). Bangalore: National Biblical, Catechetical and Liturgical Centre, 1981, pp. 579-608.

_____. "The Miracles of Jesus: Subversion of a Power Structure?" *Jesus Today.* S. Kappen (ed.). Madras: AICUF, 1985, pp. 21-29.

_____. "Radical Beginnings: The Jesus Community as the Archtype of the Church." *Jeevadhara* 15, 1985: 307-325.

_____. "The Spirituality of Jesus as a Spirituality of Solidarity and Struggle." *Liberative Struggles in a Violent Society.* J. Vattamattom et al. (eds.). Hyderabad: Forum, 1991, pp. 136-161.

_____. "The Synoptic Love-Commandment: The Dimensions of Love in the Teaching of Jesus." *Jeevadhara* 13, 1983: 85-103.

_____. "The Table Fellowship of Jesus: Its Significance for Dalit Christians in India Today." *Jeevadhara* 22, 1992: 140-159.

**Stirrat, R.L.** *Power and Religiosity in a Post-Colonial Setting: Sinhala Catholics in Contemporary Sri Lanka.* Cambridge: Cambridge University Press, 1992.

**Sugirtharajah, R.S (ed.).** *Asian Faces of Jesus.* Maryknoll, NY: Orbis Books, 1993.

_____(ed.).*Voices from the Margin: Interpreting the Bible in the Third World.* Maryknoll, NY: Orbis Books, 1991.

**Suh, David Kwang-sun.** *The Korean Minjung in Christ.* Hong Kong: CCA Commission on Theological Concerns, 1991.

**Sujita, Mary.** "Cries of the Deprived." *Jeevadhara* 21, 1991: 201-210.

**Swearer, Donald K.** *Buddhism and Society in Southeast Asia.* Chambersburg: Anima Books, 1981.

**Swearer, Donald K. (ed.).** *Me and Mine: Selected Essays of Bhikku Buddhadasa.* Albany: State University of New York Press, 1989.

_____. *Toward the Truth: Buddhadasa.* Philadelphia: Westminster Press, 1971.

**Tahtinen, Unto.** "Values, Non-violence and Ecology: Two Approaches." *Journal of Dharma* 16, 1991: 211-217.

**Tarabout, Gilles.** "Violence et Non-violence magiques: La Sorcellerie au Kerala." *Purusartha* 16, 1994: 155-185.

**Tellis Nayak, Jessie B.** *Indian Womanhood Then and Now: Situations, Efforts, Profiles.* Indore: Satprakashan, 1983.

**Therukattil, Goerge.** "Towards a Biblical Eco-theology." *Jeevadhara* 21, 1991: 465-483.

**Thomas, M.M.** "Christ-centred Syncretism." *Religion and Society* 25,1, 1979.

_____. *The Christian Response to Asian Revolution.* London: SCM, 1966.

_____. "A Christian View of Society." *Religion and Society* 7,3-4, 1960: 51-60.

_____. *Man and the Universe of Faiths.* Madras: Christian Literature Society, 1975.

_____. *New Creation in Christ.* Delhi: ISPCK, 1976.

_____. *Salvation and Humanization.* Madras: Christian Literature Society, 1971.

_____. *The Secular Ideologies of India and the Secular Meaning of Christ.* Madras: The Christian Literature Society, 1976.

_____. *Towards a Theology of Contemporary Ecumenism.* Madras: Christian Literature Society, 1978.

**Thumma, Lucas.** "The Social Teachings of the Indian Church." *Indian Theological Studies* 28, 1991: 291-321.

**Traer, Robert.** *Faith in Human Rights: Support in Religious Traditions for a Global Struggle.* Washington, DC: Georgetown University Press, 1991.

**Vadakumchery, Johnson.** "The Earth-Mother and the Indigenous People of India." *The Journal of Dharma* 18, 1993: 85-97.

**Velamkunnel, Joseph.** "Despair and Hope: Myths of the Oppressed and Their Liberative Potential." *Jeevadhara* 15, 1985: 203-212.

_____. "The Jharkhand Movement: A Response to Tribal Oppression?" *Vidyajyoti Journal of Theological Reflection* 53, 1989: 299-312.

**Venkatachari, B.V.** "Indian Mystic Approach to the Earth." *Journal of Dharma* 18, 1993: 35-41.

**Viegas, Philip and Geeta Menon (eds.).** *The Impact of Environmental Degradation on People.* New Delhi: Indian Social Institute, 1989.

**Vineeth, Vadakethala F.** "The Classical vs Liberative Approach to Indian Christian Spirituality." *Jeevadhara* 23, 1993: 291-300.

**Webster, J.** *The Dalit Christians: A History.* Delhi: ISPCK, 1992.

**Wilfred, Felix.** "Indian Social Institutions and Movements of Protest: Towards an Alternative Socio-political Conception and Praxis from Indigenous Roots." *Indian Theological Studies* 30, 1993: 220-245.

_____. *Leave the Temple: Indian Paths to Human Liberation.* Maryknoll, NY: Orbis Books, 1992.

_____. "Liberating Leadership: Towards Christian Leadership of Tomorrow." *Jeevadhara* 21, 1991: 282-299.

_____. "The Liberation Process in India and Church's Participation." *Indian Theological Studies* 25, 1988: 301-333.

_____. "Nature and Human Survival." *Jeevadhara* 18, 1988: 55-75.

_____. "New Spiritual Foundations for World in Conflict: Some Macro Perspectives." *Jeevadhara* 23, 1993: 87-92.

_____. "The Politics of Culture: Critical Reflections on Culture and Human Development from a Third World Perspective." *Jeevadhara* 22, 1992: 59-80.

**Xavier, Anthony.** "The Jharkhand Movement and the Role of the Clergy." *Sevartham* 16, 1991: 121-130.

**Zelliot, Eleanor.** *From Untouchable to Dalit: Essays on Ambedkar Movement.* New Delhi: Manohar, 1992.

# Index